CHILDREN AT RISK
Editor: V. Alan McClelland

CW00448310

ASPECTS OF EDUCATION
JOURNAL OF THE
INSTITUTE OF EDUCATION
THE UNIVERSITY OF HULL

NUMBER FIFTY
1994

First Published 1994
© THE UNIVERSITY OF HULL 1994
ISBN 0-85958-241-8

Editor
Professor V. Alan McClelland, University of Hull

Opinions expressed are entirely those
of the contributors concerned.

Aspects of Education is published by
Studies in Education Ltd., and printed
by Bemrose Shafron (Printers) Ltd. for
the Institute of Education, University of Hull.

CONTENTS

PREFACE

V. Alan McClelland

Kenneth Barnes, a Quaker schoolteacher who for many years was senior science master at Bedales, never tired of reminding educators that 'it is not true education to decide in advance what a child ought to have, what kind of person he ought to be like' (*The Involved Man*, 1969, p.26). For the student of the history of childhood, however, it is evident that a rigid subscription to such a philosophy in the nineteenth and twentieth centuries would have stultified the vision necessary for improvement in the welfare and rights of children. Indeed, a schoolmaster contemporary of Barnes, Bryan MacMahon, pointed out that while humanity is sometimes willing to accept the abnormal as normal, at the core of child adversity the pricking of societal action and desire for reform can be detected (*The Master*, 1992, p.8).

This volume of papers, read before historians at the History of Education Society gathering in Oxford in December 1993, examines the interplay of 'normality' and 'abnormality' in the nurturing of children and pinpoints some of those forces of vision, idealism and action which have led to an improvement in the lot of many children 'at-risk'.

THE RIGHTS OF THE CHILD FROM THE MID-EIGHTEENTH TO THE EARLY TWENTIETH CENTURY

Hugh Cunningham

If we think of children in the late eighteenth and nineteenth centuries our minds are likely to be filled with images of children at risk: the pauper apprentices, the climbing boys, the so-called 'free labour' of the cotton factories, and the children in mines or potteries; or the street children who became of such concern from the 1840s; or later, when the Societies for the Prevention of Cruelty to Children came into being in the 1880s, the child at risk from its own parents. Our pictures of these children come partly from campaigning literature and from the pages of Select Committee and Royal Commission reports, but also from imaginative literature, from Blake's *Songs of Innocence and of Experience* or from *Oliver Twist.* We are drawn inexorably to seeing these children as more than at risk, rather as victims. But before we launch into descriptions of the conditions in which these children lived, we need to ask in what senses they were at risk or became victims, and in whose perception.

At one level the answers are obvious. Children working in cotton factories were at risk of growing up with physical deformities. Children living in the street were at risk of drifting into a life of crime. Children neglected or abused in the home were at risk of a continuation of that neglect and abuse and of eventually visiting it on their own children. And it was campaigners and philanthropists and governments who saw these children as at risk, and who tried at the very least to reduce the level of risk. They did not, I think, use the phrase 'at risk', but they certainly saw a need for some children to be rescued or saved.

There was, however, potential for disagreement about the nature and extent of risk; for example, some people thought that factory children were at as much risk of mental and moral as of physical deformity. Moreover, if there was a variable number of children in need of rescuing or saving, or at risk, there was by implication another category of children to whom we may attach the label, 'not at risk'. It is the development of the 'not at risk' category on which I want to concentrate, for the more elaborate it became, the more it was possible to identify the opposite, the children 'at risk' or in need of rescuing and saving. In brief, the 'not at risk' children were those who enjoyed the protection of what came to be defined as 'the rights of children'. And those who asserted the 'rights of the child' were in fact engaged in a process of defining childhood itself.

I want first, however, to review briefly the legal position of children in the eighteenth and early nineteenth centuries. It is some testimony to the force with which children's rights were asserted in the late nineteenth and early twentieth centuries that scholars have accepted at face value the assertion of campaigners that children in the eighteenth century were without any rights at all. Thus in the second volume of their *Children in English Society*, covering the period from the eighteenth century to the Children Act of 1948, Ivy Pinchbeck and Margaret Hewitt start with a chapter entitled 'Childhood without Rights and Protection', and depict a situation where 'The harshness of the parent was paralleled by the harshness of the State'. The theme of their volume is the slow acquisition of legal rights for children. One mark of the harshness of the State, as they see it, was the willingness of the State to execute children.[1] In fact executions of children were extremely rare; up to 1836 children were liable to be sentenced to death, but in none of the 103 cases at the Old Bailey between 1801 and 1836 was the sentence carried out.[2] Moreover sentencing policy was decidedly lenient towards young offenders, so that the chances of being sentenced to death or transportation increased significantly for offenders in their late teens or twenties.[3] As to parental power, George Behlmer has argued that in mid-Victorian England, 'parents still enjoyed virtually unfettered power over all offspring who remained at home', and at law 'children remained defenseless'.[4] Linda Pollock, in an analysis of 385 cases of child neglect and abuse reported in *The Times* in the period 1785-1860, has shown how inaccurate is this view that children had no rights against parental cruelty. Take, for example, the case of Patrick Sheehan in 1824. Sheehan, who had beaten his 8-year-old son until the blood flowed and then thrown him on a fire so that his back was burned, argued in defence 'that he thought every father had a right to do as he pleased with his own child, and that he did not see what right other people had to interfere'. The magistrate replied that 'the law must teach the defendant that this doctrine of his was very erroneous'. The parish officers, on the advice of the magistrates, took the case forward to the Middlesex Sessions, and even though Sheehan produced evidence that the beating of the child had been as a punishment for stealing, the Chairman said that nothing could justify the dreadful treatment the boy had received, and the jury 'without hesitation, returned a verdict of Guilty'. Sheehan received a sentence of six months in the House of Correction with hard labour.[5] Nor was this case unusual. Hesba Stretton noted, before the Societies for the Prevention of Cruelty to Children were in being, that 'cases of flagrant and excessive cruelty are constantly being brought before the magistrates'. There was never any doubt that in cases of neglect and cruelty the State had a right to punish.[6]

The rights of children tended to be expressed in terms of the duties of parents. They were set out by William Blackstone in his *Commentaries on the Laws of England* (1765). By 'a principle of natural law', Blackstone wrote, 'children will have a perfect *right* of receiving maintenance from their parents'. In well-regulated states, such as England, laws enforced this parental duty. Secondly, parents had a duty to protect their children, again a 'natural duty', and one which Blackstone saw as manifesting itself in support for children in law suits or in physical defence of children. Finally, parents had a duty to provide education for their children 'suitable', as Blackstone put it, 'to their situation in life'.[7]

In some ways Blackstone set an agenda for the nineteenth century. Thus the legal duty of maintenance of a child was further addressed in the Poor Laws of 1834 and 1868, reaffirming the position as first set out in the Elizabethan Poor Law.[8] The child received some protection with the passage of an Act in 1814 which rectified the anomaly that until then there was no such crime as stealing a child. When there was a spate of such thefts in the early nineteenth century, mainly by women who had lost their own children by death or who had been unable to conceive, the only crime they could be accused of was the theft of the clothes which the babies were wearing.[9] As to education, where Blackstone acknowledged that the laws of England were deficient, in 1876 the Education Act laid down a legal duty on a parent to cause a child 'to receive sufficient elementary instruction in reading, writing, and arithmetic'.[10]

The rights of the child to maintenance, protection and education as set forth by Blackstone were relatively uncontroversial, though of course difficult to convert from theory to practice. But even if enforced, they did not of themselves provide children with what came to be thought of as their 'rights'. The emergence of the idea of a 'childhood' appropriate for all children was focused around three issues: the child at work, the street child, and the child who was abused in the home. The interplay between these three issues and romanticism led to the articulation of the belief that the child's fundamental right was a right to 'childhood'.

The first to become a matter of major attention concerned the work of children in the new employment conditions of the Industrial Revolution. It had not occurred to Blackstone that a child might have a right not to work. On the contrary, in such remarks as he made on education, he praised pauper apprenticeship for providing the kind of education that he had in mind for the children of the poor.[11] Factory work by children, however, aroused opposition almost from its outset. In part this opposition was utilitarian. It was asserted that the damage done to children's physique by prolonged early labour was so severe that it would have damaging effects on the reproduction of society. Society, or rather the state, was warranted in interfering in the market for labour in the interests of its own survival. In terms of laissez-faire, the dominant economic ideology of the time, this departure from free market principles could be further justified on the grounds that children up to the age of fourteen were not 'free agents', and could not therefore negotiate a contract. Evangelicalism provided a second source of opposition to factory labour. Wilberforce had been concerned about it, and Shaftesbury made it part of his life's work. Shaftesbury's chief concern, as he never ceased to assert, was to provide education for all children so that they could read the Bible and come within the means of salvation. These two views, the utilitarian and the evangelical, had many points of contact, and were almost certainly decisive in moulding the shape of the Factory Acts as they emerged from 1833 onwards. Moreover, the task of drawing up and implementing the Acts led the utilitarians to reflect on the role of the state in the protection of children. Thus Leonard Horner, the factory inspector, set the blame for what was going wrong in the factories at the feet of parents, and had little truck with paternal rights; 'If the father has his natural rights', he wrote, 'so has the child; and if the father robs him of these, the State must become his guardian, and restore them to him'. The Benthamite journal, the *Westminster Review*, had a similar view of the rights of the child and of the duty of the state to uphold them: 'every child has a moral right to maintenance and education, exempt from any such amount of labour as shall prevent its attaining a physical development, and a religious, moral, and intellectual cultivation, sufficient to enable it to provide for its own future wants and happiness with benefit to the community at large'. There should thus be a law 'defining generally the rights of infancy, and rendering it obligatory on the part of parents and the employers of labour to respect those rights to the extent required for the proper exercise of the faculties of mind and body. If the means of education and of a proper industrial training be wanting, let them be provided by the state'.[12]

The utilitarians, then, were anxious to see some restrictions of parental rights in order to ensure that children received that maintenance, protection and education which Blackstone had set out as their right. But in their discussions of child labour, neither the utilitarians nor the evangelicals asserted that it was an offence against the nature of childhood for children to work. It was romanticism which did that.

The Romantic poets had seen childhood as not simply innocent, but as imbued with qualities which in essence were God-given. Evangelicals like Hannah More continued to argue that it was 'a fundamental error in Christians, to consider children as innocent beings, whose little weaknesses may perhaps want some correction, rather than as beings who bring into the world a corrupt nature and evil dispositions'.[13] Wordsworth, by contrast, wrote that 'Heaven lies about us in our infancy'. However uneasily such a sentiment lies with Wordsworth's own adherence to a concept of the child as a *tabula rasa*, it became, as Coveney has put it, 'a *locus classicus* for the whole literature of childhood in the nineteenth century'. Childhood in this perspective was a privileged part of our lives, the time when we were naturally closest to God, to heaven, and to nature. Any adult who failed to respect that time of childhood committed an unpardonable sin. And adults manifestly did this, and most blatantly they did it by putting children to early hard work. Southey and Wordsworth expressed in print their outrage at child labour in factories and Coleridge campaigned actively for a Factory Act. Their view of childhood was widely disseminated and elaborated upon, and became embedded in the rhetoric of the factory movement of the 1830s and 1840s. Thus Philip Gaskell in his survey of factory conditions in his book *Artisans and Machinery* (1836) referred directly to Wordsworth's 'Intimations of Immortality from Recollections of Early Childhood' in writing that:

> It has been truly observed, and not less beautifully than truly, that 'heaven is around us in our infancy'. This might have been extended, and said, that 'heaven is around and within us in our infancy', for the happiness of childhood springs full as much from an internal consciousness of delight, as from the novelty of its impressions from without. Its mind, providing the passions are properly guided, is indeed a fountain of all that is beautiful — all that is amiable — overflowing with joy and tenderness; and its young heart is a living laboratory of love, formed to be profusely scattered on all around.

Childhood here is a fountain irrigating the arid soils of adulthood. It came indeed to be seen as some recompense to mankind for the loss of Eden. It was, or should be, 'the weary life's long happy holyday', the archaic spelling of holiday emphasising the place which childhood had in God's plan for mankind.[14]

Armed with this kind of vision, the assertion of the rights of childhood became imbued with an emotional quality lacking in the utilitarian and evangelical perspectives. Reason gave precedence to feelings, and those feelings were brought to bear on children in the factories and mines and up the chimneys. Parental rights became as nothing in conflict with the rights of children. Indeed, the issue became not children versus parents, but children versus 'the factory system', a new and unnatural mode of production, one of whose chief characteristics seemed to be an inevitable tendency to replace adult labour by child labour.[15] Whereas in nature the young devoted their time to growing and playing, in human society, or at least in the factory system, the young were put to work. As Elizabeth Barrett Browning put it in 'The Cry of the Children'.

The young lambs are bleating in the meadows,
   The young birds are chirping in the nest,
The young fawns are playing with the shadows,
   The young flowers are blowing toward the west —

But the young, young children, O my brothers,
They are weeping bitterly!
They are weeping in the playtime of the others,
In the country of the free.[16]

To the English the offence against childhood was compounded by the fact that it was occurring in 'the country of the free' — in England. But in essence what Browning and others influenced by romanticism were demanding was a childhood for all children everywhere which was in harmony with nature, and in which manual labour had no part. 'Ever a toiling *Child* doth make us sad', wrote Samuel Roberts of Sheffield in 1837. Three years later Douglas Jerrold, one of the founders of *Punch*, was to write of factory children that they were 'children without childhood'.[17] He did not need to elaborate: the romantics had helped to fix in the English mind an idea of what childhood should be. And it spread far beyond England. When American progressives set up, rather belatedly, in the early twentieth century, a National Child Labor Committee, they did so because, in the words of one spokesman, 'The term child labour is a paradox for when labour beings . . . the child ceases to be'; and in the words of another, 'To make profit out of a child was to "touch profanely a sacred thing"'.[18]

The second phase in the construction of the idea of a proper childhood came in the second half of the century when the attention of reformers turned from the factory child to the children of the poor on the street and in the home. They were engaged in an attempt to rescue children from what most of them saw as cruel and neglectful parenting. As one looks at these rescue campaigns, one cannot help noting, as in factory reform, the part played by evangelicals, and other Christians, and by utilitarianism. Shaftesbury himself, with his involvement in the Ragged School movement, was the key figure in the transition to the focus on street children from the early 1840s. His successor in many ways was Barnardo, deflected from his intention to serve as a missionary in China by his encounter with the street arabs of London. Denominational rivalry led to the establishment of another key rescue institution, the Anglican Waifs and Strays Society. Alongside, and often embedded in this Christian missionary work, there was a utilitarian mode of thinking which linked the future of the nation with the fate of children, and demanded action by the state. Gertrude Tuckwell in 1894 summarised the situation as many publicists and reformers saw it: 'Among the social problems with which the nation has to deal', she wrote, 'there is none . . . so important as the question of the children. The wise treatment of this question by us must affect the eventual solution of all other social problems. . .'[19]

Tuckwell was drawing on a body of writing which asserted the rights of children, but did so out of concern for the future of the state. Thus in 1886 Alfred Mager, in a pamphlet entitled 'Children's Rights', set out the scale of the problem. There were, he estimated (though without telling us how he arrived at this figure) 750,000 'neglected and famished children' under fourteen, 'a double line, shoulder to shoulder, reaching from Manchester to York; a procession, four abreast, a yard only between each four, stretching from sea to sea — from Preston to Hull; or say, reaching from London to Bath; or from Bolton to Birmingham, and some miles beyond. Watch this vast army of little unkempt, ragged, almost naked starvelings as they quickly march, with bare feet, past your door.' Having aroused our sympathy in the language of romance, Mager then changed his tone: if these children, he went on, continued to be 'left alone by the Church and the State, they will inevitably grow up to propagate their vile class and to inflict a terrible retribution upon the society that neglects them'. We should, argued Mager, resist 'the selfish laissez-faire policy' and 'ask our reason and conscience why Society and the State should allow these poor children to be deprived of their natural rights to proper food, raiment, warmth and comfort. . .'[20]

Even more emphatically Mary Tabor claimed that 'The mass of chronic poverty, of pauperism, disease, and crime which at this moment clogs the wheels of progress, and which forms one of the most insoluble problems of modern life, has its origin mainly in the refusal or neglect of the natural claims of children'. Every child, she wrote, 'possesses as its birthright a claim to the minimum of clothing, shelter, food, and training needed to fit it for becoming in due time a self-supporting member of the community'; the neglect of these claims was 'a menace to the peace and security of society itself'. The rights of children, she concluded, were therefore 'identical with the interests of the State'.[21]

I do not in any way wish to suggest that either the Christian mission work or the voice of utilitarianism did not influence events. Between them, for example, they seem to me to have led to compulsory schooling. But on their own they do not lead to or enforce the idea of a child's right to a childhood. It was again the imprint from romanticism which did that.

In what we may see as the second generation of romanticism, with Dickens as the key figure, the idea of the child as a messenger from God was given a natural extension: the adult who failed to keep the child in him or herself alive became twisted and embittered and could be rescued and saved most appropriately by a child. Children then may themselves need to be rescued, three-quarters of a million of them according to Alfred Mager, but children may also be instruments for the rescue of adults. Consider the miser Silas Marner who was rescued by Eppie: 'the little child', wrote Eliot, 'had come to link him once more with the whole world. There was love between him and the child that blent them into one, and there was love between the child and the world — from men and women with parental looks and tones, to the red lady-birds and the round pebbles.' Those red lady-birds and round pebbles signify the identity between child and nature, crucial to the child's

8

power. And power it is. 'In old days', concluded Eliot, 'there were angels who came and took men by the hand and led them away from the city of destruction. We see no white-winged angels now. But yet men are led away from threatening destruction: a hand is put into theirs, which leads them forth gently towards a calm and bright land, so that they look no more backward; and the hand may be a little child's.'[22]

The hand increasingly frequently was that of a little child. Christians lost their sense that original sin was the most important fact about a child; their thinking about children became infused with romanticism.[23] Children themselves, even in unlikely circumstances, took on characteristics which made them not only good but also messengers from and close to God. Missionaries learned from Ruskin who in 1867 recorded how in walks through 'the black district of St Giles's' 'I often see faces of children . . . which, through all their pale and corrupt misery, recall the old "Non Angli"', and recall it, not by their beauty, but their sweetness of expression. . .'[24] Reformers talked about 'the romance of the slums' where there was indeed beauty beneath rags, and where children exercised a curious power over adults who worked with them: 'charm' was the word used to describe the effect on them of these children.[25] If you have a restless daughter, wrote Kate Wiggin, get her to do voluntary work with poor children in a Kindergarten: 'No normal young woman can resist the influence of the study of childhood and the daily life among little children, especially the children of the poor: it is irresistible'.[26]

The Kindergarten child had been rescued from the street, and it was the street child who evoked most of this emotion and sentimentalising; who, as it were, became the emblem of a debased romanticism. A proper childhood should be spent at home or at school and in the countryside. The street child was in none of these places, but was nevertheless the child most frequently written about, painted and photographed.

The fiction about street children was produced for the children's market, much of it under the imprint of the Religious Tract Society.[27] It presented children who rescued their fellow children or adults, *Ministering Children* (1854) as Mrs Charlesworth called them. If they died, as they often did, their goodness alone would save them from the hellfire so often held out as their fate in the eighteenth century. A typical example of the genre goes under the title, *Froggy's Little Brother.* Froggy, so called because of the croak in his voice, is left an orphan and with the care of a younger brother, Benjy. His struggles to survive on the street eventually overcome him, and he dies a good death. Fortunately two concerned old Wykehamists come to the rescue of Benjy, and place him in a home, and give him a taste of country air.[28]

Visual images of the children of the poor were a matter of great concern. Ruskin, for example, in 1853 delivered a fierce attack on painting a street child like Murillo had done in seventeenth-century Spain: there were examples in the Dulwich Gallery.

Look at those two ragged and vicious vagrants that Murillo has gathered out of the street. You smile at first, because they are eating so naturally, and their roguery is so complete. But is there anything else than roguery there, or was it well for the painter to give his time to the painting of those repulsive and wicked children? Do you feel moved with any charity towards children as you look at them? Are we the least more likely to take any interest in ragged schools, or to help the next pauper child that comes in our way, because the painter has shown us a cunning beggar feeding greedily? Mark the choice of the act. He might have shown hunger in other ways, and given interest to even this act of eating, by making the face wasted, or the eye wistful. But he does not care to do this. He delighted merely in the disgusting manner of eating, the food filling the cheek . . . observe another point in the lower figure. It lies so that the sole of the foot is turned towards the spectator; not because it would have lain less easily in another attitude, but that the painter may draw, and exhibit, the grey dust engrained in the foot. Do not call this the painting of nature; it is mere delight in foulness.

Ideally the children of the people should be peasants — rough, picturesque, healthy, but this tradition was on the wane; the impact of the French and Industrial Revolutions seemed, Ruskin said, to have compelled 'our painters to represent the children of the poor as in wickedness or misery'.[29] It was misery which was to dominate. A critic in 1890, Mrs H.M. Stanley, described a tradition of depicting 'ragged life' which seemed to her 'false and made up. [The children] were all so deplorably piteous — pale, whining children with sunken eyes, holding up bunches of violets to heedless passers-by; dying match girls, sorrowful water-cress girls, emaciated mothers clasping weeping babies'.[30] By then Ruskin felt that the problem had been solved: children were being painted as beautiful: 'you have the radiance and innocence of reinstated divinity showered again among the flowers of English meadows by Mrs Allingham and Kate Greenaway'.[31] Mrs Stanley, by contrast, wanted to return to the tradition of Murillo's 'Beggar Boys' — the precise object of Ruskin's criticism — and to depict the 'merry, reckless, happy-go-lucky urchin; the tom-boy girl'. This required some ingenuity on her part, as she describes: in her walks through London, she writes, 'the first interesting object I must have seen was doubtless some dear little child in tatters'. But not quite sufficiently in tatters. Having decided on the subject matter of a picture, you needed, she advised, to collect the children from the street. 'A good supply of rags is essential (carefully fumigated, camphored, and peppered), and you can then dress up your too respectable ragamuffin till he looks as disreputable as you can wish'. An alternative method was 'to find an average boy, win his confidence, give him sixpence, and promise him another sixpence if he will bring you a boy more ragged than himself. This second boy must be invited to do the same, and urged to bring one yet more "raggety". You can in this way get down to a very fine specimen. . .'[32]

Here were three traditions of depicting children, each of them in their way thoroughly romantic. The first called forth pity; the second celebrated the innocence and divinity of the child; and the third suggested that the natural qualities of the child could survive and thrive in an urban and industrial environment. Mrs Stanley, however, would have had plenty of critics who would have told her that she was wrong. These street children, it would be admitted, had an inner resourcefulness which was lacking in adults, but in the city, it was claimed, it would burn up and be exhausted. An urban childhood was, quite simply, unnatural. Edith Nesbit, writing for children in *Five Children and It* (1902), put the matter simply: 'London is like prison for children especially if their relations are not rich . . . London has none of those nice things that children may play with without hurting the things or themselves — such as trees and sand and woods and waters. And nearly everything in London is the wrong sort of shape — all straight lines and flat streets, instead of being all sorts of odd shapes, like things are in the country. . . This is why so many children who live in towns are so extremely naughty.'[33]

It was of course impossible in the late nineteenth century to conceive of a Britain in which children were brought up entirely in the country; the desirability of so doing, however, was one reason why countenance could be given to the emigration of the 80,000 children who went to Canada in the late nineteenth and early twentieth centuries: in the name of securing them a childhood, it may be said to have been a major infringement of their rights as human beings, for they were in effect transported.[34] More prosaically there might be country holidays for children, a major philanthropic endeavour, or nature might be brought into the classroom. In all this philanthropy there was an endorsement of the romantic vision that childhood and nature should be indissolubly linked.

The children of the street were quite likely to be perceived as the victims of parental cruelty. We have seen that children did in fact have some protection against parental cruelty before the foundation of the NSPCC and the passage of the 1889 Prevention of Cruelty to Children Act. Indeed one of the initial aims of the London Society for the Prevention of Cruelty to Children was, as Cardinal Manning put it, to create 'a living, active motive-power . . . to put the statute in force'. Moreover, like the Liverpool Society which was the first to be set up in Britain, the London Society was as much concerned with prevention and with setting up a shelter for children as it was with prosecution.[35] What was new with the NSPCC was that 'the cruelty man' provided a means of bringing a case to public attention.

What is also clear is that the founders of the NSPCC were deeply imprinted with a romantic conception of the child. In their seminal article, 'The Child of the English Savage', the Roman Catholic, Cardinal Manning, and the Congregationalist, Benjamin Waugh, counterposed the savage parent to the innocent child, for a child, they wrote, 'is not only made in the image of God, but of all His creatures it is the most like to Himself in its early purity, beauty, brightness, and innocence'.[36] It was that romantic image of what a child ought to be, contrasted with the reality, which was the inspiration for the NSPCC.

In the late nineteenth century the question of the rights of children was seen almost entirely as a matter of state enforcement of what were perceived to be parental duties. These included, as we have seen, from 1876 the duty to cause a child to receive an education. It was followed by a succession of Prevention of Cruelty to Children Acts in 1889, 1894, and 1904, and by the Children's Act of 1908, each of which sought to provide legal enforcement of parental duties, and punishment of parental neglect or cruelty. The state and the child were ranged together against errant parents.

These Acts were often called 'The Children's Charter'. What they sought to do was to put into legislative form the differentiation between child and adult which was at the heart of the late romantic image of the child. If we may discern a consistent project in the work of philanthropists and publicists of the later nineteenth and early twentieth centuries, it may be said to be to drive a space between childhood and adulthood. For such people childhood was or should be a privileged time, secure, protected, defended. In the middle and upper class worlds this was indeed a reality, even if accompanied by an extraordinary distancing between children and parents. What was needed was to mark off a similar space for working-class children: to take them out of adult space — the streets and pubs and theatres — and out of the reach of adult institutions — the prison, the general mixed workhouse, the magistrate's court — so that they were insulated from the corrupting adult world. Children's rights therefore amounted to this right of insulation. It was not surprising that a 1960s response to this was to demand for children right of access to that adult world. In the nineteenth century and for much of the twentieth century the rights of children were bound up with a perception of childhood as sharply distanced from adulthood.

In 1799 the Evangelical Hannah More noted with disapproval how discussion of the rights of man, as articulated by Thomas Paine, had been succeeded by claims being made for the rights of women. 'It follows', she wrote, '. . . that the next influx of that irradiation which our enlighteners are pouring in upon us, will illuminate the world with grave descants on the *rights of youth*, the *rights of children*, the *rights of babies!*'[37] It was not a prospect which she in any way welcomed. What she feared was that the rights claimed for youths, for children and for babies would be the kind of rights which, in Paine's view, belonged to any human being as a birthright. More was correct in her forecast that people would claim rights for children, but she might have been reassured if she had lived to read these claims. For the rights to which children had an entitlement were not thought to be fundamental human rights, rights that is which might apply to people of all ages. On the contrary, they were rights which were specific to children, and in many ways the opposite of adult rights. Thus if adults had a right to work, as many people asserted at the end of the nineteenth century, children had an equal right not to work. For children, if not for adults, what we might now call 'a dependency culture' was a natural right; a child had a right 'to be a child'.[38] A person's status as a child overrode differences amongst children, whether of gender, race, class, or nationality. In Benjamin Waugh's words, 'The rights of a child are its birthrights. The Magna Carta of them, is a child's nature. The Author, its Creator'.[39] That view of childhood underlay the Declaration of the Rights of the Child by the League of Nations in 1924, and the United Nations Declaration of the Rights of the Child in 1959; the ground has shifted slightly in the 1990 United Nations Convention on the Rights of the Child, but in everyday thinking we are at one with Kate Wiggin in her assertion a century ago of the child's 'right to his childhood'. If proof is needed, it comes conveniently to hand in the *Observer Magazine*: in a feature on 'Children of our times: the end of innocence?', it drew on photographs from around the world, many of them indicating that the self-proclaimed 'Century of the Child' had failed its children; and it ended with a rhetorical question posed by Suzanne Moore: 'Who among us', she asks, 'would not insist [on] the right of every child to childhood itself?'[40] She knew that all of her readers would insist on that right; probably I was the only one to even pause. What I hope to have done in this paper is to explain how the question became uncontroversial, how it was that we have come to accept in the twentieth century that a child has an inalienable right to childhood.

I have been describing the genesis of a view of childhood which is still very prevalent, so much so that it is, as an ideology, part of the world we take for granted. It might be argued that such a view of childhood derives from nature. The historical record does not lend support to that. On the contrary, the view of childhood which I have described is a relatively recent phenomenon. And it has not simply become part of our culture at an ideological level, it has also deeply affected the way our world is organised from the building up of the welfare state to the formation and activities of the plethora of organisations which exist to rescue children from hunger, from neglect, from cruelty and from war. If we can identify and try to help children 'at risk', it is because we have inherited from the nineteenth century a sense of what it is to be 'not at risk'.

References

1. I. Pinchbeck and M. Hewitt, *Children in English Society*, 2 vols (London, 1969-73), Vol.2, pp.347-61, quoting p.351.

2. A.M. Platt, *The Child Savers: The Invention of Delinquency* (2nd ed., Chicago & London, 1977), pp.193-8.
3. P. King, 'Decision-Makers and Decision-Making in the English Criminal Law, 1750-1800', *Historical Journal*, 27 (1984), pp.34-45.
4. G.K. Behlmer, *Child Abuse and Moral Reform in England, 1870-1908* (Stanford, 1982), pp.2, 6; see also Pinchbeck & Hewitt, *Children in English Society*, Vol.2, p.611.
5. L. Pollock, *Forgotten Children: Parent-child relations from 1500 to 1900* (Cambridge, 1983), pp.91-5; *The Times*, 17 Nov., 6 Dec., 8 Dec., 1824.
6. *The Times*, 8 Jan., 1884. But see also H. Ferguson, 'Cleveland in history: the abused child and child protection, 1880-1914', in R. Cooter (ed), *In the Name of the Child: Health and Welfare, 1880-1940* (London, 1992), p.152.
7. W. Blackstone, *Commentaries on the Laws of England*, 4 vols (Oxford, 1765; repr. London, 1966), Vol.1, pp.434-42.
8. L. Rose, *The Erosion of Childhood* (London, 1991), pp.233-4; 4 & 5 William IV, c.76, s. lvi; 31 & 32 Vict. c.122, s.37.
9. H. Cunningham, *The Children of the Poor: Representations of Childhood since the Seventeenth Century* (Oxford, 1991), p.56; 54 Geo. III, c. ci. See also the 1861 Offences against the Person Act, 24 & 25 Vict. c.100, s.27, 43, 56.
10. Blackstone, *Laws of England*, Vol.I, p.439; 39 & 40 Vict. c.79, s.4.
11. Blackstone, *Laws of England*, Vol.I, p.439.
12. Cunningham, *Children of the Poor*, pp.50-96. See also J.S. Mill, *Utilitarianism, Liberty and Representative Government* (London: Everyman edn., 1910), pp.73, 160.
13. 'Strictures on Female Education', in *The Works of Hannah More*, 18 vols (London, 1818), Vol.7, p.67.
14. Cunningham, *Children of the Poor*, pp.50-96; P. Coveney, *Poor Monkey: The Child in Literature* (London, 1957), pp.1-51, quoting p.39.
15. Cunningham, *Children of the Poor*, pp.83-5.
16. 'The Cry of the Children', *Selected Poems of Elizabeth Barrett Browning*, ed. M. Forster (London, 1988), p.179.
17. S. Roberts, *A Cry from the Chimneys: Or an Integral Part of the Total Abolition of Slavery throughout the World* (London, 1837), p.35; D. Jerrold, 'The Factory Child', in *Heads of the People*, (1840; 2 vols, London, 1864), Vol.1, p.188.
18. Quoted in V. Zelizer, *Pricing the Priceless Child: The Changing Social Value of Children* (New York, 1985), pp.6, 55.
19. G. Tuckwell, *The State and its Children* (London, 1894), Preface.
20. A.W. Mager, *Children's Rights* (Bolton, 1886).

21. M. Tabor, 'The Rights of Children', *Contemporary Review*, Vol.54 (1888), pp.408-17.
22. G. Eliot, *Silas Marner* (1860), ch.14.
23. This process has not been studied in any detail for Britain. For America, see B. Wishy, *The Child and the Republic: The Dawn of Modern American Child Nurture* (Philadelphia, 1968), pp.11, 17-18, 22, 51, 96, 99, 108-9, and A.M. Boylan, 'Sunday Schools and Changing Evangelical Views of Children in the 1820s', *Church History*, Vol.48 (1979), pp.320-33. I am indebted to Dr Doreen Rosman for this latter reference. The decline in belief in hell and everlasting damnation is examined in G. Rowell, *Hell and the Victorians* (Oxford, 1974). For the 'Christian Rousseauism' of Charles Kingsley, see Coveney, *Poor Monkey*, pp.63-4. For changing attitudes in Sunday Schools, see S.J.D. Green, 'The Religion of the Child in Edwardian Methodism: Institutional Reform and Pedagogical Reappraisal in the West Riding of Yorkshire', *Journal of British Studies*, Vol.30 (1991), pp.377-98, and M.M.B. Bolton, 'Anglican Sunday Schools 1880-1914', Unpublished University of Kent MA Thesis, 1988.
24. J. Ruskin, *Time and Tide* (1867), in *The Library Edition of the Works of John Ruskin*, 39 vols (London, 1903-12), Vol.XVII, p.406.
25. Cunningham, *Children of the Poor*, pp.160-1.
26. K.D. Wiggin, *Children's Rights: A Book of Nursery Logic* (New York, 1892; London, n.d.), pp.44-5.
27. See J.S. Bratton, *The Impact of Victorian Children's Fiction* (London, 1981).
28. 'Brenda', *Froggy's Little Brother* (London, n.d. [1875]). A key writer in this vogue was Hesba Stretton, on whom see Bratton, *Impact of Victorian Children's Fiction*, pp.81-97.
29. 'The Stones of Venice', 'The Art of England', in *Library Edition of the Works of John Ruskin*, Vol.X, pp.228-9; Vol.XXXIII, pp.338-9. On the popularity of Murillo in England, and in particular of the two Dulwich pictures of boys, see A. Braham, *El Greco to Goya: The Taste for Spanish Paintings in Britain and Ireland* (London, 1981), pp.3-44, 87.
30. Mrs H.M. Stanley, *London Street Arabs* (London, 1890), pp.5-6. See also J. Treuherz, *Hard Times: Social Realism in Victorian Art* (London and New York, 1987), pp.29-35, 107-8; H.D. Rodée, 'Scenes of Rural and Urban Poverty in Victorian Painting and their Development, 1850 to 1890', unpublished Columbia University Ph.D. Thesis, 1975, pp.124-239.
31. 'The Art of England', *Library Edition of the Works of John Ruskin*, Vol.XXXIII, pp.340-2.
32. Stanley, *London Street Arabs*, pp.5-8.

33. E. Nesbit, *Five Children and It* (Harmondsworth, 1959), p.20; for the sense that the city was an unnatural environment for children, see Cunningham, *Children of the Poor*, pp.146-51.
34. J. Parr, *Labouring Children* (London, 1980).
35. R. Waugh, *The Life of Benjamin Waugh* (London, 1913), pp.144, 147, 282-3; see also Hesba Stretton's letters to *The Times*, 8 Jan., 26 May, 30 June, 1884.
36. Cardinal Manning and B. Waugh, 'The Child of the English Savage', *Contemporary Review*, Vol.49 (1886), pp.687-700.
37. *The Works of Hannah More*, Vol.7, p.170.
38. E. Rossiter, 'Child Life for Children', *Nineteenth Century*, Vol.10 (1881), p.568.
39. Waugh, *Life of Benjamin Waugh*, p.296.
40. Wiggin, *Children's Rights*, p.10; *Observer Magazine*, 25 Apr., 1993, p.42.

ENFORCING SCHOOL ATTENDANCE IN LATE VICTORIAN ENGLAND: AN INVESTIGATION INTO THE ACTIVITIES OF RURAL SCHOOL BOARDS IN THE EAST RIDING OF YORKSHIRE

Leigh M Davison

Two recent studies[1] focused attention on the work of School Attendance Committees in the East Riding during the period 1877-1903. A further paper[2] explored the policy of the Hull School Board with regard to the enforcing of school attendance in the city. Another forty-two School Boards were formed in the Riding, and it is the aim of this paper to provide an insight into their respective attitudes towards duties imposed, by statute, on each of them concerning the illegal employment of school children and the compelling of attendance within their districts. By examining these matters, the paper will shed light upon why some School Boards, for part or all of their history, neglected to deal with the problem of non-attendance. For example, it will show that a small minority of Boards repeatedly had difficulty in ensuring sufficient members were present for the meetings to be deemed quorate. In addition the relationship between the local magistracy and the Riding's School Boards, regarding non- attendance prosecutions brought by the latter, is investigated.

Fortunately, concerning these School Boards, a wealth of primary material exists, particularly in the case of minute books. However, for Sutton and Stoneferry School Board, no documents were found. A similar but not quite so desperate position is true for Burstwick School Board; the surviving minutes do not cover the years between 1882 and 1894. In the case of Newington School Board, established in 1879, the issue is not data but longevity: it being swallowed up by the Hull School Board in 1883. Five of the School Boards — Blacktoft, Langton, Langtoft, Scalby and Yedingham — were not established until the 1890s, the rest being formed in the previous two decades. With the Hull School Board serving its only city, the rural nature of the East Riding in the late Victorian period is revealed.

To be in a position to carry out fully the duties placed upon it by the 1870 Elementary Education Act a School Board had to meet regularly and, of course, have sufficient members present for these meetings to be quorate.

Within the East Riding, a small number of School Boards, though not necessarily at the same time, failed frequently over a number of years to have enough members in attendance at meetings to satisfy their respective quorum requirements. The three worst offenders were Faxfleet, Spaldington and Preston School Boards; a second division of Boards whose individual record on this matter was superior to that of the aforementioned but was still, at times, less than satisfactory comprised of Eastrington, Barmby-on-the-Marsh, Hedon, Hornsea, Holmpton, Melbourne and Atwick.

The appalling record of Spaldington and Preston School Boards, in terms of the annual number of inquorate meetings each attained during the 1880s and 1890s, is revealed in their respective minute books. Likewise, a near identical situation arose at Faxfleet in the 1890s and on into the new century. In addition, during the late 1880s, the Faxfleet Board failed to meet regularly — gaps between meetings of three and four months being common. This laxity on the part of the Board may be partially explained by the Board having no elementary school within its district; Faxfleet children attended school in neighbouring parishes, particularly at Broomfleet. In recognition of this, Faxfleet School Board was made contributory to Broomfleet School Board by the Education Department. In 1890, attempts by the Broomfleet Board to correspond with Faxfleet School Board over the latter's non-payment of monies, proved that it was no longer a question of the infrequency of the Faxfleet Board's meetings, but whether the Board met at all. The minutes of Broomfleet School Board meeting held on 17 May 1890 state:

> The Clerk stated that Mr Reed [a member of the Broomfleet board representing the interests of Faxfleet] ... had returned to him (the Clerk) the Precept issued by this board ... saying that as the Faxfleet School Board have had no meeting, therefore no Chairman or Correspondent appointed, would this Board prepare another Precept made out to the Overseers of Faxfleet instead of the Faxfleet School Board [sic][3]

Eventually the matter was passed on to the Education Department which promptly acted to bring the Faxfleet Board back to life by re-appointing its former members and giving them the power to co-opt others, if necessary. The new Board met for the first time in August 1890; prior to this the Board had met in early December of 1889, a gap of just over eight months. A similar event had taken place fifteen years earlier at Hutton Cranswick. Here again, it was the unwillingness of local inhabitants to serve on the School Board that caused the crisis. Unable to find people to fill two vacancies, the remaining members of the Board, at a special meeting held on the 30 April 1875, decided unanimously to resign and pass this fact on to the Education Department. The Department duly ordered a new election and this occurred on 27 September, with the first meeting of the Board taking place in early October. Thereafter, this Board and those that followed to serve the district of Hutton Cranswick, appear to have met regularly, with enough members present for the meetings to be quorate. The same cannot be said for Faxfleet.

Concerning the above mentioned School Boards, such failures to meet or have sufficient members present at pre-arranged meetings, as well as highlighting the apathy of the local inhabitants towards ensuring that their districts' education authority functioned properly, meant that school attendance during these periods could not be compelled. In the light of earlier comments, it is hardly surprising that Faxfleet, Spaldington and Preston School Boards appear for most, if not all, of their respective histories to have shown very little interest in school attendance matters other than occasionally having printed a notice — informing parents and employers as to the by-laws governing school attendance and the employment of children and the powers available to the board to enforce these and, of course, its apparent willingness to employ them — and the issuing of warnings to the parents of poor attenders. It is apparent, though (see appendix 1) that these three School Boards, like a number of others in the Riding, were loath to prosecute the parents of non-attenders. Faxfleet School Board summoned none, and the record of Preston School Board was only marginally better.

Spaldington School Board did very occasionally prosecute the worst offenders though it is clear that poor school attendance remained a serious problem. The minutes of the Board dated 16 August 1895 read:

> ...a letter from the Education Department dated 18 June drawing attention to the unsatisfactory state of School attendance ... That in the Spaldington School the percentage of average attendance upon the number on the books was only a little more than 66 whereas the general percentage in the country was 85.19 for older children and 90.5 for infants ...[4]

In seeking to defend the undefendable, the Board in its reply pointed out that the district 'was a very scattered one'[5] geographically and also how the 'severe winter had considerably interfered with the attendance.'[6] It rightly added that 'proceedings had been taken before the Magistrates'[7] — a case of too few to late.

As noted, the above three School Boards were not alone in their reticence or sheer unwillingness to instigate legal proceedings against the parents of non-attenders. As revealed in appendix 1, seventeen of the forty School Boards studied fit into this category. These seventeen School Boards, concerning the most severe cases of poor attendance, were usually content to issue repeatedly warning notices to the parents of these children and occasionally to threaten them with prosecution. The desired result of such threats — getting the truants to attend school regularly — must, however, have been quickly undermined when the parents realised that actual prosecutions were very rare or not authorised at all.

At Broomfleet, for example, the School Board's policy of not using the courts to deal with poor attenders ensured that truancy continued to be a major problem throughout the 1890s. In June 1895 the Board received a letter from the Education Department 'complaining of the bad attendance of scholars'[8]; two months earlier, the HMI had expressed the very same concerns. In response to the aforesaid the Board ordered that a circular be sent 'to all Parents of Children who should attend school, giving notice that if better attendances are not made in the future than in the past the Board will take steps to enforce better attendance.'[9] No prosecutions were authorised, however. Four years later, in July 1899, the Education Department passed on to the Board a letter it had received from the HMI which asserted that:

> The attendance in the whole school is bad. Several children are struck off the Rolls when under 14 and without having passed any labour Standard. There has been only one prosecution for 16 years and there is no doubt the members of the Board are, in some cases, illegal employers of labour ...[10]

In reply, the School Board asserted that when the school reopened after the harvest vacation it was 'determined to enforce more regular attendance.'[11] It failed to live up to this promise. As to the claim that some members of the Board had illegally employed children, the Board informed the Education Department: 'the members of the Board have never employed children except in [the] most urgent cases.'[12] Yet, in November of 1899, Board members were again illegally employing children 'for a fortnight or three weeks ... for the potato gathering.'[13]

Ironically, at a meeting held that very same month, the Board, for the purpose of securing an improved attendance, resolved to establish (somewhat late in the day) a system which would on a monthly basis provide it with a list of poor attenders. This information would enable the Board to carry out its unanimously agreed resolution 'to take legal proceedings against all parents of children not having made satisfactory attendances'.[14] To ensure that parents became aware of its changed position towards non-attendance, the Board authorised that 'Bills be printed and published in conspicuous places in the Village, giving notice of the steps proposed to be taken ...'[15] Of course, the Education Department was duly informed about this apparent transformation. A year later, however, the Board concurred with the Education Department concerning the latters dissatisfaction over the attendance figures at Broomfleet school during the previous quarter. Yet again, the Board promised to be tough on truants in the future; this led it to issue a circular, which was sent to every parent in its district, requesting them to see that their children attend regularly in the future — prosecutions were, as before, not on the Boards agenda.

A second group of School Boards — Barmby-on-the-Marsh, Hemingbrough, Hedon, Newport Wallingfen, East Cottingwith, Rillington, Walkington and Owthorne — which, for reasons that are not always clear, have a history of prosecutions characterised by a period of three or more years in which proceedings against truants did not occur followed by a further period when prosecutions were sanctioned, or vice versa. In turn, the pattern is then repeated once or possibility twice more, or simply reverts back to being the same as in the original phase. The history of Hedon School Board will be used to illustrate this phenomenon.

During the late 1870s and early 1880s, the Hedon School Board was plagued by inquorate meetings and it showed at best only a fleeting interest in school attendance matters. In April 1881 the HMI told the Board that 'the attendance at [its] school for the past two years has been most irregular.'[16] No prosecutions followed but further inquorate meetings did. Approximately fifteen months later, with the attendance picture not having improved, the HMI reported: 'Again the average attendance is only 92 [this] being less than 60 percent of the number on the Roll.'[17] Throughout the remainder of the 1880s the Board would, from time to time, warn the parents of truants but no prosecutions were sanctioned. Suddenly, and going against its historical trend, the incumbent Board — which had already served the township of Hedon for two years without resorting to the local police court when dealing with truancy — successfully prosecuted four parents in March 1890. In fact, prior to this, no parent had been prosecuted on account of their offspring's non- attendance. Excepting 1893, proceedings were authorised by the Board in each and every year during the period from 1890 up to and including 1897. Another manifestation of this newly found zeal on the part of the Board to tackle truancy surfaced in July 1891 when it actively sought to have a very poor attender committed to an industrial school in Hull. In 1898 and 1899 no legal action was taken against the parents of poor attenders. Thereafter, however, further prosecutions occurred in 1900, 1901 and 1903. The surviving evidence fails to provide the reason(s) behind the Boards *volte-face* on its use of the local magistracy to compel the worst cases to attend school.

In general, factors such as external pressure from the Education Department or an HMI could trigger a School Board into taking a tougher line with truants, even resulting in prosecutions. However, as already revealed, a significant number of the School Boards studied in this paper were seemingly immune to such pressure and made little or no attempt to enforce attendance. Owthorne School Board failed to authorise proceedings against irregular attenders in 1881 and 1882; however, complaints from the HMI in each of the following three years about the irregularity of attendance resulted, every time, in the Board instigating legal proceedings. At Hemingbrough, in 1890, it was a change in three of the five members of the School Board, as a result of the triennial election, which directly led to a different approach to the compelling of school attendance within its district. The new Board , unlike its immediate predecessor, was not prepared to resort to the local police court when dealing with non-attenders. Thus, a significant change in the membership of a School Board, on account of the triennial election rule or other factors, could possibly have a positive, negative or no effect on the existing policy towards compelling school attendance.

The attitude of a School Board, in terms of whether or not it should prosecute poor attenders, could be shaped to some degree by the judgements of the local magistracy in such cases, and secondly, by the possible cost involved to a Board of taking out a summons against the parent of a truant. The experience of Wold Newton School Board illustrates the latter point. The Board authorised its first prosecution of a truant in July 1882, which went before the nearest magistrates court at Bridlington, but the expense to the Board was high: 9 shillings (45 pence) costs, plus 5 shillings (25 pence) expenses on behalf of the attendance officer, who represented the Board at the hearings. Thereafter, with the possible exception of a prosecution in 1895, the School Board for the remainder of the century refrained from using legal proceedings in its attempts to enforce school attendance.

For Holme-on-Spalding-Moor School Board a clash with the clerk of the local bench at Market Weighton in December 1879, over being charged 8 shillings costs as a consequence of its successfully prosecuting the parent of a truant — an attendance order being granted — did not deter it from instigating proceedings in future years. The School Board seriously considered taking the matter up with the Home Office. Over the very same issue Burstwick School Board corresponded with the Education Department in August 1880. The Board informed the Department that 'the Justices fine the parent 1s[hilling] whereas it cost the Board seven or eight shillings each summons taken out and asking their instruction upon this matter.'[18] The response of the Education Department reveals that it was not blind to this matter and had 'already communicated with the Home Office in the hope that that Department may be able to promote some measure for effecting a reduction in the amount'[19] of the fees charged.

In the said letter to the Education Department, Burstwick School Board also asserted that it was 'unable effectually to carry on the school in consequence of the Justices in the District not fining the Parents of Children the full penalty for non-attendance at shool[sic].'[20] Two months earlier, in June 1880, Keyingham School Board resolved that: 'the Clerk write to the Education Department to inform them that the magistrates do not sufficiently assist the Board in their prosecutions under the Bye Laws.'[21] Likewise Owthorne School Board, in the spring of 1890, informed the Education Department, by letter, that the outcomes of truancy cases it had taken before the local bench 'frequently fail to assist...[it] in enforcing the regular attendance of children at school.'[22] The Board went on to claim that as a rule a first offender in a truancy case was likely to receive an attendance order, with any subsequent prosecutions resulting in 'a small fine.'[23] All three above mentioned School Boards fell within the South Holderness petty sessional division of the Riding, with the sittings of the magistracy being held at Patrington.

In June 1883, the Patrington School Attendance Committee(SAC) wrote directly to the clerk of the local bench, pointing out that during the past year the committee had 'taken out 19 summonses and had 17 cases heard without obtaining a conviction.'[24] In attempting to defend the reputation of the local magistracy, the clerk stated that every non attendance case 'has been decided on its own merits',[25] though he went on to admit that the 'excuses' given by parents — 'poverty and inability to pay school fees, . . . illness of child, mother'[26] — received due consideration 'when the cases have been heard'.[27]

The evidence against the bench at Patrington appears damming, but to be in a position to fully comment upon the nature of the response of the said magistracy in school attendance cases — brought by local School Boards and the incumbent SAC — a complete record of judgements made in these prosecutions is required; however, the judgements made in truancy proceedings instigated by only Owthorne School Board and Patrington SAC are available, for 1883 to 1895 and 1885 to 1902 respectively (see appendix 2). What immediately stands out in both cases is the low dismissal rate and the fact that by far the most common judgement was the giving of an attendance order — around 45 percent of prosecutions ordered by the SAC and a colossal 74.4 percent for those brought by Owthorne School Board. This explains the earlier mentioned claim by the Board that first offenders tended to receive an attendance order, but it also suggests that a number of parents, who were subsequently prosecuted at least one more time on account of their children's truancy, were the recipients of a second attendance order instead of a fine. The minute books of the School Board by documenting a number of such instances provides support for this view.

On the question of the monetary value of fines given in attendance cases brought by these two local education authorities, the evidence shows the most common fine to be one shilling. Prior to 1890, no prosecution ordered by Owthorne School Board led to a fine that exceeded this figure and, concerning the years thereafter, the maximum penalty given in such cases was two shillings. These judgements can in no way be viewed as aiding the Board in its attempts to tackle the most severe cases of non-attendance. However, by far the majority of the prosecutions instigated by the Board were heard during the 1880s, 1890 and 1892; in other words, the prosecution data for cases brought by Owthorne School Board does not provide an insight into how the Patrington bench dealt with attendance prosecutions through out the 1890s — the Patrington SAC prosecutions data does.

It reveals that, despite the SAC regularly bringing truants before the magistracy, a fine of five shillings in such a case was not given until 1893; by the end of 1902 this fine had been the penalty received in a further 15 prosecutions. Moreover, of the 56 cases which received a fine of two shillings 51 of them went before the bench in the 1890s or early in the new century. Similarly all the cases given a three or four shilling fine took place within this time-frame as well as over two-thirds of the prosecutions which ended with the parent receiving a fine of two shillings and six pence. During the 1880s the most frequently given monetary penalty was the one shilling fine. Accepting that this evidence is based upon only one source, the results of the non-attendance prosecutions instigated by the said SAC nonetheless suggest that the local bench were willing to fine more heavily the parents of truants in the 1890s than was the case in the previous decade. The factor(s) which brought this about cannot be stated with any degree of accuracy.

Moreover, when attempting to assess the response of a particular bench serving a petty sessional division, with regard to its attitude towards school attendance prosecutions, the aforementioned analysis of the activities of the magistracy sitting at Patrington demonstrates most clearly the dangers of just relying on the surviving qualitative contemporary material; quantitative data, if available and of the necessary quality, by adding that extra dimension, can substantiate, qualify or challenge the view painted by other sources. In addition, the said analysis highlights the possibility that the nature of the response of a local bench, in such cases, could change — more severe fines, a greater use of fines relative to the granting of attendance orders and so on — over time. In turn, for the local education authorities bringing truancy cases before it, this had implications concerning their individual success or failure in enforcing attendance; Patrington SAC, in its attempts to deal with poor attenders, for example, can only have benefited when the local magistracy, from the early 1890s onwards, started imposing higher fines in a number of such cases.

In general, with the exception of a number of the judgements made by the magistrates at Patrington during the late 1870s and the 1880s, the picture that the surviving evidence reveals is of a magistracy based within the Riding which, for the most part, was supportive of both School Boards and SACs when hearing non-attendance cases.

Appendix 2 details the outcome of proceedings instigated against poor attenders by seven School Boards -Bridlington, Walkington, Hornsea, Driffield, Hedon, Hemingbrough and Owthorne — as well as five SACs: Beverley Union, Skirlaugh, Patrington, Howden and Pocklington. It clearly reveals that the local magistracy serving the Riding infrequently dismissed non-attendance prosecutions; an exception seems to have been the cases brought by Skirlaugh SAC before the magistrates sitting at Leven. For Skirlaugh SAC the extraordinarily high dismissal rate, accounting for around 36% of the attendance prosecutions it instigated in the period 1881 to 1902, is partly explained by its own ineptitude. With 15 of these 42 prosecutions being dismissed because the School Attendance Officer failed to arrive at the court at the appointed time. Moreover, of the remaining 27 prosecutions, 18 were dismissed in August 1883 'by the promise of amendment in the future'[28] on the part of the parents. Other than this judgement, and when the cases were dismissed because of the non-attendance of the School attendance officer, the Leven magistrates very rarely dismissed an attendance case brought by Skirlaugh SAC. Moreover the Leven magistracy, in truancy prosecutions authorised by Hornsea School Board during the period 1889 to 1902, dismissed less than 14 percent.

Table 1: Attendance orders as a % of known judgements given in non-attendance cases.

School Board	%	Local Bench
Owthorne, 1883-1895	74.4	Patrington
Hemingborough, 1880-1900	69.6	Howden
Driffield, 1883-1888	30.2	Driffield
Hornsea, 1889-1902	3.4	Leven
Bridlington, 1888-1899*	59.2	Bridlington
Walkington, 1878-1885	20.	Beverley
Hedon, 1890-1903	57.5	Hedon
SAC		
Patrington, 1885-1902	45.	Patrington
Howden, 1885-1902	41.8	Howden
Pocklington, 1896-1902	42.5	Pocklington
Skirlaugh, 1881-1902	18.	Leven
Beverley Union, 1882-1900	3.7	Beverley

* This figure ignores the prosecutions of truants ordered by Bridlington School Board in 1891 and 93, on account of the frequency with which the judgement given in these cases is not available.

Table 1, based upon information given in appendix 2, indicates a somewhat uneven picture concerning the granting of attendance orders by the region's magistracy when dealing with attendance prosecutions. Under section 11 of the 1876 Elementary Education Act, a first-time offender could reasonably expect to be given an attendance order and the stated evidence concerning judgements made by the Patrington, Pocklington, Bridlington and Howden courts, and those of the Driffield bench, supports this contention. The same is true regarding the attendance prosecutions ordered by Hedon School Board during the period 1890-1903. This, however, would not be an accurate interpretation of the evidence relating to how the magistracy based at Beverley and Leven dealt with non-attendance prosecutions.

According to the surviving data, the magistrates at Beverley, when deciding attendance cases instigated by both Beverley Union and Beverley Borough SACs, usually imposed a monetary penalty. However, the prosecutions brought before them by Walkington School Board, given that the data relates only to the years 1878-85 and that it concerns a relatively small number of summonses, shows a greater willingness on their part to grant attendance orders — though with only 20% of these cases resulting in such an order, the majority by far came away with a financial penalty. Similarly, the judgements made by the Leven based magistracy, in attendance cases initiated by Skirlaugh SAC and Hornsea School Board, reveal that a financial penalty, with or without an attendance order, was far more common than just giving the offender an attendance order.

Though far from complete, the evidence from across the Riding, excepting the Patrington data, on the monetary value of the financial penalty given to non-attenders, suggests that the majority were not let off lightly. In other words, fines of one shilling, or less, were the exception rather than the norm. Of course, as earlier commented upon, the magistrates at Patrington, when dealing with attendance cases brought by Owthorne School Board and Patrington SAC in the 1880s, having decided to impose a financial penalty on the parent, usually gave a fine of one shilling. Other than this, the Riding data reveals that the two most frequently given financial penalties were the two shillings and six pence fine and the five shillings fine, the latter being the maximum that could be imposed.

For Beverley Union SAC and Hornsea, Walkington and Driffield School Boards, the five shilling fine was the most common financial penalty given in the attendance prosecutions they authorised. The record of Beverley Union SAC, for example, for the period 1882-1900, shows that in nearly 44 percent of attendance prosecutions the parent came away with a fine of five shillings while only about 18 percent were fined two shillings and six pence. The attendance prosecution data for Pocklington SAC only deals with the period 1896-1902, but here again by far the most common fine was five shillings. The same appears to be true regarding cases brought before the magistracy sitting at Howden by the local SAC, although, on the grounds that a fine imposed on the parents of a truant was not always given, this cannot be stated with certainty. The Eastrington School Board attendance prosecution evidence, only covering the years 1892- 96, does show, when a financial penalty was imposed, that the Howden magistracy usually fined the guilty parent five shillings.

The surviving material reveals that by the 1880s and 1890s the local magistracy was quite prepared to use the 'last resort' in what can be termed the 'stick' approach to tackling the problem of non-attendance. Namely, the parents of the most severe cases of non-attendance — who probably had already been the recipient of one or more attendance orders as well as being repeatedly fined — were cautioned that if the child in question did not return to school forthwith and attend regularly in the future, then the child would be taken from his/her home and sent to an industrial school. However, as the following extract from the By Laws committee of the Hull School Board (dated 21 September 1880) reveals, the Riding in the late 1870s and early 1880s had insufficient industrial school places to meet demand:

The Clerk reported that the Police Magistrate had requested him to represent to the Committee the difficulty he experienced in granting summonses against persons who had been repeatedly fined, and whose children ought to be committed to Industrial Schools, but for whom there exists at present no Industrial or Truant school accommodation.[29]

Within the Riding, the city of Hull was the only provider of industrial school places. The Hull School Board provided the local industrial school with financial support; support of this nature was also provided by the Board for the industrial ship, the *Southampton*. The ship, moored on the River Humber, was deemed unsuitable for girls, but the industrial school located at Marlborough Terrace accepted both sexes at first; however, on the recommendation of the HMI of Industrial and Reformatory schools, the school in 1875 changed its policy to one of taking boys only. The result of this was that the Riding had increased provision for boys but had no industrial school places for girls — the nearest being at Leeds or Sheffield. Nearly ten years on, in 1884, the Board itself provided such accommodation for girls. Initially the school functioned in a rented house, but in June 1888 the girls were transferred to the newly erected industrial school located in Park Avenue. Also in 1884, the Board took control of Marlborough Terrace industrial school, so it became the sole provider of industrial school accommodation in the Riding. The Board, after building Park Avenue school, seems not to have taken steps to further expand the overall provision of industrial school places.

The giving of books or money as prizes for high attendance throughout the school year can be viewed as the 'carrot' approach to improving school attendance. Another variant of this being the awarding of a medal or certificate to a scholar who had met or exceeded the required number of attendances as set down by the School Board. Burton Fleming School Board, in June 1885, introduced what it termed the 'bonus' system; if a scholar made over 400 attendances, he would benefit from a reduction in school fees. Three years later, July 1888, the Board ended the system believing it to be illegal. Of course, whether such measures simply rewarded those scholars who were likely to attend well anyway is another matter. Several Boards, despite the awarding of prizes and/or certificates, still noted that irregular attendance remained a concern. Nonetheless Melbourne School Board, in March 1902, felt it necessary 'to place on record its complete satisfaction with the success of such prizes in securing a more regular attendance on the part of scholars.'[30] (It is not now possible to confirm or refute this claim.) A similar view was held by the HMI, who, in 1882, told Hedon School Board, on account of average attendance being below 60%, that 'if a fixed sum were given in prizes to the most regular scholars it would no doubt help to improve the attendance.'[31]

The minutes of thirteen of the said School Boards make no reference to the establishment of attendance prizes for scholars. Of the remainder, only around five boards — Rillington, Holmpton, Keyingham, Burton Fleming and Barmby-on-the-Marsh — sanctioned the giving of such prizes in the 1880s. In April 1881, Barmby-on the-Marsh School Board, using funds offered by a local charity, decided to give a prize to all those children who had made 'not less than 250 attendances upto the end of this month.'[32] In the following years, the Board appears to have lost interest in using the awarding of prizes as a means to improve scholars'attendance. A few other Boards acted similarly. Rillington School Board in January 1887 determined that 'a system of giving prizes to be introduced to induce the children to attend school better.'[33] This system operated up to and including 1893, but thereafter until 1897 no attendance awards were presented. The entry in the minutes of the Board for 27 May 1897 reads: 'No prizes given for sometime.'[34] A new scheme was introduced in July of the same year. Similarly Burton Fleming School Board, in July 1891, four years after the demise of its 'bonus' system, awarded prizes for good attendance. This continued until 1893; from then onwards up to the election of a new Board in May 1897 the annual giving of attendance prizes ceased. The new Board, consisting of not one member from the previous Board, reintroduced attendance prizes.

For reasons that are not clear, the 1890s and the early 1900s witnessed at least seventeen of the Riding's School Boards either introducing or re-introducing prize schemes for good attenders. East Cottingwith, in line with a request from the schoolmaster, set aside three pounds for the most regular attenders in 1893; this giving of monetary prizes continued on an annual basis into the new century. Broomfleet School Board rather late in the day, April 1900, decided to present scholars who had made 400 or more attendances in the current year with a book prize. Given, as noted earlier, that the history of the Board prior to this date was one of neglect, this desire on the part of the Board to award books as prizes for excellent attendance is clearly out of character. In November of the said year, the Board was told by the Education Department that the recent school attendance record of children in its district was not satisfactory. The promise of prizes in the form of books was obviously not in itself sufficient to ensure regular attendance; but this is hardly a surprise.

Finally, this paper turns its attention towards how the said School Boards dealt with those employers who illegally employed scholars. At least thirty of the Boards were not prepared to prosecute such employers of children. In the cases of Broomfleet, Faxfleet, South Duffield, Preston, Spaldington, Holmpton, Atwick, Thwing, Withernwick, Langtoft, Wold Newton, Skerne and Blacktoft School Boards this is not out of character, for it has already been established that these Boards, with regard to the prosecution of non-attenders, either decided against such a policy or did so very rarely. Another group of School Boards — including Cottingham, Great Driffield, Holme-on-

Spalding-Moor and Rillington — who each have a superior record in terms of prosecuting the parents of poor attenders, likewise limited their efforts in cases of illegal employment to issuing warnings and/or the putting up of notices pointing out the law on the employment of children and threatening proceedings against any party who broke it.

In October 1887 Burton Fleming School Board, having previously that year held a special meeting to discuss the issue of poor attendance, resolved that 'Notice be given to all whom it may concern that legal proceedings will at once be taken against any person who thereafter employs any child under ten years of age unless such child holds a labour certificate.'[35] This threat was never translated into action on the part of the Board even though, at times, attendance was low; in November 1890, for example, the average attendance reached only 71%, neither illness nor inclement weather being the cause. Likewise Bridlington School Board, in July 1888, determined that 'in future when the non attendance of any child is caused by such child being employed, the employer be proceeded against as well as the parent.'[36] In October of the following year, the Board duly prosecuted six people for illegally employing scholars: one case was dismissed, the remainder each received a fine. Prior to these proceedings, Bridlington School Board had often resorted to the local police court when dealing with the parents of non-attenders but the most an employer had received from the Board was a written warning . The Board went on to prosecute at least another five employers.

Like Bridlington, Bubwith, Reighton, Barmby-on-the-Marsh, Fridaythorpe, Eastrington and Hutton Cranswick School Boards authorised proceedings against individuals accused of employing scholars. For these Boards, with the possible exclusion of Bridlington School Board, it was the exception rather than the rule to instigate proceedings against employers of child labour. Fridaythorpe School Board's decision, in June 1895, to prosecute four employers is clearly out of character: the Board previously having made no such prosecutions and also having shown very little interest in compelling school attendance within its district; post June 1895 the Board authorised no further prosecutions of employers. Similarly, it appears that Hutton Cranswick, Eastrington and Barmby-on-the-Marsh School Boards each ordered the prosecution of local employers on one occasion only.

With regard to the illegal employment of scholars, Eastrington and Barmby-on-the-Marsh School Boards are worthy of attention for a second reason. Namely, their respective minutes reveal that one or more of their members illegally employed scholars. In the case of Barmby-on-the-Marsh, the minutes of a Board meeting held in March 1882 reveal that the Education Department, in responding to a claim by the Board that children employed by Mr W Fox, a Board member, 'all held or were entitled to hold certificates enabling them to work'[37], declared:

Their Lordships found however from the examination Schedule that in accordance with sec 4 of the Act of 1880 none of these children had obtained or were entitled to certificates enabling them to be employed and that 3 of them were absolutely prohibited by reason of their age. [And] that it also appeared the Board acquiesced in their employment....[38]

The Department added that 'before considering whether they should not declare the School Board in default under Sec. 27. of the Elementary Education Act 1876, [it] wished to be furnished with any observations which the Board might have to make on the subject ...'[39] Two months later, in May, the School Board was duly declared to be in default. Sixteen years later, and again on account of illegal employment of scholars, the Board was told by the Education Department that 'if they fail to perform the duty which is imposed upon them their Lordships may have to declare the Board in default ...'[40] Contemporary material also reveals that scholars were at one time employed by a member of the Thwing School Board. The same was true at Broomfleet, as noted earlier. Other than these instances, however, it is not possible to say how common or uncommon this practice was in the Riding during the given period.

In conclusion, it has been shown that a significant minority of the School Boards studied failed to properly carry out their duties regarding the enforcing of school attendance within their respective districts. Concerning the illegal employment of children, the picture is even worse as all but a very small number of School Boards were unwilling to prosecute such employers; there is, however, evidence to suggest that certain Boards were prepared to prosecute the parents of those illegally employed non-attenders. The surviving contemporary material does not provide the necessary information for an accurate assessment of the extent to which School Board members themselves employed scholars. It does, however, reveal that, with the possible exception Patrington Bench, the local magistracy were not hostile to the work of School Boards, when the latter prosecuted non-attenders.

References

1. L.M. Davison, (a) 'School Attendance and the School Attendance committee: the East and North Ridings of Yorkshire, 1876-1880', Journal of Educational Administration and History, xvii,1, January 1986.
    (b) 'Rural education in the late Victorian era: School Attendance Committees in the East Riding of Yorkshire, 1881-1903', History of Education Society Bulletin, 45, Spring 1990.
2. L.M. Davison, 'Compulsory Schooling in a Northern City: The Policies of the Hull School Board regarding school attendance, 1871-1902', History of Education Society Bulletin, 39, Spring 1987.
3. Broomfleet School Board Minutes, Humberside County Record Office, Beverley (HCROB) SB 5/1

4. Spaldington School Board Minutes, HCROB, SB 33/1
5. *ibidem*
6. *ibidem*
7. *ibidem*
8. Broomfleet School Board, *op cit*
9. *ibidem*
10. *ibidem*
11. *ibidem*
12. *ibidem*
13. *ibidem*
14. *ibidem*
15. *ibidem*
16. Hedon School Board Minutes, HCROB, SB 15/1
17. *ibidem*
18. Burstwick School Board Minutes, HCROB, SB 7/1
19. *ibidem*
20. *ibidem*
21. Keyingham School Board Minutes, HCROB, SB 21/1
22. Owthorne School Board Minutes, HCROB, SB 26/1
23. Owthorne School Board, *ibidem*.
24. Patrington School Attendance Committee Minutes, HCROB, PUO, uncatalogued.
25. *ibidem*
26. *ibidem*
27. *ibidem*
28. Skirlaugh School Attendance Committee Minutes, HCROB, PUS, uncatalogued.
29. Report of Bye-Laws Committee, 21st September 1880; in Hull School Board Minutes 1880-1883. L.379.153. Local Studies Library, Central Library, Hull.
30. Melbourne School Board Minutes, HCROB, SB 24/1
31. Hedon School Board, *op.cit.*
32. Barmby on the Marsh School Board Minutes, HCROB, SB 2/1
33. Rillington School Board Minutes, HCROB, SB 29/1
34. *ibidem*
35. Burton Fleming School Board Minutes, HCROB, SB 8/2
36. Bridlington School Board Minutes, HCROB, SB 4/2
37. Barmby on the Marsh School Board, *op.cit.*
38. *ibidem*
39. *ibidem*
40. *ibidem* SB 2/2

Appendix One: Truancy Prosecutions authorised by selected School Boards, 1875-1902

School Board	75	76	77	78	79	80	81	82	83	84	85	86	87	88	89	90	91	92	93	94	95	96	97	98	99	1900	01	02
Preston	–	0	0	0	0	0	0	0	0	0	0	0	0	0	0	0	0	0	0	1	0	0	0	1?	0	0	0	0
Holmpton	–	–	0	0	0	0	0	0	0	0	0	2	1	0	0	0	0	0	0	0	0	0	0	0	0	0	0	0
Atwick	–	–	0	0	0	0	0	0	0	0	0	0	0	0	1	0	0	0	0	0	0	0	0	0	0	0	0	0
Faxfleet	–	–	–	–	–	–	0	0	0	0	0	0	0	0	0	0	0	0	0	0	0	0	0	0	0	0	0	0
Broomfleet	–	–	–	–	–	–	0	0	0	0	0	1	0	0	0	5	0	0	0	0	0	0	0	0	1	0	0	0
South Duffield	–	–	–	–	–	–	–	–	–	–	–	–	0	0	0	0	0	0	0	0	0	0	0	0	0	0	0	0
Blacktoft	–	–	–	–	–	–	–	–	–	–	–	–	–	–	–	–	–	–	0	0	0	0	0	0	0	0	0	0
Skerne	–	0	0	0	0	0	0	?	0	1	0	0	0	0	0	0	0	0	0	0	0	0	1	0	0	0	1	2
Thwing	–	–	–	–	–	–	1	0	0	0	0	0	1	0	1	0	0	0	0	0	0	0	1	0	0	0	1	–
Wold Newton	–	–	–	–	–	–	0	0	0	0	0	0	0	0	0	0	0	0	0	3	1?	0	0	0	0	0	1?	0
Fridaythorpe	–	–	–	–	0	0	0	0	0	0	0	0	0	0	0	0	0	0	0	3	1	1	0	3	0	0	0	0
Reighton	0	0	0	3	1	0	0	0	0	0	0	0	0	1?	0	0	0	0	0	1	2	0	0	0	1	0	0	0
Withernwick	–	–	–	–	–	–	–	–	–	–	–	–	–	–	–	–	–	0	0	0	0	0	0	?	0	0	0	0
Spaldington	0	0	0	4	4	0	0	4	0	0	0	?	?	0	0	0	4	0	0	0	+	0	0	4	0	0	0	0
Willerby	0	0	0	0	0	0	0	0	0	9	0	0	0	0	0	0	1?	0	0	0	0	0	0	0	0	0	0	0
Yedingham	–	–	–	–	–	–	–	–	–	–	–	–	–	–	–	–	–	0	0	0	0	0	0	0	0	0	0	0
Langtoft	–	–	–	–	–	–	–	–	–	–	–	–	–	–	–	–	–	–	–	–	–	0	0	0	0	0	–	–

Key

? Possible prosecution(s)

+ Prosecutions ordered but the number cannot be given.

Appendix Two (i): Judgements given to prosecutions brought by seven School Boards concerning truants.

School Boards

Driffield (1883-1888)

	Fines			AO	AO (2s.6d. in default)	Cautioned	W	NG
	5s.	2s.6d.	1s.					
	24	26	10	14	18	3	1	8
%	32.1	24.5	9.4	13.2	17	2.8	0.9	

Hornsea (1889-1902)

	Fines						AO	Adj	dis
	NS	10s.	5s.	2s.6d.	1s.	2s+3sC			
	3	2	10	4	2	1	1	2	4
%	10.3	6.9	34.5	13.8	6.9	3.4	3.4	6.9	13.8

Hemingborough (1880-1900)

	Fines		AO	Fine (unless MC produced)	NG
	5s.	2s.6d.			
	13	1	39	3	7
%	23.2	1.8	69.6	5.4	

Owthorne (1883-1895)

	Fines			AO	Adj 1 month	Dis
	1s.	1s. suspended for 1 month	25			
	4	1	2	32	1	3
%	9.3	2.3	4.7	74.4	2.3	7

Appendix Two (i) continued

Hedon (1890-1903)

	Fines						Respited with C	Respited	Dis	Ind Sch adj 1 month	Ind Sch	NG	AO
	1s.	1s+AO	1s+3sC	2s.	2s+3sC	5s.							
	1	1	2	3	1	2	1	2	1	2	1	1	23
%	2.5	2.5	5	7.5	2.5	5	2.5	5	2.5	5	2.5	1	57.5

Walkington (1878-1885)

	Fines		AO	AO+5sC	W	dis
	NS	5s.				
	1	8	4	3	3	1
%	5	40	20	15	15	5

Bridlington (1882-1899*)

	Fines						AO	Adj	dis	In Sch	NG
	5s.	3s.6d.	3s.	2s.6d.	1s.	6d.					
	46	4	1	57	24	2	219	2	2	13	11
%	12.4	1.1	0.3	15.4	6.5	0.54	59.2	0.54	0.54	3.5	

Key

Dis	Dismissed
W	Withdrawn
AO	Attendance Order
C	Costs
MC	Medical Certificate
S	Shilling(s)
NS	Fined but amount not specified in minutes
Adj	Adjourned
NG	Judgement not given in School Board minutes
*	Non-attendance prosecutions authorised by Bridlington School Board in 1891 and 1893 are excluded, on account of the majority of the judgements received not being given in the minutes.

34

Appendix Two (ii): Judgements given to prosecutions brought by five East Riding SACs concerning School Attendance Cases

SAC

Beverley Union (1882-1900)

	AO	AO+C	AO+2C	AO+3C	AO+5C	Cs	1sF+C	3sF+3C	1sF+3sC	W	Dis	NG
	6	1	3	8	1	2	3	1	2	1	12	2
%	3.66	0.61	1.83	4.88	0.61	1.22	1.83	0.61	1.22	0.61	7.32	1.22

Fines

	5s	3s6d to 3s	2s6d	1s6d	1s3d	1s	6d
	72	7	30	2	3	6	2
%	43.9	4.27	18.29	1.22	1.83	3.66	1.22

Skirlaugh (1881-1902)

	NS	AO	AO+2s6dF	5sF+C	3sF+C	3sC	1sF+C	Adj	NG	Dis
	2	21	1	2	2	2	2	1	1	42
%	1.71	17.95	0.85	1.71	1.71	1.71	1.71	0.85	0.85	35.59

Fines

	5s	3s	2s6d	2s	1s6d	1s
	9	5	19	4	3	3
%	7.69	4.27	16.24	3.42	2.56	2.56

Patrington (1885-1902)

	NS	AO	AO+C	5s+C	MT	Adj	W	NG	Dis
	1	205	3	2	3	7	4	5	33
%	0.22	44.96	0.66	0.44	0.66	1.53	0.88	1.1	7.24

Fines

	5s	4s	3s6d	3s	2s6d	2s	1s6d	1s
	16	4	1	9	21	56	4	82
%	3.51	0.88	0.22	1.97	4.60	12.28	0.88	18

Howden (1885-1902)

	NS	AO	Cs	Ind Sch	5s+C	Cautioned	No Quorum	Dis	W	Adj
		135	3	1	2	·	1	12	5	7
%		41.79	0.93	0.31	0.62		0.31	3.71	1.55	2.17

Fines

	5s	2s6d	1s	6d
	63	87	1	1
%	19.5	26.93	0.31	0.31

Pocklington (1896-1902)

	AO	Adj	W	Dis
	350	14	13	17
%	42.53	1.7	1.58	2.06

Fines

	10s	7s6d	5s	3s6d	3s	1s
	11	3	374	30	6	5
%	1.34	0.36	45.44	3.64	0.73	0.61

Key

AO	Attendance Order	W	Withdrawn
MT	A Month's Trial	Dls	Dismissed
C	Costs	NG	Judgement not given in the SAC minutes
F	Fine	NS	Fined but amount not specified in minutes
s	Shilling(s)	Adj	Adjourned

CHILD EMIGRATION TO CANADA IN LATE VICTORIAN AND EDWARDIAN ENGLAND: A DENOMINATIONAL CASE STUDY

V. Alan McClelland

When Philip Bean and Joy Melville published in 1989 their somewhat emotive book, *Lost Children of the Empire*,[1] Mgr. Michael Connelly, Secretary of the Catholic Welfare Council, felt constrained to point out that 'judgments made with the benefit of hindsight can be too condemnatory — the work of the agencies has to be seen in the social context within which they were operating at the time, particulaly as regards emotional desolation and social and economic deprivation.'[2] The authors of the book made no reference at all to the work of Fr. Thomas Seddon, the Westminster priest who perhaps did as much as any other single person to humanize the whole process of child emigration in late Victorian England and they did not consult the series of the folio volumes of Seddon's correspondence and reports, covering the period from 1867 to 1891 which are available in the Westminster Diocesan Archive. The source is a rich mine of primary material, extending to some twenty-three volumes.

This paper is an attempt to locate the emigration issue within the context of a case-study of Roman Catholic endeavour which, even for its entrepreneurial nature, was remarkable for the crusading zeal and single-minded dedication brought to bear upon the spiritual and material welfare of orphaned children.

First of all, we need to be aware of the context and scale of the problem. Although exact statistical data is not available, John Bossy has argued forcibly that in the metropolis there was a growth in the Roman Catholic population of something like 90,000 between 1767 and 1851.[3] Basing his estimates upon the parliamentary returns of 1767 and 1780 and the Census of 1851, he argues from the distribution of the parishes of Catholics returned, that more than half of the Catholics in London in the first half of the nineteenth century were either Irish or of Irish descent. He is inclined to agree with Bishop Thomas Griffiths who, in the year of his death, 1847, maintained that something like three-quarters of his London flock were of Irish origin, perhaps some 80,000 out of about 100,000 practising their faith. This, however, must be a highly conservative estimate. In London, the Irish population in 1851 was given as 156,000: in the following decade it rose to 178,000. Furthermore, F.H. Wallis in a recent study, published in 1993, *Popular Anti-Catholicism in Mid-Victorian Britain*,[4] has argued that Irish Catholics were staunch Church attenders, comparing them with their Anglican and Dissenting neighbours. The population of Liverpool, for instance, in 1851 was 376,000 and, on Census Sunday, of all Church attendances, 40% was made up of Anglicans but 33% of Roman Catholics and only 27% of Dissenters.

Where employment was concerned for the London Irish, most of it took the form of unskilled or semi-skilled labour and, while this helped to generate a certain cohesion and urban sub-culture, 'replacing the peasant sub-culture of their ancestral land,'[5] it brought its own problems. Sheridan Gilley has shown how ambivalent were English Protestant attitudes towards their pauperized Irish neighbours.[6] The latter were despised for their religious and Celtic characteristics, condemned for inebriation, violence and superstition, suspected of harbouring an alien political culture. Yet, on the other hand, the Irish community was also admired for its piety, for its fundamental sense of purity, for its industry, generosity and conviviality.

The first attempt by English Catholics to provide for the education of these poor people in London was originated in 1764 by the philanthropic involvement of Catholic merchants and traders in the metropolis, galvanized into action by a chaplain of the Sardinian Embassy. Out of this grew the Society for Educating Poor Catholic Children which, by 1815, was teaching and clothing around 700 children. A second charity was formed in 1784 for the apprenticing of the children of poor Catholic parents and yet a third charity, in 1796, was dedicated to the task of the maintenance of destitute orphans. All three societies were supported by annual subscriptions and, in 1812, were amalgamated into one, known as the Associated Catholic Charities, the precursor of the modern Crusade of Rescue. The enterprise was put on a sounder organizational and financial footing, first by Charles Butler (the nephew of Alban Butler, author of the *Lives of the Saints*, 1745) and then by Joseph Booker, a London publisher, who remained Secretary of the Associated Catholic Charities for twenty-six years.[7] In the first three years of the merger, the Associated Catholic Charities succeeded in raising donations of £2,000. In addition, there was a fourth charity established in 1803, St. Patrick's Benevolent Society, which soon established one of the largest schools in London. Under Bishop Griffiths in 1837, it was educating 450 children and caring for 14 orphans. Many of these children were girls.

Such limited and, of course, inadequate provision, was a mere drop in the ocean when compared with the need to cope with the consequences of the Irish potato famines of the 1840s. Frank Wallis has estimated that in 1847 over 296,000 Irish arrived in Liverpool alone, somewhat less than half of them being transhipped to America, 50,000 going on to other destinations in Britain: 'the remaining hundred thousand were destitute and applied for poor relief.'[8] Between 1847 and 1853, 1.4 million Irish arrived in Liverpool and 585,000 of them sought public assistance. The social deprivation which lay hidden beneath such a demographic problem was well-nigh intractable but it ensured than an emphasis was placed upon elementary education in general and 'rescue' work in particular — described by Bernard Sharratt as 'the sociologically central component of specifically English Catholicism.'[9]

The *Dublin Review* argued in 1843 that 'the first step to be taken should be to get together accurate statements of the extent of the wants of the Catholics of their respective dioceses [*sic*] as to education and religious instruction.' When the Roman Catholic hierarchy was established in England and Wales in 1850, it was estimated there were about 600,000 Catholics in the two countries but only about 25,000 were 'traditional' Catholics, that is descended from survivors of penal days.[10] The rest, apart from recent Oxford Movement converts, were of Irish origin or descent. The new Cardinal Archbishop, Wiseman, had the vision to appreciate that to weld together his diverse community and to keep alive the sense of the euphoric solidarity of the 1850s, the development of elementary schooling and its associated social works was a key factor. Such concentration which angered some members of the local Catholic gentry and squirearchy, brought together priests, people, middle-class benefactors, rich and poor in a tightly-knit social and religious enterprise.'[11]

The establishment of the Catholic Poor Schools Committee in 1847 (when Wiseman took up office as Pro-Vicar-Apostolic of the, then, London District) to receive government grants for elementary education and to be the mouthpiece of the bishops in their dealings on education with government, marked a significant watershed in the growth of the Catholic population. Roman Catholics had become eligible in 1839 for the grants of the Committee of the Privy Council, six years subsequent to the National Society and the British and Foreign School Society receiving their grants for elementary education from the Treasury.[12] Between 1848 and 1863, the Catholic schools, through the medium of the Poor Schools Committee, received £239,757 in grants and earned the right to have Catholic school inspectors paid by government and set up reformatories and industrial schools. In 1855, Wiseman opened the first Catholic reformatory for boys at Hammersmith and the first industrial school for them at Walthamstow, both receiving Home Office certification.[13] The need was great. It was estimated that in the manufacturing districts the Irish poor were building up a sturdy Catholic population: the problem lay in the slums of London, Birmingham, Liverpool, Manchester and Leeds. The people needed not only religion 'but salvation from the blight of casual employment, and the depravity begotten of squalor.'[14]

Two years before he was appointed to succeed Wiseman as Archbishop of Westminster, Henry Edward Manning had identified education for the poor and middle classes as one of the six 'wants', as he evocatively called them, of the Roman Catholic Church in England. He identified the need for new elementary schools to provide for at least 20,000 Catholic children in 1863 and, he wrote 'to find funds sufficient for this purpose a system is needed which will not only gather or ask alms of Catholics, but so address the intellect, heart, and will of the faithful as to move them to deny themselves for the accomplishment of this great and vital work.'[15] Two weeks after his consecration as Archbishop of Westminster in 1865, Manning reverted to the theme in his first Pastoral Letter to the diocese, seeking help 'in gathering from the streets of this great wilderness of men, the tens of thousands of poor Catholic children who are without instruction or training.' 'It is our first appeal to you,' he wrote 'but it will not be our last. Year by year we hope to labour for this end, and year by year to remind you of your share in this work of love.'[16] Six months later he wrote to the diocese a second time emphasizing the provision of education was to be the chief preoccupation of his episcopate. Referring to the spiritual dangers confronting Catholic children in workhouses and 'corrupted in the streets of Liverpool,' he asked 'how is it that Christians who believe in the supernatural grace of Baptism can neglect the Christian education of their children, and can even endure to see helpless unconscious souls robbed of their faith, and cast down from the grace of children of God?'[17] It was a powerful and emotive appeal and eschewed the palliative tone which had penetrated many of Wiseman's addresses to the faithful. 'In the Name of God, then, and for the love of Jesus and of His Blessed Mother, we call upon you,' he declared 'to give us the help of all your strength, and prayers, that we may never slacken until the name of every Catholic child is inscribed in the books of our schools, and not one shall grow up, so far as we are answerable, without a Christian and Catholic education.'[18] Six months later, again, he drew attention to the numbers of Catholic children in workhouse schools and, in London, he estimated the total at over a thousand. 'Hunger and thirst and nakedness drive them to the workhouse,' he declared, and, thus, 'a thousand Catholic children detained by hunger and practical maladministration of the law, are defrauded of their education in the faith, and are educated in doctrines contrary to their faith.'[19]

Manning established the Westminster Diocesan Educational Fund in 1866, a fundamental purpose of which was to 'rescue', as he put it, as many Catholic children as possible from workhouses and accommodate them in Catholic schools and orphanages. The fund was launched with a certain aplomb at a public meeting in St. James's Hall on 14 June, 1866, Manning being accompanied on the platform by a number of scions of the 'old Catholic' families. Three objectives were set before the gathering: to provide for about seven to twelve thousand Catholic children in London who were receiving no elementary education at all and who would need at least thirty new schools; to build two new reformatories and two new additional industrial schools to accommodate the numbers of Catholic children under the Law and, finally, to undertake the 'rescuing' of Catholic children in workhouses. Manning's vigour, leadership and sincerity led to the Fund being able to open twenty new day schools for children both sides of the Thames within the first year of its operation and to make provision for a thousand children in them who had not enjoyed schooling before.[20] An annual general meeting of the Fund was to be held in June of each year henceforward to help to raise money for the Fund and to report on progress.

It is with the process of 'rescue' that we are particularly concerned in this paper. It will be recalled that the Poor Law Amendment Act of 1834 had eschewed outdoor relief, poor relief now being obtained in the workhouse provision. Parishes were grouped together into 'Unions' for the purpose of workhouse provision. The Board of Guardians administered them and sought their support from the rates. Centrally the Poor Law Board was in charge until 1871, then the Local Government Board.

Under the Poor Law Act of 1864, Catholics could remove their children from the workhouses provided their own Homes held a certificate of suitability and no government financing was involved. The Guardians, however, would have to pay a suitable maintenance allowance in respect of each child so removed.

The nature of Manning's task is evident. The workhouse was reluctant to lose money as a consequence of the transfer of Catholic children and Manning had to rely on alms to support his own Homes and industrial schools. He relied, often, on private benefactions and the free services of congregations of Religious brothers and sisters. There was also a reluctance on the part of the workhouses to transfer children on religious grounds. By the 1866 Act it was laid down that a close relative of a child 'relieved in a workhouse or district school . . . may make application to the said/Poor Law/Board . . . and the Board may, if they think fit, order that such a child shall be sent to some school established for the reception/maintenance and education of children of the religion to which such child shall be proved to belong.' Records of the religious affiliation had to be kept by each workhouse. The task of securing Catholic children was often a lengthy exercise and a separate application had to be made for each child. Reactions of workhouses were varied. Some yielded children without much opposition, others fought bitterly against the idea, yet others were prepared to face litigation.

The fee laid down in 1866 to be paid in regard to each child transferred from the workhouses was 6/ — a week which many workhouses, who said they could keep a child for about 3/6d or less a week, were reluctant to pay. The Poor Law Amendment Act of 1882 reinforced this payment of 6/ — but it was made possible for London workhouses to seek help from the Metropolitan Common Poor Fund if they needed it. Even so, payment for transferred children was often sporadic or insufficient. The Seddon papers at Westminster give a comprehensive picture of the difficulties the diocese experienced in gaining access to a sufficient income to which it was entitled for the support of ex-workhouse orphans.

There are four leading clerical figures in the history of developing responsibility in the nineteenth century for orphaned children in the Westminster diocese. The first and most important is Thomas Seddon, a native of Liverpool from 1836, who was educated at St. Edmund's College at Old Hall Green in Hertfordshire, where he remained to study for the priesthood for the Westminster diocese. He was ordained in Soho in 1862 and spent five years in parochial work there before being selected by Manning to be the first Secretary of the Westminster Diocesan Education Fund, a task he was to retain, while remaining in Manning's household (and, then, that of Cardinal Vaughan) until his death in 1898. Seddon was retiring, dedicated, single-minded and friendly. He was capable of forming good relationships with government ministers and civil servants on the one hand and with young children, parents and Poor Law guardians on the other. He was well-fitted to take responsibility for the Canadian emigration venture when the process began.

For a third of his time, Seddon worked closely with the second of the priests referred to, the Rev. Lord Archibald Edward Douglas, the third son of the seventh Marquess of Queensberry, a convert to Roman Catholicism, and uncle of the poet Lord Alfred Douglas, 'Bosie', whose connection with Oscar Wilde was to achieve notoriety in the 1890s. Douglas was ordained under his own patrimony by Cardinal Manning in 1876 and immediately was recruited by Manning to take charge of St. Vincent's Home for Boys which he was to relocate in the Harrow Road. There he remained until 1887 before retiring to parochial work in his native Galloway. St. Vincent's Home had been in existence for sixteen years when Douglas took it over and had already 'rescued' 700 boys. It had been administered originally by a committee made up of members of the lay confraternity of St. Vincent de Paul. The qualification for entry to St. Vincent's was that boys should be orphans and destitute or otherwise experiencing danger to their faith and morals. Douglas had private financial resources and was willing to lavish his wealth upon the Home, impoverishing himself in the process. His was a volatile and vibrant personality, the very antithesis of Seddon's quieter make-up. He was the idol of the young men in his care and St. Vincent's soon had the reputation of being one of the happiest and caring Homes in the diocese. Douglas established an apprenticeship scheme for the older boys and he instituted workshops, a press, a bakery, and a selling-out shop as part of the foundation. He built a votive Church there, too, and dedicated it to Our Lady of Lourdes. His example was able to awaken in the Catholic community a renewed consciousness of personal responsibility and he was to be involved with Seddon in attempting to make the Canadian emigration scheme humane, efficient and well-ordered.

The remaining names that have place in the *saga* are those of the Hon. Rev. Douglas Hope, O.S.C., a cousin of Lord Archibald Douglas and a great grandson of the second Earl of Hopetown. He was a convert of 1877 and he too had private means. Hope took over responsibility for St. Vincent's Home, then acquired by the diocese, when Douglas returned to Scotland in 1887, having worked with the latter at St. Vincent's for some time prior to that date. After only three years in the post, Hope had to resign because of an attack of rheumatic fever which led to his death. Fr. William Barry, who had been successful in establishing Homes for waifs and strays in the East End of London, succeeded Hope as administrator of St. Vincent's and retained control of the Homes in Enfield and Stepney. The final name is that of Father Emanuel Bans who assisted and then succeeded William Barry in maintaining nearly 1,000 orphans and destitute girls and boys in Homes in the diocese before becoming administrator of the new, consolidated Crusade of Rescue under Cardinal Vaughan in 1902.

There were several reasons why an emigration scheme to Canada was thought to be desirable. As to the location, the Roman Catholic Church had strong roots in the country and was, indeed, the major educational force in French-speaking Canada. It had freedom to function. There was a general acceptance that the moral conditions of life in Canada were better than they were in the slums of industrial and commercial London and that rural locations in Canada would provide healthier conditions for work and a more stimulating environment. Work opportunities were better, wages reasonable and the possibilities for career development and advancement greater. *The Tablet* considered that emigration to Canada 'removes from (children) the stigma of pauperism, and enables each (child) to consider himself an individual with certain personal prospects for the future, and not mere units in some large barracks or workhouses.'[21]

Canadian families were usually receptive to children from England and, as often as not, treated them as their own. Apart from these positive issues, there were the negative ones of the impossibility 'of settling satisfactorily in life in England those children who had been brought up in (Catholic) Institutions.'[22] The latter problem was exacerbated as the century progressed by the practical abolition of the apprenticeship system and the crowding of the labour market. Canada was a healthy land and, it was argued, the children rapidly developed into strong, big men and women.

In writing to Provost James Spencer Northcote of the Birmingham diocese in April, 1884, Seddon outlined some of the problems with which he was confronted:

'In our poor law schools (in London) we have about 1,800 pauper children. They are passing as a stream through these schools to such a degree that we have had nearly 7,000 on our hands since 1867. It will be evident at once the great question respecting the children is their disposal for future life.

The girls are scattered in seven certified schools. Each school is under the care of Religious. Now these Religious bodies are extremely useful in solving the difficulty of disposal of the girls. They train the children for domestic service: and do it well. The result is that each School has as many applications for good servants as they can turn out. There is, therefore, no question here of emigration for the girls. The nuns know them and keep an eye upon them until they are settled down in life. Of course, this system is not perfect, but it approximates to it. And I am as certain as I can be that it is a far more wholesome outlet than sending them to Canada . . .'[23]

'With the boys,' he went on 'we have a difficulty. They are divided into three certified schools. In one they remain from infancy to seven years of age: and in the two others until 15 or 16. In the former there are 170 boys. In the two latter schools there are 780. Here is where the difficulty crops up. To keep finding suitable places for them as they are being discharged when of age for work is almost beyond us. And to meet this congestion, which seems a pet word nowadays, I send the boys to Canada, generally on to farms away from the contamination of the towns.

'The rule I have formed is this: 1. Not to send out girls at all except in cases where the places are bespoken by persons recommended by their clergy: and where I know the girls will be safe. 2. To send out boys to places prepared for them but this only as a means of meeting the home difficulty of scarcity of suitable arrangements . . .'

Because the scale of Seddon's Canadian enterprise was limited — indeed the Catholic involvement was to remain small, by 1902 only about 5,000 Catholic children having been emigrated compared with some 50,000 from Dr. Barnado and other agencies — he was in a privileged position to ensure the quality and establish proper monitoring arrangements. Indeed, his organization was drawn to the attention of the Local Government Board in 1874 because of the inadequacies of the entrepreneurial arrangements of certain other bodies which had led to concern.

John Lambert, Secretary to the Local Government Board, had commissioned an enquiry into the emigration of pauper children into Canada, headed by Andrew Doyle, a Local Government Inspector. The report, laid before the House of Commons on February 8th, 1875 was greatly welcomed by Seddon. Doyle was an elderly barrister who had spent his life as a civil servant working on the Poor Law. His brief was to follow-up and inspect those children sent to Canada at the ratepayers' expense and he was a keen advocate of the workhouse system. Abuses relating to Canadian emigration had come to light and Doyle's report was a devastating indictment of the bad organization and haphazard management of the enterprise on the part of many of the emigrating bodies.

The main scandal related to the activities of two ladies, Maria Rye and Annie Macpherson who had been sanctioned by the Poor Law Board in

1870 to emigrate pauper children to Canada. Doyle examined how children were selected, collected and sent out to Canada by the ladies, the arrangements for their conveyance and reception, the mode of placing them and the nature of the employment, the character of the homes in which they were placed and, importantly, the extent of the supervisory arrangements in Canada. The investigation covered a four-year period since the official approval of the Rye-Macpherson involvement. Doyle, in the process of his investigation, visited some four hundred of their children widely distributed throughout Quebec and Ontario. He had frequently 'to drive forty or fifty miles a day' through a rough country to see only half a dozen children.

The children placed out in Canada by Maria Rye and Annie Macpherson were pauper children sent out at the cost of the rates and children rescued from the streets — 'waifs and strays', 'arab children', 'gutter children' as they were variously called. Maria Rye was forty years of age when she began emigrating children to Canada. A formidable woman,she was an early advocate of improving the lot of women and girls in English society. She firmly believed that by emigrating young pauper girls to Canada, she was improving the social position of women generally both there and at home. She had an unfortunate manner in dealing with others and Bean and Melville have described her as at times 'positively hostile to the children in her care,' a woman 'difficult to deal with (but) often well in advance of her time.'[24] Annie Macpherson was less idealistic than Rye and more warm in personality. Born in 1833 and educated in Glasgow, she was an evangelical Christian and seems to have been driven by religious motives, reinforced by her close contacts with Dr. Barnado, with whom her organization was eventually to be amalgamated. These ladies, of course, were only two of many philanthropical entrepreneurs concerned with child emigration operating at the time.

Doyle discovered that Rye had distributed about 800 pauper children in Canada and Macpherson 350, but that the proportion of 'arab' children distributed by the latter was greater than the former. He found the children had been deposited 'over the Dominion, from New Brunswick to the remotest "concessions" in the West' and 'although he considered Macpherson's work to be marked with greater care and liberality' than that of Rye, the activities of the two women did not differ materially from each other. Rye had a Home at Peckham into which she received waifs and strays professing to train them for Canada, Macpherson had a similar one at Hampton where she received orphans and deserted children for removal to Canada. She also had a network of Homes in Liverpool, Edinburgh, Glasgow and Dublin for the same purpose. The exercise for both ladies was financially lucrative. Doyle noted 'for the collecting and training of these children, and the subsequent emigration of a portion of them, very large sums, several thousand pounds a year, have been and continue to be contributed by private individuals.' Considerable pecuniary assistance is also afforded by the Government of the Dominion and of the Province of Ontario, in addition to a payment of £8. 8s. for every pauper child taken by them to Canada.[25] Macpherson had even invited children, incredibly, to repay the cost of their emigration to assist in the emigration of others.

Doyle found the preliminary training to be neither methodical nor systematic and the process of selection to be not always honestly operated. The law required the consent of the children themselves to be given before two magistrates in the case of workhouse children but this rule was often not followed by the ladies in the case of orphans or deserted children. He had found 'several cases of children sent out as "orphans" who had one, if not both, parents living.' The authority of legal guardians should have been obtained formally. Doyle, as a consequence, was to recommend that if the emigration of pauper children was to continue it should be separate from that of other classes of children.

On arrival in Canada, the children were located in distributing Homes where they were received and lodged for a few days before being placed out in service. Each of the ladies had establishments with which they dealt. In the case of one of these, used by Macpherson, Doyle reported 'under its present management the shorter time children are allowed to remain in it the better.'

On the placement of children in Canada by the ladies, Doyle expressed great dissatisfaction. He found that as many as a hundred children had been placed out in service without more than merely formal reference to Miss Rye. 'For the disposal of a large proportion of the girls,' he wrote, 'both Miss Macpherson and Miss Rye depend upon what they term "adoption" . . . Although I have seen several such cases of real adoption they constitute, and will always constitute but a small percentage of children who may be placed out under any system of emigration.'[26] The more common way of proceeding was by 'indenture of service' or apprenticeship. 'Though generally kind and just,' Doyle found 'the Canadian farmer is often an exacting and unthoughtful master. Bound to make the most of his short season, he works through seed time and harvest from daylight to dark, and expects every hand that is capable of work to do the same. Many of the children who have been placed out in service at 13 or 14 years of age have certainly a hard time of it.'[27] He was not happy with the placement of many children and noted that some of Rye's had been placed in service in the United States. Furthermore, 'Miss Rye does not profess to have any regular or organized means of supervision at all' and although the system was better in Miss Macpherson's case, there remained loopholes.

Doyle's recommendations included greater care and discrimination in selecting and preparing children for emigration and the provision of industrial training for those children about to be placed in service, which training should in the case of children of 12 and upwards be of two or three year's duration. He considered the mode of transit needed attention and the numbers involved in one transit operation should not exceed 50, Miss Rye having been accustomed to sending parties of 150. They should be better supervised with a more adequate ratio of attendants to children than had been the case. Above all, better provision needed to be made to receive the children. The receiving Homes should be certified as industrial schools and certified in England and they should be inspected periodically, as were workhouses in England. Similarly, 'it appears to be but reasonable that up to a certain age every child should be entitled to admission to, and support, when "destitute", in the Home from which it may have been sent into service . . .'[28] Better placement arrangements should be devised until more could be learned about matching the abilities and dispositions of children to those of their new employers. Doyle commented: 'if Miss Rye and Miss Macpherson were less anxious to get the children off their hands immediately upon their arrival, not only would they be able to exercise greater discrimination in seeking places, but they would be able to get them out upon better terms.'[29] Several employers complained to him 'that no-one seemed to take any interest in the children after they were placed out; that no-one visited them or inquired about them.'[30] Although he did not come across any cases of gross cruelty, he did hear of many cases of ill-treatment and hardship. The system of indenture, as operated by Rye, should cease: it led to many abuses and provided no protection for a young man or woman against a hard taskmaster. Even by the standards of comfort of an average English agricultural labourer, the conditions of hired service on a Canadian farm were, for man or boy, hard and rough. Boys, however, who were sent into this sort of service without some previous preparation for it were at a great disadvantage. He argued strongly that 'if they could have had a few years of preliminary training in some well-organized industrial establishment in Canada, there would be no limit, within reason to their finding suitable employment in farm service.'[31]

With reference to girls, Doyle was decidedly of the opinion 'that they ought not to be sent out at a later age than from *seven* to *eight*: all the better if still younger. Girls who are sent out at ages from *nine* to *fifteen* are at once placed in service. By whatever name that service may be called, though disguised as "adoption", it is in fact domestic service, quite as hard as, and in some respects more uninviting to the children than the service in which at the same age they might be placed out in England . . .' He added he was often painfully struck in speaking to children of that age 'with the sense of loneliness manifested by them . . .'[32]

Fr. Seddon welcomed Doyle's report as calculated to stem many abuses, shortcomings and malpractices. Sending a copy of it to R.H. Froude he called it 'an able document', adding 'he grapples with the subject and its difficulties in a masterly manner. His knowledge of it is acquired by personal investigation. You will find his suggestions and remarks thoroughly practical. The pamphlet bears evidence of immense and conscientious paintstaking . . .'[33] Doyle, as his name might indicate, was a Roman Catholic and use was made of this fact in attempts by opponents of his recommendations to discredit his evidence. Indeed it was to be twenty-five years before his report was treated with seriousness.

In October 1884, Sir Charles Dilke asked Seddon[34] to put in writing for the information of the Local Government Board his views and conclusions on the work of sending out, placing and superyising emigrant children in the Canadian operation. In reply, Seddon informed Walter Sendall, through whom Dilke had contacted him, that he had been engaged since 1874 in sending out at various intervals poor Roman Catholic children as emigrants to Canada. The total number sent out was 463. He said: 'the first point which struck him, looking at the emigration scheme as a whole and thus embracing all those who were engaged in it' was the importance of eliminating from it every element of personal gain. If the work is undertaken with a purely philanthropic motive, it may be safely encouraged within certain limits but, he added 'if it can be shown that there are pecuniary rewards attached to it, I am strongly of opinion it should receive no sanction or approval whatever . . .'[35]

Emigration should also be backed up by a proper organization and management. Dr. Barnado was a good example in the Protestant sphere and, with Roman Catholics, the main agencies were Seddon's own Canadian Catholic Emigration Committee of which he was Secretary for the metropolitan area and for which he also acted from time to time for other areas of the country and other dioceses and, secondly, the Children's Catholic Protective Society based in Liverpool under the lay management of Richard Yates, which acted for the north of England.

Seddon's own committee had established three working centres in Canada, at Rimouski, Ottawa and Toronto. The Liverpool Society had established a similar one at Hamilton. 'I should propose,' Seddon wrote 'that whilst these two Roman Catholic agencies are working in their respective sphere for the same end, there should be issued regulations by the Local Government Board which would be acceptable to both. The London agency would deal with children who are inmates of the Certified Roman Catholic Schools for the Metropolitan District. The Local Government Board should authorize the several Boards to pay out of the Rates a sum of ten pounds per head for children over ten years of age and eight pounds for those under that age on condition that the Committees rendered a detailed account showing the name of the child, its ultimate destination and the several items of expenditure in connection with the emigration and likewise produce the vouchers as far as practicable.'[36] Expenditure above the authorized sum should be carried by the agencies, any shortfall leading to a corresponding abatement of claim against the Guardians. The committees, however, would have at their free disposal the capitation allowance of 8/ — per head made by the Federal Government. This would cover the stock of bedding, its washing and repairing and its replacement as necessary in respect of the voyage to Canada. Any saving from this sum could be used to further the work or assist in the support or provision of the several Homes in Canada 'into which the children are received after landing in that country previous to their being placed out . . .'[37]

On the matter of visiting the children, Seddon pointed out that his present role was to visit them once a year (he and Archibald Douglas going to Canada alternately) and he added 'whether it would not be wiser to appoint an official in each township or county to visit twice or even three times for the first year only and not afterwards, except in rare instances where the special circumstances of the case might need it, is a matter for the Dominion Government and the Local Government Board.' He recommended its adoption if it could be carried out. He was in favour, too, that a formal agreement should be drawn up with the receiving Homes in Canada and their respective committees in London and Liverpool in which the former engage to receive the children temporarily, to place them out in suitable Roman Catholic families, to receive them back if it should prove necessary, and to engage to have them visited by a trustworthy person of the district in which they are placed and at least three times within the first six months, the supervision to end there except when special circumstances might require it.' This should be possible 'considering the fair allowance made to the receiving Homes in Canada.' A Register should be kept at each Home, giving the particulars in connection with each child, similar to that used in the reformatory schools in England.[38] Seddon advocated appropriate arrangements for Protestant children, indicating how they might be dealt with.

As for the class of children to be emigrated, Seddon told Sendall that it was his experience that it was undesirable to send out to Canada any girls 'over eight years old, or nine as a very outside figure. . .' As to boys, he would permit infant boys 'up to eight years, or nine as an outside one, and those over fourteen but still keeping to 15 or 16 as near as possible. In the former case there could be no possible temptation to turn the child's labour to profit. In the latter, if there was undue pressure by the master, the boy could leave and look out for work elsewhere for himself. In some instances this would be sure to happen, but a grown-up boy would not be long out of employment. Under no circumstances whatever should there be indentures of agreement between the Committee and the recipient of the child, either boy or girl.'[39]

He concluded his statement on a somewhat sombre note: 'If it really is a fact that the Dominion is a gainer by child immigration and the Local Government Board desire its continuance, I trust that what I have said may direct the stream into a channel beneficial alike to the children and the

Dominion but I earnestly pray that if the scheme is to be left in the hands of those who would turn it to personal gain, it may cease altogether.'[40]

Seddon's three Homes in Canada to oversee the arrival, training and placement of Catholic children were well-organized. One was at Rimouski, about 180 miles from Quebec on the south bank of the St. Lawrence. The second was St. Patrick's Asylum in Ottawa and the third St. Nicholas's Institute in Toronto. All were run by nuns who dedicated their vocation to the service of the poor and had no other work.[41] Concerning the reception of reports on the children, Seddon wrote: 'these have been gathered at Rimouski with the most scrupulous and painstaking care by the Very Rev. Edmond Langevin, brother of the Hon. Hector Langevin, one of the Ministers at Ottawa. At Ottawa, the Sisters visit in the winter months most of the children placed out by them in the summer. If their visits do not extend to all, it is by reason of the distance. At Toronto most, if not all, the boys remain at the Homes whence they go out to work in the city at some suitable occupation. Their interests are carefully watched over by the sisters. Sometimes they send the boys to persons in the country with whom they are acquainted, but the rule seems to be that the boys return after a while to the Home . . .'[42] Undoubtedly, through the association of convents, Religious houses, diocesan and parochial organizations in Canada, a network of supervision was constructed that was more difficult to achieve for other agencies. At Toronto, for instance, Seddon was immensely pleased with the success of the work. He wrote after one of the annual visits: 'I found the boys happy and contented. They give a portion of their wages (I forgot what amount) to the sisters for their board and lodging. The rest is banked for clothes and a rainy day. I wish we had Homes like that in London. The sisters do not find the situations for the boys but they insist on the boys (aged over 14) obtaining them by their own efforts. The working of the place is thoroughly sound. I should mention that some few, but very few indeed, have gone to farm in the country around Toronto but have invariably found their way back to the Home where they always receive a hospitable welcome so long as they behave themselves properly.'[43]

The annual visits paid by Seddon or Douglas were eagerly looked forward to by the emigrants. Both men sustained a substantial correspondence with emigrant children and youths and tried to deal promptly with the cases of unhappiness, cruelty or grievance that came to their notice. It is not unfitting that Seddon, who devoted his sacerdotal life to helping disadvantaged children, should have died suddenly when surrounded by a group of emigrant children on board ship for Canada in 1898.

After Seddon's death, the management of the Canadian Catholic Emigration Society passed to a Southwark priest, Edward St. John, who was to work closely with Archibald Douglas in the Canadian enterprise, learning much from the latter's personal knowledge and contacts. On April

20, 1893, St. John took a party of 40 boys to Canada whose ages ranged from 16 to 20, perhaps the first attempt by a Catholic organization to help young *men* to start afresh. He found places for them in the farming districts around Montreal. Reporting on the venture six years later, St. John found that at least a quarter of this 1893 party were in positions and earning wages they could not have hoped for in England. Another quarter had each improved their position but, in doing so, had moved away from the district where they had been originally placed. Ten had not done well and had returned to England. Two had died. With the help of Fr. Douglas, St. John decided to put his new work for young men on a better footing and, in 1894, they both established for the purpose their own farm in Manitoba, which they called *New Southwark*. Here, it was intended, London youths could farm for a year and get used to Canadian life before finding their own farms upon which to work. In 1903, St. John wrote 'the result of this venture in Manitoba, has been that not one of the lads that have passed through the farm have had any wish to return to London life as far as we can ascertain, and all have become determined to make their way in the world in Canada.'[44] The farm was managed by a Frederick O'Connor from St. Vincent's Home in London, a protégé of Douglas. In 1896, the first issue of *Across the Sea* was printed, edited by Douglas, with the dual purpose of attracting support at home for the Canadian venture but, more importantly, of keeping the emigrants in touch with the old country. The magazine regularly printed letters and articles from the boys at New Southwark and elsewhere and gave detailed accounts of the visits paid to them by priests from England. It is a mine of information on the day-to-day life of the emigrant colony. A reception centre, New Orpington Lodge, was also opened in Ottawa and a similar one in Montreal. St. Anne's, Montreal, became a centre for girls' education. The girls went to Canada with a Miss Proctor who remained there with them and St. Anne's acted as a social centre where emigrant girls could congregate each week. Emigration to Canada continued until 1933 when the widespread economic crisis brought it to an end.

In April 1895, Douglas received a letter from a boy who had left *New Southwark* to farm on his own in the North-West Territory. It is worth quoting because it gives the flavour of the pioneering spirit necessary for survival in such an outpost of Empire:—

'I am still holding down on my claim: my crop did not turn out as well as I expected, it was a very dry year. I had 500 bushels of oats, 150 of barley and 60 of wheat, but I had to sell the most of mine off early last winter. I have thirteen pigs now, but they have gone down in price on account of the scarcity of grain, but I think they will rise again. My cow presented me with a calf the other day, so that gives me five horned cattle. . . . We had a very fine winter. We will soon be starting to plough.

. . . I have to wash my own clothes, bake my own bread, and wash the dishes, etc. I do feel very lonesome here sometimes, and think to myself what keeps me here in this wild North-West, nine miles from a church and all alone — and then something seems to tell me to have patience, and that the wheel will change, etc., etc. I remain one of your old boys.'[45]

The letter heightens the pathos and the achievement of the pioneer, while indicating too, the warm relationship sustained between Douglas, in particular, and his 'old boys'.

At the beginning of this paper I quoted from Michael Connelly to the effect that the work of the agencies had to be seen in the social context within which they operated, a context of both social and economic deprivation, one of abandonment and, often, of emotional desolation. When the future Cardinal Vaughan, then Bishop of Salford, said farewell to sixty Lancashire Catholic orphans on their way to Canada on September 12, 1889, he said he had asked them to come and see him to wish them 'goodbye' and give them God's blessing: 'They were going on a long voyage across the ocean, but they need not be afraid, because Father Rossall (a Salford priest) and two good Sisters would accompany them and remain with them until they were placed in bright and happy homes which had been provided for them. A great deal of trouble had been taken, he said, and a great deal of money spent in finding out for them good and happy homes, where they would have good Catholics all round them, and plenty of work to do, and, when they grew older, good wages to win. They were not going to poor miserable cottages, or to the bad low slums of some large towns: but they were going to live with good, respectable, and well-to-do farming people, who were anxious to have boys and girls to make their homes bright and happy. They were going to be raised in the social scale and to live under conditions far superior to any which would fall to their lot in this country . . .'[46]

Such, then, was the perceived social and educational context, as held by contemporaries. Such, then, was the hope: such, then, was the dream which contemporaries placed before twenty young girls, dressed in dark red capes and blue caps, and forty young boys, dressed in tweed suits and check ulsters as they prepared to leave for Canada. The reality was, perhaps, not quite so idyllic!

References

1. Philip Bean and Joy Melville: *Lost Children of the Empire* [Unwin Hyman, London, 1989].
2. *The Universe*, 14 May, 1989.

3. John Bossy: *The English Catholic Community, 1570-1850* [Darton, Longman and Todd, London, 1975], p.312.
4. F.H. Wallis: *Popular Anti-Catholicism in Mid-Victorian Britain* [Edwin Mellen Press, Lampeter, 1993], p.215.
5. Lynn H. Lees: *Exiles of Erin: Irish Migrants in Victorian London* [Ithaca, N.Y., 1979], pp.46-57; 246-249.
6. Sheridan Gilley: 'English Attitudes to the Irish in England, 1780-1900' in C. Holmes: *Immigrants and Minorities in British Society* [Allen & Unwin, London, 1978], pp.81-110.
7. Joseph Gillow: *A Literary and Biographical History or Bibliographical Dictionary of the English Catholics, etc.* [Burns & Oates, London, 1885], I, p.226.
8. Wallis, *op. cit.*, p.214.
9. Adrian Hastings (ed.): *Bishops and Writers* [Anthony Clarke, Wheat-hampstead, 1977], p.128.
10. Joseph L. Altholz: 'The Political Behaviour of the English Catholics, 1850-1867' in *The Journal of British Studies*, November 1964, pp.89-103.
11. See my chapter: '"Sensus Fidelium"': The Developing Concept of Roman Catholic Voluntary Effort in Education in England and Wales' in Witold Tulasiewicz and Colin Brock: *Christianity and Educational Provision in International Perspective* [Routledge, London, 1988], pp.61-88.
12. Chapters II and III of my *Cardinal Manning: His Public Life and Influence, 1865-1892* [O.U.P., London, 1962], pp.26-86.
13. *Ibidem*, p.30.
14. N. Waugh: *'These, My Little Ones': The Origin, Progress, and Development of the Incorporated Society of the Crusade of Rescue and Homes for Destitute Catholic Children* [Sands & Co., London, 1911], p.51.
15. H.E. Manning: 'The Work and the Wants of the Catholic Church in England' [*Dublin Review*, July 1863] in his *Miscellanies* [Burns & Oates, London, 1877], vol. I, pp.45-46.
16. The *Pastoral* is quoted at length in Edward St. John: *Manning's Work for Children* [Steed and Ward, London, 1929], p.13 *et seq.*
17. *Ibidem*, p.18.
18. *Ibidem*, p.19.
19. *Ibidem*, p.31.
20. V.A. McClelland: 'The Making of Young Imperialists': etc. in *Recusant History*, vol. 19, no. 4, pp.509 *et seq.*
21. *The Tablet*, 5 November, 1887.
22. Emanuel Bans & Arthur Chilton Thomas: *Child Emigration to Canada*. Report of 17 November, 1902. Printed *in extenso* as Appendix II of Waugh, *op. cit.*, pp.215 *et seq.*

23. Westminster Diocesan Archives [W.D.A.]. Thomas Seddon to Provost James Spencer Northcote, Stoke-on-Trent, 7 April, 1884.
24. Bean & Melville, *op. cit.*, pp.50-51.
25. *A Report to the Right Honourable the President of the Local Government Board, by Andrew Doyle, Esquire, Local Government Inspector, as to the Emigration of Pauper Children to Canada*, 8 February, 1875.
26. *Ibidem*, p.11.
27. *Ibidem*, p.13.
28. *Ibidem*, p.18.
29. *Ibidem*, p.20.
30. *Ibidem*, p.26.
31. *Ibidem*, p.31.
32. *Ibidem*, p.35.
33. *W.D.A.* Seddon to Froude, 19 March, 1884. Froude was interested in developing an emigration scheme of his own. Seddon was disapproving of all such ventures not supported by a well-founded committee and organization.
34. *W.D.A.* Walter Sendall [acting on behalf of Dilke] to Seddon, 31 October, 1884.
35. *W.D.A.* Seddon to Sendall, 13 November, 1884.
36. *Ibidem*.
37. *Ibidem*.
38. *Ibidem*.
39. *Ibidem*.
40. *Ibidem*.
41. *W.D.A.* Seddon to the Secretary, Local Government Board, 28 March, 1887.
42. *Ibidem*.
43. *W.D.A.* Seddon to R. Hedley, 26 October, 1888.
44. Southwark Diocesan Archives (*S.D.A.*), *Boys and Girls*, 1903, pp.7-8. Edward St. John's report on 'Emigration'.
45. *S.D.A.* 'Across the Sea', letter to Douglas, April 1895.
46. Salford Diocesan Archives *The Harvest*, October, 1889, pp.5-6.

NOISELESSLY AND CALMLY:
NUNS AND SOCIAL RESPONSIBILITY FOR CHILDREN IN NINETEENTH-CENTURY IRELAND

Caitríona Clear

In 1898 the archbishop of Dublin, Dr. Walsh, praised the women Religious of the city for going about their 'extensive and useful work' among the poor 'noiselessly and calmly', and around the same time Fr. Vaughan, a prominent Jesuit, marvelled at the versatility of nuns: 'You can switch a Sister of Charity or Mercy on to anything'.[1] Their capacity for hard work, and their ability to get the job done without apparent fuss, were the qualities most prized in nuns in late nineteenth-century Ireland. By this time not only is the Irish Catholic Church impossible to imagine without nuns, so too is the Irish landscape of social administration. Nuns ran projects that were entirely voluntary and partly State-subsidised, and they also worked, from the 1860s, in public institutions such as Uniion workhouses and their infirmaries. Nearly all convents had some kind of daily contact with children and teenagers, through schools, hostels, sick visiting, orphanages, reformatories, workshops and other projects. The exclamations of delight and gratitude which greeted the novelty of socially-active communities of women in the first decades of the nineteenth-century subsided to a low murmur of approval by the century's end. This approbation had a strong political dimension; 'Look at the Sisters of Mercy', eulogised Daniel O'Connell in 1840, '. . . O such a country is too good to continue in slavery'.[2] Throughout this period the strongest and most popular brand of nationalism was identified clearly with the resurgence of the Catholic Church after a century and a half of oppppression under the Penal Laws. Women were an integral part of this resurgence, and the four biggest and most widely-distributed female Religious Congregations were founded before Catholic emancipation on the initiative of middle and lower-middle class women; Nano Nagle, Teresa Mullaly (the Presentation), Mary Aikenhead (the Irish Sisters of Charity), Frances Ball (the Loreto), and Catherine McAuley (the Sisters of Mercy). (No individual female foundress is identified with the east midlands-based Brigidines, founded in the early century.) The much older Poor Clares, Carmelites and Dominicans also began to run schools and orphanages. This kind of work was seen by almost all of these early foundations as part of a broadly-based movement among the poor which, like much of the social work carried out by all denominations at this time, combined a religious mission with belief in the urgent need to discipline and control the ever-growing army of rootless poor — for their own good and for the good of society as a whole.[3] For most Irish nuns, however, the provision of schools and other institutions for children came to be the most important aspect of their work. Demand for nuns to set up schools and through them, it was hoped, to 'reform' or 'civilise' entire communities, was so great that home-grown congregations could not keep pace with demand and foreign institutes began to be imported even before the Famine.[4] The number of convents in Ireland increased from 12 or 13 in 1800 to approximately 368 in 1900, and the number of nuns multiplied by 8 between 1841 and 1901, a sixty-year period when the Catholic population almost halved because of famine, emigration and changing marriage patterns.[5] All over Europe at this time, the number of nuns grew significantly, and residential communities of single women devoted to social and political aims of various kinds were also common.[6] Community life offered middle and upper-middle class women the challenge of hard work without the loss of social status, at a time when ladies who worked outside the home risked losing caste. Entering a convent in nineteenth-century Ireland was also a public affirmation of social and political identity — apart altogether from the spiritual motivation, which was immeasurably important in an evangelical age.

There was little if any debate in early nineteenth-century Ireland about whether or not effort should be expended upon the children of the poor. Liberal reformers and social conservatives, those in favour of Catholic Emancipation and those against it, nationalists and unionists all agreed, if for different reasons, on the political and social utility of schooling and training. Smouldering Catholic resentment at government subsidising of the Kildare Place Society, seen as a proselytising agency, was eventually appeased by the setting-up of the National Board of Education in 1831. The Board provided considerable funds for voluntary bodies who wanted to set up schools, provided these bodies consented to certain rules, regular inspection and so on.[7] Catholic organisations applied for funds for Catholic schools, Protestant organisations for funds for Protestant schools, and thus was set in place the denominational primary State school system still in place today. By the late 1850s 75% of convent 'poor schools', as they were popularly known, were affiliated to the National Board; although several individual communities had grave reservations about affiliating to a non-Catholic government agency, and some convents and congregations stood aloof altogether from it, most convents managed to operate the kind of schools they wanted within the system. Usually they could not do without the money.[8] The Reformatories Act of 1858 and the Industrial Schools Act of 1868 provided government support for custodial institutions and orphanages run by nuns, and the provisions of these acts were rapidly availed of. Also, Catholic-dominated Boards of Poor Law Guardians were often very sympathetic to applications from nuns who wanted to work in Union workhouses, especially when three or four nuns elected to work for the price of one or two, which was what usually happened. Seventy-three Union hospitals — there were 163 Poor Law Unions in the country as a whole — were under the care of nuns by 1898. Nuns usually took a particular interest in the workhouse children.[9]

Observers, even non-Catholics, usually approved of the 'moral training' given by nuns in the 'poor'/National schools. According to the *Presentation Directory* of 1850 this consisted of, as well as Christian doctrine of course, 'decency, cleanliness, and correctness of manner'; deference to parents and to social superiors was also stressed. The Mercy *Guide* of 1865 believed 'neatness, industry, mutual forbearance, and self-control' to be the most important qualities to be inculcated. Teaching the children to *work* was considered very important; Nano Nagle's early schools in Cork in the late eighteenth-century taught the girls sewing and knitting, the syllabus for the Loreto Free School, opened in Dublin in 1822, was 'the three "r"'s, needlework, knitting and the platting of straw'; the Poor Clares school in Harold's Cross in Dublin in 1840 taught the girls 'various kinds of needlework', and as late as 1878 Mother Genevieve of the St. Louis congregation in Ireland was reminding her colleagues that needlework 'must at all times rank next in importance to religious instruction'.[10] Since at least the 1830s earnings from home-based textile and garment work were, throughout most of the country, either very small or non-existent; work-training in general, however, was seen as an important part of moral training, and it was considered crucial for girls to learn 'female' skills which might be useful to them in later life as wives and mothers. The National Board inspectors in 1864 noted that where convents were not enclosed (i.e. where the members were free to leave the convent *environs*) attendance at the schools was much higher, because the nuns were able to use sick and poor visitation as a means of encouraging the children to come to school. This could explain the high attendance rates of girls in particular at National Schools; compulsory education was not introduced until 1892. In Athlone, in a school run by the Sisters of Mercy, 'children are sought and brought to school, are fed and clothed'. The very numerous and widely-distributed Presentation nuns were enclosed, so they could not actually seek children out like this, but like the Mercy and almost all other Congregations running poor schools, they provided breakfast for children every morning. As far as general instruction was concerned, the 1864 inspectors remarked that the convent schools were usually very good at reading and writing, and often poor at arithmetic — this probably reflected the bias in the education that the nuns themselves had received, although if the business acumen of some legendary Reverend Mothers (e.g. Mother Agnes Bernard Morrogh of Foxford Woollen Mills) is anything to go by, some nuns must have developed a competence at sums. Extras like music and drawing were often laid on for the children at no extra cost, reflecting the talents of community members — this was the case in the Presentation National Schools in county Kerry in this period. The inspectors also commented, curiously, that the nuns were, on the whole, 'infinitely better-educated' than ordinary National School teachers; this is likely to have been automatic deference on their part to the social origins of the nuns, as they provided no evidence to back it up.[11]

It was also remarked with great approval that the nuns were 'disinterested and devoted', and that they often followed up their ex-pupils' progress in the world. In Bagenalstown Presentation convent, for example, a nun used her connections with wealthy Catholic families on the continent to obtain governess work for the ex-National School pupils. Governesses, ladies' maids, shopgirls, 'respectable apprentices' and teachers were the occupations of some of the past-pupils of Charleville Mercy convent in 1864, while the past-pupils of the Irish Sisters of Charity National School in Tramore became nursery governesses, and acquired positions in houses of business. Most of the past-pupils of all National and 'poor' schools, however, became domestic servants.[12] As domestic service was the largest of all female occupations in Ireland at this time, this is hardly surprising.

Nuns also operated paying schools/pension schools/superior schools or whatever they were called; as early as 1821 such schools were considered very important by the Catholic authorities — the Loreto order, a variant of the English Institute of the Blessed Virgin Mary, was set up for this specific purpose. Immortalised in the novels and writings of Kate O'Brien and Mary Colum, the more expensive of these schools came to be viewed with some suspicion by Irish nationalists, though this did not in any way detract from their popularity. A nationalist newspaper in early twentieth century Ireland criticised Laurel Hill convent in Limerick, run by the Faithful Companions of Jesus, a French order, for turning out women fit to be wives of colonial governors and bank managers. Kate O'Brien, an ex-pupil of the school commented in later years that bank managers would have been considered a very low social target indeed by the Reverend Mother of her day.[13] Laurel Hill was one of the more expensive schools; far more common were the 'superior schools' set up by convents alongside their National/poor schools, in order to cater for parents who did not want their children to mix with those of the poorest, but who could not afford the prohibitive fees of the more exclusive schools. The Sisters of Mercy in particular ran this dual system, which won praise from observers like James Kavanagh in 1859; 'all are nurtured according to their special necessities . . . the children of the beggar and the burgher, the little ones of the man of toil and those of opulent trade'.[14] The rules of the

Presentation nuns forbade them to set up paying schools and consequently their National/poor schools attracted children from a wide variety of backgrounds — in Kerry towns and in Limerick city towards the end of the last century for daughters of middling to large farmers were taught alongside those of small farmers and labourers. In theory some nuns did not consider social mobility to be either possible or desirable; 'Besides manual work they are taught to read, write and make up accounts', an 1881 publication describes the regime in the Houses of Mercy, hostels for unemployed teenage girls run by the Sisters of Mercy: 'Save in extraordinary cases — and genius, like murder, will out — Mother McAuley was no advocate for over-educating, so as to unfit them for their station in life, girls who as servants of rich men or wives of poor men must earn their bread by the labour of their hands'.[15] In practice, a girl who went to a well-equipped National School, and whose parents could afford to do without her earnings for some years, could embark on an on-the-job course in teacher-training, followed by a subsidised year in a training college in Dublin. Even if her school was not affiliated to the Board, the experience and the references gained from working with the nuns would stand her in good stead for seeking teaching work. When formal school-leaving examinations were introduced in 1878 many convents prepared girls from the National Schools for these examinations. However, as Anne O'Connor points out, where there was already a 'paying school' in existence, the Intermediate department was situated there, rather than as an adjunct to the National school, so social divisions as to opportunity might have been reinforced by the nuns, at least as often as social mobility was encouraged.[16] It cannot be denied, though, that whatever their varying opinions and practices, nuns' interest in their pupils extended beyond the imparting of skills in a school setting.

The emphasis on preparing children for life was most marked in orphanages, reformatories and Industrial schools. The Acts of 1858 and 1868 which provided funds for the last two types of institutions were, in effect, a recognition of existing trends in the kind of care already being offered by nuns and by other philanthropic bodies, Catholic and otherwise. In 1850 Mount St. Vincent's orphanage in Limerick, run by the Sisters of Mercy, trained orphan girls as nursery governesses and housemaids, and familiarised them with farm-work and lace-making; the provision of funds under the Industrial Schools Act 18 years later did not change the character of the school, but enabled the nuns to add on a fully-equipped dairy and piggery.[17] The Mercy *Guide* of 1865 recommended that as many orphanage pupils as possible be trained as teachers; the Irish sisters of Charity's orphanage in King's Inn St. in Dublin remarked in 1866 that many ex-pupils became governesses, schoolmistresses, and paid musicians — there was a particular emphasis on music in that school. Many of the girls who left the Mercy Industrial school in Galway city, according to a report of 1870, 'have developed vocations and make very good lay sisters at home and abroad'.[18] Lay sisters were professed religious, who, although they took vows and consecrated themselves to God, could never rise to positions of authority in the convent and held a position roughly analogous to that of servants in large households. They did not, as a rule, have to bring any dowries to the convent with them. Most convents in nineteenth-century Ireland had lay sisters — there would usually have been about 2 or 3 lay sisters to maybe 15 or 20 'choir' nuns.[19] Ex-industrial school pupils could not usually aspire to becoming 'choir' nuns, though they could, if considered suitable for training, become teachers. (This gives us an idea of the relative 'respectability' of lay teachers and teachers/carers in the religious life.)

Under the terms of the Industrial Schools Act, orphans, children considered to be vagrants, and young criminal children under 14 were to be committed to Industrial schools by the courts. The Reformatories were for older children and teenagers; putting young people into jail with adults was frowned upon by a society which believed more and more in the environmental causes of crime. Industrial schools and reformatories run by nuns and religious brothers have in Ireland in recent times become identified with harshness and emotional neglect probably because the system established in the mid-nineteenth century survived, and was allowed to survive, virtually unchanged up to 1970, into times when a different set of values about child-care prevailed.[20] If religious-run places of refuge and detention for children were criticised at all in the nineteenth-century, it was usually, as Jane Barnes points out, for being too soft, maintaining 'little beggar children' at the public expense, and bolstering up 'dependency'.[21] Were nuns themselves alive to such criticisms? An orphanage, says one source, 'should never assume the character and appearance of a boarding-school, but should continue to be and to seem, in every way, a charitable institution, a place of refuge for the needy little ones of Christ'. The manner of the nuns should be 'maternal . . . firm and vigilant' but neither 'severe nor suspicious'. Practices and priorities differed from one convent to another — the Sisters of Mercy *Guide* enjoined that illegitimate children not be admitted to the orphanages, presumably so as not to encourage 'vice', but this injunction was heavily crossed out in the copy held in the Limerick convent — was this because it was considered unfair, or because, under the terms of the Industrial Schools Act, the nuns had little choice about admitting illegitimate children?[22] Some Congregations kept Industrial school children and National School pupils strictly separate, others, like the Sisters of St. Louis, for example, mixed them in classroom and playground alike, to the approval of the government inspectors. This latter detail, like many other 'positive' ones, is gleaned from an inspector's report quoted in the Congregation's history;[23] examination of Reformatory and Industrial school reports for the period does not uncover any horror stories of abuse and neglect, although criticisms are often made.[24] An insight into the internal organisation and values of one convent-run reformatory is given in a letter from Sister Genevieve Beale to Cardinal Cullen in 1861; she was a member of the Sisters of St. Louis, who had recently opened a reformatory in Monaghan. Each child, says Sister Genevieve, should be treated 'according to her individual disposition and propensities'. The sentence should be as long as possible, because 'even a clever child of 13 or 14, and that child a female, could scarcely be expected to earn its own living'. (This was at a time when children, boys and girls, of this age were being sent out of Union workhouses to work for farmers, and many children from the labouring class went into service as early as 11 or 12.) The daily régime for the inmates was laid out; the day began at 6 a.m. and ended at 9 p.m.; more time was spent on sewing, laundry work and gardening than on literary instruction, but Sr. Genevieve justified this by pointing out that reading could lead to novel-reading, and that out-door exercise was particularly important for criminal children 'who are, perhaps, more sensitive than others'. Food deprivation was never used as a punishment, because the girls were growing. The aim of the reformatory was to make the girls into good servants, and good wives and mothers.[25]

The Sisters of St. Louis were only 3 years in Monaghan at this stage; a French Congregation founded in the early nineteenth-century, they had been invited to Monaghan by interested local Catholics, and within three years had set up a boarding-school, a National School, a reformatory and a sick mission. There were about six nuns in the community at that time. This multiplicity of projects was typical of communities which settled in areas where there was no convent already in existence; city convents were in more of a position to specialise. The nuns had not been very long in Monaghan when Dr. McNally, bishop of Clogher, presented them with an ultimatum — to break their organisational links with their Mother-house in France, or to clear out. All along his manner to the young community had vacillated between indifference and hostility. After much deliberation the nuns decided they could not abandon the projects they had taken on, so they broke their ties with France.[26] It is impossible to evaluate or to judge nuns' work with children at this time without understanding nuns' structural position in the Church. Small, vulnerable foreign Congregations were not the only victims of interference and dominance. The Sisters of Mercy were well-established, and highly-valued, by 1865, yet when some nuns in this congregation conceived the idea of drawing up a Guide for internal circulation, to standardise work practices and to establish guidelines for new projects, many bishops refused to allow the convents in their dioceses to attend the meeting which was held in Limerick to discuss the proposed guide. Other bishops thought it was a great idea and encouraged attendance.[27] Similar stories abound; the Good Shepherd nuns in Limerick city were forced, in the 1860s, to stop sending aspiring members to France for their novitiate; Loreto convents founded from Dublin to Navan, Fermoy, Letterkenny, Omagh and Killarney between 1833 and 1861 had to sever ties with the Dublin convent, and so on.[28] The two largest and most widely-distributed Congregations in the country — making up, between them, 52% of all convents in 1864 — the Presentation and the Mercy, had no centralised structures, but were under the authority of the local bishop wherever they settled. The Presentation order was also enclosed, which prevented even the kind of informal inter-community visiting carried on by the Sisters of Mercy. Even Congregations with supposedly centralised organisations were not immune to interference — the outgoing, socially-active congregation of women was such a canonical novelty that often not even the nuns themselves knew the extent of their rights or the limits which could be placed on outside interference. Partly because of this, formal co-ordination, co-operation and even the sharing of ideas and strategies among the largest single identifiable group of child-care workers in the country was almost impossible. Nuns rarely published critical accounts of their work or contributed articles to contemporary periodicals, even Catholic ones. (There is hardly any mention of nuns at all, let alone of their work, in the contemporary *Irish Ecclesiastical Record.*)

One of the few nuns to speak out in public about the work in hand was Margaret Anna Cusack, the Nun of Kenmare, who wrote historical and geographical works under the name M.F. Cusack (Mary Francis was her name in religion) between the 1860s and the 1880s. She also wrote several books and articles on nuns' work, particularly their work with girls; her views were if anything socially conservative, and well within the range of orthodox Catholicism. A member of the Poor Clare community in Kenmare, she received permission from the relevant bishops to set up a new Congregation, the Sisters of Peace, in Knock. This new Congregation's activities were very much in line with the kind of work already being carried out by nuns, running a school and a training centre for girls. However Cusack fell foul of her local bishop and parish priest — why, it is not very clear — and when she went to America to set up her Congregation there, she was subjected to persecution by bishops and priests all down along the eastern seaboard. She eventually abdicated control of her Congregation and left not only the religious life, but the Catholic Church. Her story is a long and confusing one, because, as one historian points out, no bishop or priest ever said exactly why they wished to be rid of her, but lack of humility was probably the most tangible of the charges levelled at her.[29] Humility as a moral virtue is considered important for all consecrated Religious, from the Pope down. It was given added weight, for nuns, by their structural position at the bottom of the ecclesiastical ladder (as non-ordained Religious, like brothers) *and* by the fact that as women, they were irrevocably barred from aspiring to any higher position in the

Church.[30] Did a strong Victorian social convention against women speaking out in public reinforce nuns' silence? Partly; but this convention was being challenged on a large scale throughout the nineteenth-century by 'respectable' middle-class women involved in voluntary work. Frances Power Cobbe, Mary Carpenter, Florence Nightingale, Octavia Hill, Isabella Tod and many more Irish and British women, claimed that by finding a public voice for women in matters to do with poor relief, health, education, housing and care of youth, they were merely exercising maternal, innately feminine functions, in the public sphere. This extension of their nurturing work, they argued convincingly, was in no way incompatible with the self-effacement required of women, because they were not asking anything *for themselves*.[31] Nuns in nineteenth-century Ireland, many of them strong, able women by all accounts, confident in their social standing and also in their active (if junior) membership of a Church whose political and social power was increasing day by day, were ideally placed to contribute to the ongoing debate in the statistical journals on such questions, all of which have a direct bearing on children's welfare. Because of the structural constraints under which they operated, however, they found it almost impossible to extend the power they undoubtedly held in their own fields, into collective action and public statement. Therefore debate on child welfare and on many other aspects of 'social work' was not developed to its fullest potential in Ireland, because of the silence of the largest single group of workers with children.

Another reason why nuns did not develop in this way might have been because they were too busy to spend time on reflection and analysis. Sixty-three per cent of all convents in 1900 operated more than one project, and demands were particularly heavy on convents in rural areas. It was not necessarily the case, either, that the larger the convent the more work it undertook — 110 Loreto nuns in Rathfarnham, Dublin, in 1882, operated a large day-and-boarding-school, and a National school, while eight Sisters of Charity in Benada, Sligo, ran a sick mission, a National school of equivalent size to the Loreto one, and a large Industrial school.[32] Convents were always being called upon to make foundations in other areas, calls which they rarely refused. Ill-health and early deaths from consumption and other wasting diseases were common among nuns, despite the fact that a clean bill of health was one of the requirements for entry, which suggests that many women's health broke down after they entered convents.

As far as social responsibility for children was concerned nuns in nineteenth-century Ireland were not pioneers — or if they were, then they shared this title with other non-religious, non-Catholic reformers. Nano Nagle, like Hannah More, was wary of teaching girls how to write; the early schools of the Irish Sisters of Charity operated on the Bell and Lancastrian systems;[33] training orphan children to be useful members of society was an ideal shared by most people of all persuasions. Nuns were quick to examine new approaches to the work and to take advantage of new developments, and they shared many of the social values of their contemporaries. The following extract is from a government inspector's report on the Reformatory run by the Sisters of St. Louis in Monaghan in 1865:

> About eight months ago two girls, cousins, were to be released by expiration of sentence on a certain day. Their relatives, a gang of wandering tinkers, had been prowling around the reformatory and were driven off by the constabulary. Mrs. Beale (Mother, formerly Sister, Genevieve) was determined to rescue the girls if possible. A steamer was to sail from Londonderry three days before the expected day of discharge. She telegraphed me to obtain a pardon from the Chief Secretary, which he kindly granted, and three days before the day of discharge the two girls were sailing for New York, where careful friends and safe employment were secured for them.[34]

Here nuns collaborated with government virtually to kidnap two girls; we are not told whether the girls themselves wanted to leave Ireland. The girls' families are described in terms appropriate to wild animals — 'prowling', 'driven off' — and their rights over the girls are held to be of no account whatsoever because they are 'wandering tinkers'. Mother Genevieve's actions would have been applauded by all enlightened contemporary opinion for whom 'vagrancy' was a social and moral pathology. Many of the children committed to Industrial schools were not really orphans, but children of 'vagrants' and therefore considered to be virtual orphans, and as mentioned earlier, if contemporaries raised their voices in protest at all, it was at Industrial schools' apparent facilitation of a life of ease and comfort for the parents of these children, and their 'indulgence' toward the children themselves. M.F. McCarthy, a relentless and indiscriminate critic of Catholic power in Ireland, quoted with approval the following remarks from a meeting of the Wexford Board of Poor Law Guardians in 1902. The Guardians were discussing whether the workhouse children should be sent to the Industrial school run by the Sisters of Mercy:

> Mr. John Lambert said — 'He was opposed to sending the children to the convent, and anyone who had any experience of the children trained there would not be in favour of the proposition. He asked Mr. Ennis if he had had any servant from the Convent of Mercy? If you get one, do not let her see the moon, or she will want to get it'. (Laughter)
> Lady M. Fitzgerald — 'I had often girls from the Convent of Mercy and I found them most satisfactory'.
> Mr. John Lambert said — 'He was satisfied to send the children outside to board with private people, but he objected to sending them to

the Sisters. The Convent of Mercy was the means of taking work out of the hands of many of the honest labouring families in Wexford. Why should these workhouse children be trained up for fine situations? There should be some one to do the rough work, and why should they not do it? . . . I had one of the convent girls minding a child at the fire, and she never let the child get burned. Right enough; she was too near the fire herself for that — (Laughter) — and she always wore gloves for fear the coal would ruffle the skin of her hands.[35]

Perhaps the servant in questiion had ambitions to become a lady's maid — which would have been a step up from general servant — and wanted to keep her hands soft for this reason. What Lambert and McCarthy find amusing and outrageous is that the nuns have managed to instil in this girl and others like her, 'notions' about comfort and beauty, and aspirations inappropriate to somebody reared at the public expense. Were nuns because of the full-time nature of their work, and their long-term commitment over years, in a unique position among care-workers to provide continuity of care and interest over a long period, continuity which might well have imparted a sense of personal worth to those under their care? Were they also because of this in an unique position to inflict equally long-term damage? It is about as difficult to judge and to generalise about nuns' day-to-day informal contact with children as it is to judge the work of mothers rearing children in the home. Individual personalities and resources varied widely from one convent to another, so the question which must be asked is, whether the structures of care operated for the most part for children's 'good' or against it. Nuns certainly, through their work, affirmed the worth of 'friendless' and poor children, though they fixed this worth firmly on an hierarchical scale of social value. They replicated social distinctions through their projects, but also opened up avenues for individual mobility for some of their charges, and rejoiced at such 'success stories'. They taught children and young people essential survival skills, and if deference occupied an important place among these skills, then it is easy to understand why. Nuns, of all people, knew the value of keeping on the right side of authority. The Sisters of Mercy in Sligo, whose bishop, Dr. Gillooly, had refused to allow them to attend the 1865 convocation in Limerick, made him a present in 1882, on the occasion of his Silver Jubilee, of oak furniture, 'rich hangings in antique style' and a carpet. The Limerick bishop Dr. Butler who forced the Good Shepherd nuns to break their links with their native France was their most consistently generous patron.[36] Even the willingness to take on more and more work can be seen in this light; often the easiest way for a young and struggling Community to remain in existence was to make itself as indispensable as possible as quickly as possible. Taking on a heavy workload was tactical as well as practical.

Care of the weak and defenceless is always the province of those whose power is limited — in our own time one has only to look at the pay and workload of nurses, childcare workers, teachers and social workers, to say nothing of the working conditions and consistent undervaluation of carers of the very young and very old at home. Social care of children in nineteenth-century Ireland was for the most part delegated to women who, though they held considerable authority in their own spheres, were severely hampered when it came to the exercise of the kind of transforming, executive power necessary for the growth and development of the work. On the other hand we know, and can know, very little about the day-to-day empowerment that nuns' work with children might have meant for all those involved in it. Like all caring and human-maintenance work, it is immeasurable and invisible.

References

1. *Irish Catholic Directory 1900* (Dublin 1900), p.363.
2. Quoted in Mary P. Cryan, 'The Sisters of Mercy in Connacht 1840-1970' M.A. thesis, University College, Galway 1963, p.1.
3. The main accounts of the founding of the modern Irish female Congregations, and the regeneration of the older Orders, can be found in the following secondary works; Sara Atkinson, *Mary Aikenhead, Her Life, Her Work and Her Friends* Dublin 1879; A Member of the Order of Mercy, *Leaves From the Annals of the Sisters of Mercy* New York 1881; Helena Concannon, *The Poor Clares in Ireland* Dublin 1929; Margaret Gibbons, *Life of Margaret Aylward* Dublin 1928, and *Glimpses of Catholic Ireland in the Eighteenth Century* Dublin 1932; R. Burke Savage, *A Valiant Dublin Woman: the story of George's Hill* Dublin 1940; Brigidine convent, Tullow, *Gleanings from the Brigidine Annals* Naas 1945; M.B. Degnan, *Mercy Unto Thousands* Dublin 1958; T.J. Walsh, *Nano Nagle and the Presentation Sisters* Dublin 1959; A Loreto Sister, *Joyful Mother of Children: Mother Mary Frances Teresa Ball* Dublin 1961.
4. The Sacred Heart nuns came to Roscrea, Co. Tipperary in 1840, the Faithful Companions of Jesus and the Good Shepherd sisters settled in Limerick city in the mid-1840s. Useful information on the foreign Congregations can be found in Irish Messenger Publications, *Religious Orders and Congregations* Dublin 1933, which, like most of the titles referred to, can be found in the Central Catholic Library, Merrion Square, Dublin 2.
5. *Battersby's Catholic Directory 1840* Dublin 1840, *Irish Catholic Directory 1900, Religious Orders and Congregations*, and the works mentioned in note 3, above; on nuns increasing eight-fold, see Tony Fahey, 'Female Asceticism in the Catholic Church: a case study of nuns in nineteenth-century Ireland' PhD thesis, University of Illinois

1981, p.56.

6. For a review of writing on women Religious, amongh others, see Caroline Ford, 'Religion and Popular Culture in Modern Europe' *Journal of Modern History* Vol.65, No.1, March 1993, pp.152-175. On nuns in England, see Susan O'Brien, 'Terra Incognita: the Nun in nineteenth-century England' *Past and Present* No.121, November 1988, pp.110-140; on France, see Claude Langlois, *Le Catholicisme au Feminin* Paris 1984. On women and communities see, e.g. Martha Vicinus, *Independent Women: Work and Community for Single Women* London 1985.

7. D.H. Akenson, *The Irish Education Experiment* London 1970.

8. Walsh, *Nano Nagle*, p.216; see *Special Reports of Convent Schools in Connection with Board of National Education* 1864 (405) XLVI.

9. Patricia Kelly, 'From Workhouse to Hospital: the Role of the Irish Workhouse in Medical Relief to 1921' M.A. thesis University College, Galway 1972, p.171, p.245; Jane Barnes, *Irish Industrial Schools 1868-1908* Dublin 1989.

10. *Presentation Directory 1850*, pp.17-18, p.20; *A Guide for the Religious Called Sisters of Mercy 1865* pp.1-13. These two publications were put together by nuns themselves and circulated to some of the convents. See also Walsh, *Nano Nagle*, passim; A Loreto Sister, *Joyful Mother*, pp.125-6; Sr. Mary Pauline, *God Wills It: the Centenary Story of the Sisters of St. Louis* Dublin 1959, pp.210-11.

11. On efficacy of visitation, see *Special Reports convent schools 1864*, passim; Sr. M. Vincent Keane, *A History of the Presentation convents in Kerry in the nineteenth-century, and their contribution to education in that period* M.Ed. thesis, University of Dublin 1976, p.57; on 'education' of nuns, *Special Reports convent schools 1864*, pp.10-11.

12. *Special reports convent schools 1864*, pp.12-3, pp.31-2; Atkinson, *Mary Aikenhead*, p.452.

13. Kate O'Brien, *The Land of Spices* London 1941; Mary Colum, *Life and the Dream* New York 1928; Kate O'Brien, 'Memories of a Catholic Education' *Stony Thursday Book* No.7 (1981), pp.28-32.

14. A Catholic Layman (James Kavanagh), *Mixed Education: the Catholic Case Stated* Dublin 1859, p.236.

15. Keane, *Presentation in Kerry*, p.67; *Special reports convent schools 1864*, p.16, pp.159-60; A Member of the Order of Mercy, *Leaves*, p.246.

16. Anne V. O'Connor, 'The revolutiion in girls' secondary education in Ireland 1860-1910' in Mary Cullen (ed.) *Girls Don't Do Honours: Irish Women in Education in the 19th and 20th centuries*, Dublin 1987, pp.31-54.

17. Annals, St. Mary's Convent of Mercy, Limerick, 1850, (Vol.I, pp.231-153); 1868, (Vol.2, pp.294-30).

18. Mercy *Guide*, pp.20-1; Atkinson, *Mary Aikenhead*, pp.447-9; Annals, Mercy convent, Newtownsmyth, Galway, p.27.
19. Lay sisters were described by one nineteenth-century Catholic source as 'those who have the religious but no ecclesiastical vocation'. (W. Addis & T. Arnold, *A Catholic Dictionary* London 1884, p.507.) These Religious wore different dress and had less time-consuming prayer and observance than choir nuns. The whole idea of lay sisters was reviewed in most Congregations after Vatican 2, and the distinction seems to have died out. For a more detailed discussion of lay sisters in nineteenth-century Ireland, see C. Clear, *Nuns in 19th-century Ireland* Dublin 1987, pp.69-99, and 'Walls within Walls: convents in nineteenth-century Ireland' in C. Curtin et al (eds.) *Gender In Irish Society* Galway 1987.
20. This was acknowledged by the 1970 *Report on Industrial schools* (commonly known as the Kennedy report) E.68.
21. Barnes, *Industrial Schools*, pp.118-47.
22. Mercy *Guide*, pp.15-17.
23. Sr. Mary Pauline, *God Wills It*, p.169.
24. Barnes, *Industrial Schools*.
25. Letter from Sister Genevieve Beale, Sisters of St. Louis, Spark's Lane, Monaghan, to Cardinal Cullen, 25 March 1861; Cullen Papers 340/2 (Laity), 340/2/44, Dublin Diocesan Archives, Clonliffe College, Dublin.
26. Sr. Mary Pauline, *God Wills It*, pp.146-51.
27. Annals, Mercy convent Limerick, 1865, (Vol. 2, p.78-116).
28. Ms. synopsis of annals, Good Shepherd convent, Limerick; A Loreto Sister, *Joyful Mother*, pp.267-70, pp.273-5.
29. The main source of information on Cusack is her own highly melodramatic *Authobiography* London 1889, and Irene French Eager, *Margaret Anna Cusack: the Nun of Kenmare* Dublin 1979. A list of her publications can be found in the latter work, e.g. *Advice to Irish Girls in America* (1872), *Woman's Work in Modern Society* (1874), and several works of historical interest, including a life of St. Patrick, (1871) for which she received a letter of congratulations from Pius IX and actually made it into the *Irish Ecclesiastical Record*. Liam Bane, whose work on John MacEvilly, archbishop of Tuam in Cusack's time, is shortly to be published ('John MacEvilly 1816-1902' M.A. thesis, University College Galway 1979), is as puzzled as Cusack herself claimed to be at the archbishop's harassment of the nun.
30. 'No religious superior who is a woman can possess power of jurisdiction in the proper sense of the word. Ecclesiastical jurisdiction implies the power of spiritual rule over the faithful insofar as they are members of the Church. Hence it descends directly from the spiritual power which Christ granted to his disciples, by means of holy orders, to their

67

successors, the ministers of the Church.' L. Fanfani and K. O'Rourke, *Canon Law for Religious Women* Iowa 1961, p.59. For a nineteenth-century perspective, see Addis and Arnold, *Dictionary*, p.73.

31. Nineteenth-century middle-class and upper-middle class women turned the ideology of 'separate spheres' to their own advantage, using it to legitimate their own activity outside the home. Historical works on this phenomenon are too numerous to mention, but see, for a start, M. Vicinus (ed.) *A Widening Sphere: changing roles of Victorian women* Indiana 1977, and J. Rendall (ed.) *Equal of Different: women's politics 1800-1914* Oxford 1987.

32. *Irish Catholic Directory 1900; Irish Catholic Directory 1882.* Lists of religious houses in each diocese throughout the country, giving details of projects and occasionally, numbers of religious.

33. Walsh, *Nano Nagle*, pp.48-50; Atkinson, *Mary Aikenhead*, passim.

34. Sr. Mary Pauline, *God Wills It*, pp.168-9. The extract is taken from a government inspector's report of 1865.

35. M.F. McCarthy, *Priests and People in Ireland* London 1902, pp.455-7.

36. *Irish Catholic Directory 1882*, p.230-1; Ms. synopsis of annals, Good Shepherd convent, Limerick.

CHILDREN AT RISK IN THE NETHERLANDS IN THE NINETEENTH CENTURY: THE PHILANTHROPICAL CONNECTION

Jeroen J.H. Dekker

The relation between 'Children at risk' and the role of philanthropy in nineteenth-century Holland is an intriguing one. In this article, we shall examine this philanthropical connection by asking the following questions.

Firstly, how and with the help of which methods did Dutch philanthropists approach the problem of 'children at risk'? Special attention will be given to one very popular approach, namely that of residential re-education (Section 2).

Secondly, was Dutch philanthropy itself transformed as a result of her engagement with children at risk? More concretely, can we claim that philanthropy, after paving the way for legal arrangements for child protection, decreased in influence, or was philanthropy merely changing its shape? We shall demonstrate our view on this by means of the birth of the Children Acts of 1901 (Section 3).

A third question arises out of the choice by philanthropists of 'children at risk' as one of their main areas of concern. Is it the case that the philanthropical approach would never have achieved such a high degree of success if this choice had not been made? Such a counter-factual question can of course never be answered conclusively. In any case, we can only ask ourselves whether the philanthropical movement was more or less dependent on engagements with 'children at risk', in the light of the examination of the first two questions (Section 4).

Preceding this, we must, of course, clarify the meaning of 'children at risk' and also of 'philanthropy'. Is philanthropy a modern phenomenon, originating in modern times, characterised by industrialisation and urbanisation? Is 'children at risk' a concept, shaped by the philanthropists? Or does this concept refer to individual and social realities, to a special social group, living in slums and belonging to Benjamin Disraeli's second nation (Section 1)?

1. Philanthropy and Children at Risk: Concepts and Realities

Philanthropy and Charity

'It is not easy to decide what constitutes philanthropy, what topics must be included. and what may be safely left out', sighed David Owen in his classic *English Philanthropy 1660-1960*[1]. His answer is a 610 pages long, impressive book on the history of English Philanthropy which does not, however, provide a clear definition. Charity and philanthropy both play a role in his book, but the differences between them, if they are of importance, remain unclear. Kirkman Gray, on the other hand, author of another classic on English Philanthropy mentioned with respect by Owen, gives a very clear definition: Philanthropy 'proceeds from the free will of the agent, and not in response to any claim of legal right on the part of the recipient'[2]. In fact, philanthropy is defined here in contrast with modern social policy of the Welfare State, in which it is true that recipients possess certain claims under well-defined conditions, while the representatives of the State cannot proceed from their own free will, but from Acts and Arrangements decided by parliament. Kirkman Gray's definition is charming of course, but is it representative of the manifestation of such a different, sometimes even contradictory form of so-called philanthropy in nineteenth-century Holland?

Perhaps, it is a good idea to consult some encyclopaedias and dictionaries on philanthropy, thereby distinguishing between two categories, namely religious and lay ones; categories which always occur in histories of philanthropy[3]. When doing this, we find ourselves in the centre of fierce debates about the meaning and the value of philanthropy and charity. Moreover, we find an idea of history, with, at its core, the idea that philanthropy and charity succeed each other in clear directions. In other words, history is divided into charitable and philanthropical periods. At the same time, however, we find different, sometimes even contradictory, opinions as to the meaning and periodisation of of these two elusive terms. After presenting these opinions, we shall try to draw up a balance and give our own interpretation on the differences and similarities of philanthropy and charity.

The Dutch Protestant *Christelijke Encyclopedie* (Christian Encyclopaedia), mentions both charity and philanthropy[4]. Philanthropy is limited to human beings, and their mutual relations. Charity is much more important, since it differs principally from philanthropy, having divine inspiration and divine origins[5]. Matthew, 25: 35, mentions the six (later completed to seven) acts of charity. These acts of charity, however, do not form its essence. They only function as a means of realising that fundamental goal of charity which is God's love in his son Jesus Christ. In short, it is charity which counts, philanthropy having only a human dimension.

In another Christian encyclopaedia, the American *The New Catholic Encyclopaedia*, the word philanthropy is not even used; here it is also only that charity counts. Charity is defined as follows: 'the state of being in and responding to God's love and favour [...]. The dominant theme is that God first loves us (lJn4.9) and commends His charity toward us in the death of His Son (Rom 5.8-10). Our love in return springs from the new man who is now dead to sin and born afresh to life in Christ [...] This is charity, that we walk according to God's Commandments'[6].

In short, only charity really counts in these Christian texts, Roman Catholic as well as Protestant ones. Philanthropy is considered either as a preliminary stage of charity (and of a rather primitive character) or even as a deviation from its more fundamental relative.

Lay dictionaries reflect a different mentality. In the *Algemeene Nederlandsche Encyclopedie voor den beschaafden stand* (General Dutch Encyclopaedia for the Civilised Class)[7], it is charity which is not even mentioned. This encyclopaedia propagates the goals of modern and liberal philanthropy, namely education and integration of the poor and the marginals by way of schooling, well-doing, etcetera. 'Philanthropy means humanity' (menschlievendheid)[8].

Two famous general encyclopaedias, the *Encyclopaedia Britannica* and the French *Grande Encyclopedie*[9], also distinguish between the two concepts, but with another intention. According to these dictionaries, the use of charity occurs already in Stoic circles, an idea which is completely incompatible with the idea of the birth of charity with the beginnings of Christianity, an interpretation to be found in the above-mentioned Christian dictionaries.

In the *Encyclopaedia Brittanica*[10], charity is defined very broadly, as 'the principle of the good life. It stands for a mood or habit of mind and an endeavour'. Therefore,' [t]the history of charity is a history of many social and religious theories [and not only the Christian religion], influences and endeavours, that have left their mark alike upon the popular and the cultivated thought of the present day. The inconsistencies of charitable effort [inconsistencies contested by the Christian interpretation] and argument may thus in part be accounted for. To understand the problem of charity we have therefore (1) to consider the problem of charitable thought- the primitive, pagan, Greek and Roman, Jewish and Christian elements, that make up the modern consciousness with regard to charity, and also the growth of the habit of 'charity' as representing a gradually educated social instinct. (2) We have also to consider in their relation to charity the results of recent investigations of the conditions of social life. (3) At each stage we have to note the corresponding stage of practical administration in public relief and private effort; for the division between public or 'poor-law' relief and charity which prevails in England is, comparatively speaking, a novelty, and, generally speaking, the work of charity can hardly be appreciated or understood if it be considered without reference to public relief. (4) As to the present day, we have to consider practical suggestions with regard to such subjects as charity and economic thought, charity organisation, friendly visiting and almonership, co-operation with the poor-law, charity and thrift, parochial management, hospitals and medical relief, exceptional distress and the 'unemployed', the utilisation of endowments and their supervision, and their adaptation to new needs and emergencies. (5) We have also, throughout, to consider charitable help in relation to classes of dependants, who appear early in the history of the question-widows and orphans, 'the sick and the aged, vagrants and wayfarers'.

With reason, therefore, the *Encyclopaedia Brittanica* does not need to treat *philanthropy* in its 1910 edition, since charity includes both concepts. However, the 1947 edition[11] does treat philanthropy: 'Various groups of the modern social order resent the idea of alms, regarding such forms of assistance as undemocratic. So the use of the word charity is often avoided. [...] Between 1775 and 1800 there were significant beginnings of that notable philanthropic activity which was to characterise the nineteenth-century. Conspicious among its forerunners in England were John Howard, pioneer in prison reform, and Sir Samuel Romilly, who sought to abolish the barbaric feature of British criminal law. [...The] rapid and unparalleled transfer of people from rural to urban conditions [...] gave rise to problems in social adjustment of immense range and complexity. Accompanied by the progress of democracy, the advance of popular education, the increasing sense of civic responsibility, the application of scientific methods and above all, the ever-widening permeation of the humanitarian spirit, these social transformations formed the background for the development of the great outstanding philanthropies of our time. Most notable among the results of the philanthropic spirit were the great advance in industrial welfare, the abolition of human slavery, improved housing in cities, enlightened care for the defective classes, immense extension of free public education, the organisation of the Red Cross society, the charity organisation movement, the social settlement movement, the child welfare movement and the establishment of scientifically equipped hospitals'.

In other words, philanthropy is, on the one hand, a modern phenomenon, belonging to the industrial society of the nineteenth century, on the other hand, it is simply another word for charity for those people who do not like the Christian connotation of this term.

For the *Grande Encyclopédie*, however, written in the context of the struggle between Laics and Catholics in nineteenth-century France, this vague and even pragmatic distinction between charity and philanthropy is unthinkable. In volume 10, under the reference to *charity*, we see the first transformation of charity, namely from stoic charity, *caritas generis humani,* into Christian charity. 'Tout autre est la charité chrétienne. La charité exprime une grâce [...], c'est-à- dire un don gratuit d'une personne à une autre, qui ne peut avoir sa raison que dans l'amour désintéressé de la première pour la seconde. La charité a donc le don pour moyen, l'amour pour principe et pour but [...]. Dieu est charité'.

In the eighteenth century, the *Grande Encyclopédie* illustrates another transformation of charity, namely into benevolence and into *philanthropy*: 'la charité pratique s'est appelée la bienfaisance et surtout la philanthropie [sic]. Ce qui répugnait le plus à la philosophie du XVIIIe siécle, dans l'idée chrétienne de la charité, était l'idée de la dépendance où l'homme se trouve constamment dans ce systéme vis-à-vis de la gratuité des dons divins'.

It is still, however, no pure philanthropy, because dependency (that enemy of liberty) had yet to be eliminated. 'Il y a là quelque chose qui sort des pures relations de droit et qui fait revivre les anciens privilèges, l'ancienne charité [...]. C'est pur caprice de la part du bienfaiteur, c'est un privilège dont jouit celui qui a reçu le bienfait'. Therefore, another transformation took place, namely of philanthropy into *solidarity*. '[L]a société moderne [...] ne veut plus admettre que la justice, les relations juridiques réciproques entre tous ses membres [...] ni charité, ni fraternité, mais solidarité'. In fact, we see here the birth of social politics, considered as the such-and-such transformation of philanthropy, which was itself a transformation of charity.

In volume 26 of this encyclopaedia, *philanthropy* is treated separately. Surprisingly, the philanthropy of the Enlightenment is now seen as the renaissance of the philanthropy of antiquity, and not of the transformation of Christian charity. 'La philanthropie proprement dite renaît au contraire avec le naturalisme de la Renaissance et triomphe avec le XVIIIe siècle anglais et français. Elle y apparaît comme un sentiment essentiellement laïque, qui s'adresse à l'humanité seule et non à Dieu' [...]. Par là, l'idée stoïcienne est retrouvée, mais devenue, grâce au Christianisme, plus efficace et plus humble, plus ardente et plus profonde.[...] Cette morale philanthropique et humanitaire, qui est celle du xviiie siècle, est d'origine anglaise[12][..]. D'Angleterre, cette philosophie, dégagée de tout mysticisme chrétien et même de toute métaphysique, se répand en France, en Italie, en Amérique, inspire Voltaire, Montesquieu, Diderot, Rousseau, Beccaria'.

So, for the *Grande Encyclopédie*, real, i.e. non-Christian, philanthropy is different but also superior to charity, which was mostly considered as a Christian phenomenon, notwithstanding the non-Christian varieties[13].

The mother of all Encyclopaedia's, the famous *Encyclopédie* of Diderot and d'Alembert, however, does not demonstrate this ideological bias. The two concepts are treated neutrally. 'Charité [...] on la définit une vertu théologale, par laquelle nous aimons Dieu de tout notre coeur, et notre prochain comme nous-mêmes. Ainsi la charité a deux objects matériels, Dieu et le prochain'. Philanthropy is defined as 'vertu douce, patiente, et désintéressée, qui supporte le mal sans l'approuver'[14].

In short, philanthropy is a very ancient phenomenon indeed, whilst charity is a relatively modern one. Therefore, it is an illusion to try to trace the birth of philanthropy in modern times. Nevertheless, the philanthropy of the Enlightenment differed from ancient philanthropy in a fundamental way. The philanthropy of the Enlightenment is founded on the idea of the elevation of the poor, including their children, by a pedagogical and educative strategy. Antique philanthropy was focused exclusively on the individual, while charity, being a Christian virtue, was founded on performing the seven acts of charity for the marginals, in order, eventually, to reach God.

The first traces of modern philanthropy can be found at the end of the Middle Ages. Together with the development of commercial capitalism, the integration of marginals in society becomes a major social challenge[15]. Eventually, two different phenomena emerged. On the one hand, a variety of philanthropy which was inspired by the antique philanthropical tradition, while becoming the precursor of the philanthropy of the Enlightenment. On the other hand, Christian philanthropy was born, being a combination of ancient charity and modern philanthropy. It becomes clear then, that Christian philanthropy unites the vertical goals (directed to God) and intentions of the traditional charity with the horizontal goals (directed to the well-being of other people) of modern philanthropy.

Children at Risk in Nineteenth-Century Europe: Social Reality and the Construction of a Category

In nineteenth-century Europe, a new phenomenon appeared, which went by the name of residential re-education for deprived and criminal children, in other words for children at risk[16]. In France, a sharp distinction had first been made between child and adult criminals in the revolutionary Constitution of 1789. The French example strongly influenced legal developments in countries such as Belgium and the Netherlands, both during and after the Napoleonic era. The 'Era of philanthropists'[17], the rule of the Citizen-King Louis-Philippe between 1830 and 1848, was of crucial significance for the philanthropical involvement with re-education in France, Belgium and the Netherlands. In this period, residential re-education was born in Western Europe. The revolution of 1848 provided a further catalyst for change[18]. The bourgeoisie's increasing fears of public disorder made it possible to finance the extension of the residential solution for the problems posed by delinquency.

Notwithstanding this social and political background, the residential solution was, from the beginning, also characterised by pedagogical intentions. To cite De Montbel, the last minister of Home Affairs under King Charles: 'Young inmates, detained under articles 66 and 67 of the Penal Code, need our special care. [...] Thus it is their education to which we must pay particular attention'[19].

Re-education in reform houses of children at risk was adopted as a solution in France, England, Belgium, Germany, the Netherlands, and elsewhere. In France, the innovations of Charles Lucas (the Inspector General of the Prisons of the Realm) and of the judge Frédéric-Auguste Demetz, became famous. Originally Lucas favoured cellular prisons for children and juveniles (i.e. an organisation based on cells) but went on to stimulate the foundation of agrarian colonies for the re-education of criminal or potentially delinquent children. In England this development occurred against the background of radical economic, social and political modernisation, illustrated by the New Poor Law of 1834, the reform of the electoral system in 1832 and many acts and regulations in the area of child labour and education. Mary Carpenter, a leading protagonist in the reform movement, greatly influenced by John Stuart Mill, managed perfectly to combine two major successes in an effort to achieve the ultimate philanthropical aim: the improvement of the national economy, and the means, therefore, for the establishment of 'Reformatory Schools' and 'Industrial Schools' for children and deliquents[20].

In both France and England informed observers of social and economic conditions were obsessed with the notion of the 'dangerous class'. In France the issue was posed by the Academy of Moral and Political Sciences, and H.A. Frégier responded with the prize-winning solution[21]. Benjamin Disraeli's description of the problem of the 'Two Nations', the rich and the poor, in unambiguous and lively terms[22] and Mary Carpenter's establishment of her 'Schools for the Children of the Perishing and Dangerous Classes' indicate how seriously the issues were viewed in England.

However, the first residential re-educational institutes were established in Germany and it was on these that the attention of the French, English and Dutch was focused. The most famous Home was the Rauhe Haus of Johann Hinrich Wichern, established near Hamburg in 1833. This home was to serve as an example for a series of other model homes such as Mettray in France, Mettray in the Netherlands, Ruysselede in Belgium and Red Hill in England[23]. The 'Nederlandsch Mettray', founded by the philanthropist Willem Suringar, began its work in 1851, as we shall see below[24].

In short, children at risk formed a social reality: a result of the effects of the Napoleonic wars in continental Europe, of the rapid economic development in England, and of the social and economic crisis of the forties. At the same time, however, children at risk became a category, and not a very clear one. For this group of children was described in very different terms, such as dangerous children (criterion: social order), children in danger (criterion: pedagogical care), criminal children (criterion: juridical), fallen children, especially girls (religious criterion), finally, at the end of the century, non-normal children (in terms of the new child-science, pedagogical pathology). Choice of category depended on the choice for the interpretation of social reality. For the Dutch liberal philanthropists, in the beginning it was the juridical and social criteria which were dominant, while Christian philanthropists made all criteria dependent on religion. At the end of the century, the impact of the scientific criterion was increasing, and it is interesting to analyse the effects of this.

Pedagogical pathology was strongly influenced by medical terminology. Pedagogical theory on educational problems (special pedagogics) was not available in the nineteenth century, and general pedagogics was in fact part of, mainly German, philosophy. Within medical pathology, however, casuistry and nomenclature were well developed[25]. At the end of the century, pedagogics became more focused on empirical questions[26], especially about children at risk and child deficiencies, and to make it a more scientific activity, medical nomenclature was put in pedagogical concepts and theories. While making use of medical nomenclature, the differences between medical and pedagogical pathology were stressed, that is to say by the pedagogues themselves. The Leipzig professor Adolf Heinrich Ludwig von Strümpell (1812-1899) was of great importance in the development of Dutch pedagogical pathology. The title of his book, *Die Pädagogische Pathologie oder die Lehre von den Fehlern der Kinder. Versuch einer Grundlegung für gebildete Altern, Studirende der Pädagogik, Lehrer sowie für Schulbehörden und Kinderärzte*, already gives us an idea about his intention to write a book for pedagogues and doctors at the same time. Pedagogical science had to be more empirical, less philosophical, he argued. Pedagogical pathology was, in the words of Von Strümpell '[d]ie Lehre von allen denjenigen Zuständen und Vorgängen, welche erfahrungsmässig während der Entwicklung des geistigen Lebens im Kindheitsalter von solcher Beschaffenheit sind, dass sie der Abschätzung und Werthbestimmung, nach denen der Pädagoge sie im hinblick auf sie von ihm gedacht und erstrebte Jugendbildung auffast und beurtheilt, sie entweder nicht als genügend oder als bedenklich oder schädlich, überhaupt als irgendwelcher hinsicht der Besserung bedürftige Fehler darstellen'.[27]

In nineteenth-century Holland, systematic inventarisation of child deficiencies, especially deficiencies of the moral kind, was realised by school teachers in particular. Child deficiencies were considered to be fundamentally different from adult deficiencies, in so far as a child's character and behaviour could be changed, while changing an adult's behaviour and character was considered far more difficult, not to say virtually impossible. Children's deficiencies were formulated in normal, non-scientific language. Hundreds of them were formulated, such as stubbornness, a propensity to steal, disobedience. Jan Geluk, a schoolmaster, published a real inventory on that subject within his *Dictionary of Education* (1882), in which he summed up a tradition beginning with Father Cats, the famous moralist and *Landsadvocaat* of the Golden Age[28].

Within a few years, however, everything changed. Pedagogical pathology, with its own nomenclature, different from the ordinary language of Geluk and his tradition, developed further. Its fathers were Jan Klootsema and K. Andriesse. They took over the existing medical nomenclature and introduced the new terms enthusiastically into their pedagogical theories. They wrote texts like 'Introduction to pedagogical pathology and therapy' (the first handbook on pedagogical pathology written in Dutch) in which they tried to establish an independent position and a domain of its own for the pedagogical pathology. They found it necessary to overstress its differences with the medical pathology, a normal phenomenon in the history of the genesis of new scientific disciplines. A naive sort of arrogance was not strange to these representatives of the new discipline, of whom Von Strümpell considered his pedagogical pathology as even more difficult than the existing mother discipline, the medical pathology. Was it not the case that only one hundred childhood diseases were known, whilst more than three hundred moral and pedagogical deficiencies could be mentioned?[29].

2. Philanthropy and Children at Risk in the Netherlands in the nineteenth-century

Two Philanthropies

A national philanthropy? The pedagogical mission of Nut

Together with the growth of poverty around 1800 and onwards, new forms of philanthropy were developing[30]. The struggle against poverty was entered via pedagogical and educative strategies directed at the poor and their children. The most famous philanthropical society became the *Maatschappij tot Nut van 't Algemeen* (The Society for the General Good), abridged as *Nut,* founded in 1784 in Edam. This philanthropical society was focused on the elevation and education of children of the poor and their parents. This philanthropical society, liberal and Christian at the same time, was a good example of the mentality of the Dutch Enlightenment: not anti-Christian, but characterised by a tempered Protestantism[31]. In the words of Simon Schama:

'Of far greater significance was the principal agency of Christian sociability, the Society for the General Good. Quite apart from its independent importance as a disseminator of new educational and philanthropic ideas, the 'Nut' [...] was different, both in kind and degree, from the other learned societies which mushroomed in the Netherlands towards the end of the century and from which the Batavian Republic had drawn many of its leaders. [...] it remained less a gentlemen's club or debating society than a kind of social church. [...] Its literature was vernacular, earthly and simple, preoccupied with the ethics of everyday life and designed to catch the imaginations of the 'brede middenstand' who were the principal victims of the events which overtook the Netherlands after 1780 [...] It meant, above all to be popular. And so indeed it was'[32].

According to Mijnhardt, *Nut* was the first Dutch society without formal relations with the State, which held itself responsible for actual social problems, and was seen in terms of national unity and national civilisation (in contrast with the local or regional identities, defended by the traditional societies before 1795)[33]. National identity, a concept born in the Dutch Enlightenment, founded the objectives of *Nut*. Its organisational structure, however, was a typical compromise between national and local identities, characterised by its locally rooted departmental structure[34].

At the outset, *Nut* represented a real cultural revolution. After the Batavian Revolution, however, the social and political respectability increased at the expense of the revolutionary élan[35]. The intensification of informal relations between Society and State made that clear. Thus, an illusion was born: the idea of a national civilisation, which was shared by the whole nation, and not merely by some regions, some cities, some social groups. Mijnhardt shared this idea, or this illusion: 'Around 1815, the formation of the nation on the cultural level was completed, and, for the first time in Dutch history, an era started which was characterised by a national culture, shared by all parties'. According to him, that idea of national civilisation, represented by *Nut*, remained dominant during nearly the whole of the nineteenth-century, notwithstanding the tensions between 1830-39 around the Southern Netherlands (the future Belgium) and the influence of the Dutch Réveil[36].

It is my opinion that this is an illusion of philanthropists as well as of historians, because *Nut* represented the moderated, Protestant Dutch Enlightenment, and not national identity, which, on the contrary, was already very heterogeneous[37]. Catholics (numbering around 40 percent of the population) were nearly unrepresented in this society, and orthodox Protestants were totally absent, being a denomination which should play a key role only in Christian Philanthropy. Jews were even formally excluded from membership until 1864. In short, *Nut* was a very influential philanthropical society, characterised by its pedagogical and educative goals, but it was not a national one.

Christian Philanthropy: between Charity and Philanthropy

Besides this 'national' philanthropy, Catholics and orthodox Protestants developed their own philanthropy, i.e. Christian philanthropy. This philanthropy united the goals of traditional charity with the methods of its more modern counterpart. Protestant Christian philanthropy was linked closely to the Protestant Réveil, influential in Germany, in Switzerland, in the Netherlands, and in England[38]. This Revival Movement was a reaction against modernism; a result of the Enlightenment. Under the Batavian Republic (1795-1806), clear separation came about between the Dutch Reformed Church (once winner of the struggle between Arminians and Contra-Arminians in seventeenth-century Holland) and the State. Through it, two different movements were stimulated. On the one hand, the emancipation movements of non-Calvinist religious groups, beginning with the Roman Catholics. On the other hand, the modernisation of the Dutch Reformed Church itself.

The Dutch Réveil was against such modernisation. She departed from the Regulations of the Synod of Dordrecht of 1619, when the victory of the orthodox Protestants was confirmed[39].

The leading figures of the Dutch Réveil were Guillaume Groen van Prinsterer, founder and ideologue of the Dutch political anti-revolutionary movement Isaac Da Costa, a former Jew, and Otto Gerhard Heldring, founder of several re-education houses for deprived boys and girls in danger. In the first 'interior' phase, followers of the Rveil were mostly occupied with their own spiritual agony, philanthropical effects being almost absent as a matter of fact. After 1830, however, the followers of the Réveil began to look more outside of themselves, focusing on the spiritual agony of the other, trying to save sinners. Christian philanthropy as we know it, was born. In the sessions held by the Christian Friends in Amsterdam, leading figures like Groen van Prinsterer and Heldring discussed concrete projects, such as elementary education, benevolence and slavery (which was abolished in 1863 in the Dutch colonies)[40]. Notwithstanding this new concreteness, it was not the free will of the philanthropists conducting this agenda: God Himself engineered these philanthropical activities.

Dutch Catholic philanthropy (charity, however, is perhaps the better term in the beginning) could develop fully with the separation between the Dutch Reformed Church and the State, and the emancipation of the Catholic Church. A leading figure in this period of origins was J.G. Le Sage ten Broek, author of *The Excellence of the doctrine of the Catholic Faith* (1815). In 1853, the episcopal hierarchy was restored and as a consequence, the emancipation of Dutch Catholics was accelerated. Catholic philanthropy entered in to a new, dynamic phase.

Philanthropical Societies

Nineteenth-century Dutch philanthropy flourished in a new political and legal context: a centralised régime, the separation between the Dutch Reformed Church and the State, and last but not least, the introduction of the Napoleonic Code. The new Dutch State, however, modernised and centralised though it was, took no responsibility whatsoever for children at risk, with the exception of criminal children. This expanding field was left to philanthropical movements. Their activities were further promoted by the 1848 constitution of Jan Rudolf Thorbecke (1796-1872), a constitution which was decisive for the Dutch State, inaugurating the constitutional monarchy. Through this constitution, new possibilities of organisation and association became possible. The philanthropist made use of them willingly.

Dutch philanthropists organised themselves in philanthropical societies and circles, like their counterparts in England and France. Moreover, the orthodox Protestant and the Catholic philanthropical movements succeeded in using philanthropical activities for their own particular goals, i.e. the emancipation of their supporters and the extension of political influence. Before examining some of these societies, it is beneficial to pay attention to some Enlightenment-oriented, more moderate Protestant societies.

Amongst them, *Nut*, already considered, is by far the most important one. For the members of this society, the distance between the poor and the rich was the main problem, solutions being education and schooling. Therefore, one needed to develop a system of patronage of the poor, including control and supervision. The famous philanthropist Willem Suringar published a book along these lines, entitled *The patronage of the poor* (1842)[41].

Another society with a slightly more liberal character was founded in 1823 under the name of the *Society for the moral amelioration of prisoners*; a society comparable with its French counterpart the *Société royale pour l'amélioration des prisons*[42]. Willem Suringar was among the three founders. The main goals of this society consisted in visiting the prisoners and trying to influence them morally. Willem Suringar published another book, which was a *Religious and Moral Manual for prisoners*, and was explicitly intended to be read by the prisoners themselves (including the young criminals, for whom some special sections were written[43]).

The *Society of Benevolence* became famous but also attracted some ill-repute. This society was founded in 1818 by Johannes Van den Bosch, ancient general of the Dutch army, participant in the battle against the Napoleonic army in 1813, and touched by the expansion of poverty after that war. By founding agrarian colonies in the north of the country (the principal activity of his society) he tried to reach three goals together: growth of the national production; the definitive solution of the poverty problem by means of forced participation of certain categories (i.e. the poor, the beggars, the vagabonds, in sum the real marginals[44]); finally, the elevation of the moral level of the population. This society was a private one, but sustained by the State. By several Acts and Royal Decrees, local and regional governments were forced to send their orphans to the colonies, which consequently also became child-saving institutions, at least nominally, as we shall see in section 4. At first, reactions were positive, from inside the Netherlands, and from abroad. L.-F. Huerne de Pommeuse, adherent of the idea of agrarian colonies in France, visited the Dutch colonies in 1829 and back in France, he wrote enthusiastically: 'La société de Bienfaisance aura rendu, chaque année, à l'ordre social, comme lui devenant désormais utiles, plusieurs centaines d'individus qui, précédemment, n'y apportaient que la honte, l'inquiétude et des charges d'une progression effrayante'.[45]

Some decades later, however, opinion was to change drastically, in the Netherlands as well as abroad. In 1869, the colonies were closed and replaced by a prison, which still functions to this day[46].

The Protestant Réveil did not form real societies, but assembled in philanthropical circles. Notwithstanding their rather loose organisational structure, the results of this philanthropical movement were impressive. Inspired by this movement, several reeducation houses were founded, which I shall examine below. To this were added several deaconesses' hospitals, for example in Utrecht[47]. In any case, at the end of the nineteenth century,

80

the orthodox Protestants around the future prime minister Abraham Kuyper developed a well-organised Christian philanthropy.[48] The periodical *Bouw-steenen. Tijdschrift voor inwendige zending*[49] became the mouthpiece of this Christian-philanthropical movement.

Finally, the Catholics did become more important, but their activities were more charitably than philanthropically oriented. *The Catholic Society for Good Morals in the Kingdom of the Netherlands,* founded by Le Sage Ten Broek, became the first important Catholic society as a result of the new constitution. It served the Catholic emancipation movement. In 1846, a Dutch department of the international society of *St. Vincent de Paul* followed. The Catholic emancipation movement only attained its full development, however, in the second half of the nineteenth-century. the *Pius Almanak* functioned as the organ of this Catholic version of Dutch Christian philanthropy[50].

Dutch philanthropy was first of all characterised by a pedagogical, moral and evangelical mission. We shall now pay attention to the philanthropical connection with children at risk. Especially the creation of a vast system of re-education houses in the Netherlands in the second half of the nineteenth century which formed concrete evidence of the success of that pedagogical and moral mission[51].

Philanthropy and Children at Risk in the Netherlands

Willem Hendrik Suringar (1790-1872) was the most important pedagogically oriented philanthropist of his time. Suringar, a moderate Protestant, was a member of the established Calvinist Dutch Reformed Church. At first, he was an adherent of the cellular method for re-education of criminal minors, like his French counterpart Charles Lucas. He wrote a handbook on religious and moral questions (including texts for minors) to be used daily by prisoners[52]. Child criminals attracted his special attention. After his visits to agrarian colonies in France (the French Mettray), Belgium (Ruysselede), and elsewhere, he became convinced that agrarian colonies were, in fact the solution, and was to maintain this position for the rest of his life; defending a solution that was fashionable throughout Europe at that time[53].

Strikingly, all philanthropically oriented ideologies, and not only Suringar's, although very different in outlook and ends to be realised, and being in competition with each other and sometimes even hostile towards others, realised the same ultimate solutions of residential re-education for the punishing, rescue or education of deprived and criminal children. Despite this, however, they remained in competition with each other over this specific philanthropical area. Before examining in more detail one of the most important results of this residential re-education movement, the agrarian colony 'Nederlandsch Mettray', we shall briefly mention other important models of residential re-education, present in the Netherlands.

It was the agrarian colonies of the *Society of Benevolence* which served as a catalyst for the foundation of other agrarian colonies in the Netherlands and abroad. Meanwhile, the *Society for the amelioration of prisoners* (founded by, amongst others, Willem Suringar) influenced strongly the decision, taken by the State, to found a prison for criminal boys in Rotterdam (1833) and for criminal girls in Amsterdam (1837). The Principal of the Rotterdam prison, J.W. Schlimmer, a former schoolmaster, became in 1851 the first Principal of the Dutch Mettray, of which we shall give more details below.

The re-educational houses founded by the Reverend Otto Gerhard Heldring served as paradigmatic models for the orthodox Protestant philanthropical movement. The houses for the rescue of fallen girls, called 'Heldringgestichten' or 'Zettense Inrichtingen', were founded in 1848, and the re-education house for deprived boys in Hoenderloo in 1851.

The Catholics founded their first modern re-education houses at around he same time: 'Aloysius' in Amsterdam, founded in 1848 by the Jesuit A. Frenthof, and the agrarian colony Heibloem, situated in the southern province of Limburg, in Heythuizen.

The example of 'Nederlandsch Mettray'

In 1880, the American E.C. Wines wrote: 'Holland boasts one of the model reformatories of the world, under the name of 'Netherlands Mettray'[54]. Willem Hendrik Suringar was very impressed by his visit to the agrarian colony for child criminals in Mettray, near the French town of Tours. He therefore decided to found such an agrarian colony, another Mettray, in Holland. Many Dutch philanthropists, including the King himself, supported Suringar's project. The official opening of the colony, which was situated in the countryside, in the province of Gelderland, along the river IJssel about five miles north of the city of Zutphen, took place in January 1852.

Most of the two thousand boys who crossed over the threshold of the colony between 1851 and 1914 were already living on the periphery of society and were badly brought up children according to the informants, who often included the parents of these children. They did not attend school regularly, they did not express themselves in an acceptable way and their behaviour was sometimes dangerous. Nevertheless it was hoped that it would prove possible to eradicate these childhood faults.

The colony had been specifically designed with re-education in view. This was a luxury. Few institutions were able to construct a residence to the specifications of the founder as in the case of 'Nederlandsch Mettray' for whom an isolated site was bought in the east of the country. This move was carefully thought out in accordance with the objectives of the association. Isolating the boys from the dangers of city life in the west of the country was a precondition for moral regeneration. This was the general opinion in the first years of the existence of the colony[55].

The Situation around 1900

The Dutch re-education movement began as a private, philanthropical activity, laying the foundations for a large system of re-education houses in the second half of the nineteenth-century. This was achieved through the realisation of their main models, i.e. the agrarian colony, the cellular prison for criminal children, and the family house. Towards the end of the nineteenth century, more than one hundred re-education houses had been founded, the vast majority being Protestant or Catholic, while half of their capacity was destined for fallen girls.[56]

This very heterogeneous philanthropy obtained similar results in the field of residential re-education for many different societies. In short, the same practice, re-educating outside the family, proved to be the success of different philanthropical movements, including the Laic philanthropy, the Protestant Christian philanthropy, and finally, the Catholic philanthropy.

3. The Children's Acts: both Philanthropy and Social Policy

Child protection before the Children's Acts: a Private Enterprise

Initially, the protection of the young including residential re-education, was a private affair, with only one exception: punishment of criminal children being the task of the State. This situation remained unchanged until the end of the nineteenth-century. Both parties, the State and the philanthropical movements, were uninterested in augmenting the influence of the State over the protection of deprived children.[57] After all, orthodox Protestants and Catholics alike were completely outside the political centre of power until 1888. They tried, instead, to expand their private and philanthropical power, while the liberals, dominating the government between 1848 and 1901 (with only one exception, the government of Mackay from 1888-1891), were not interested in expanding State influence on the field of the protection of deprived children for ideological reasons.

Nevertheless, a series of Acts, stimulating the protection of children, were formed; a series which, retrospectively, can be considered as significant legislative preparation for the concluding Child Acts of 1901.

In 1806, under the Batavian Republic, the first National School Act created the public school. It was followed in 1857 by the first Primary School Act under the Kingdom, known as 'Van der Brugghen'.[58] In 1810, under the then French dominated Kingdom of Holland, the Napoleonic Penal Code became effective and remained so until 1886.

In the twenties, a series of Royal Decrees on the treatment of marginal children was issued. The Decree which became effective on November 6 1822, was one of the most notorious of the group. It prescribed that all orphans and all abandoned children aged 6 years and over, had to be transported to the agrarian colonies of the Society of Benevolence in the

83

northern part of the country. With the Royal Decree of 24 March 1824, the Decree of 1822 was also enforced, by ordering that regional and local governments give subsidies to orphanages, since the agrarian colonies were available. In any case, in 1865 the orphanages, which formed part of the agrarian colonies of Veenhuizen, were evacuated after a long period of bad treatment and high mortality rates.

More instantly successful were the laws against child labour. In 1874, such a law first came into effect, although its principal importance was more important than the practical effects. In 1889, however, real enforcement became possible, for example with the creation of a system of inspection[59].

In 1884, the laws on the 'Rijksopvoedkundige Gestichten', i.e. the 'Pedagogical Houses of the State' (the former correction houses) became effective. In practice, this was merely a change of name. Notwithstanding this, such pedagogical naming of an already existing institution could, and should have had symbolic meaning. Two years later, in 1886, the Napoleonic Penal Code was replaced by a new Code, named after its author 'Modderman'. This bought to an end a series of prior propositions in 1827, 1839, 1842-46, 1847 and in 1859, which had all failed in their attempts to replace the existing Code.[60]

In 1889, a new School Act came into force, the principal change being that partial subvention of the denominational school became possible. In 1901, at last, the School Act enforcing obligatory schooling, became effective[61].

In short, on the eve of the realisation of the Child Acts for the protection of criminal and deprived children, a series of laws was already available, excluding children from the factories and sending them to schools. In that climate, a call for a comprehensive Child Act could easily be answered, if other factors would join forces and help[62].

The Children's Acts of 1901: a Marriage between the Private and the Public

At the end of the century, several other factors were to prove very helpful indeed. Three developments stimulated the birth of the Child Acts: a changing political situation, a number of studies on children at risk, and finally the philanthropical practice of protecting children at risk itself.

Firstly, the political and ideological positions had changed. In the last quarter of the nineteenth-century, liberals dominated the Government. Orthodox Protestants and Catholics remained outside the Cabinet. From 1888, however, this situation changed. Between 1888-1891, religious parties dominated the Cabinet. At the same time, the liberals developed more progressive ideas about State intervention regarding social problems. It became necessary for a compromise. On the one hand, the influence of the State on child protection (a typical left-wing liberal wish) could grow. Private, mostly religious, philanthropy, was eager to receive money from the State in exchange for the re-education of children at risk[63].

Secondly, a great number of studies appeared on the situation of children at risk, on the relation between juvenile criminality and education, on the legal situation in a number of other countries, and on the need for new legislation[64]. Perhaps the study of the philanthropical society *Nut* was the most influential one. In 1898, *Nut* published a report with the results of a comprehensive examination of the practice of child protection, especially child protection in residential institutions (mostly private ones)[65]. The editors shared the main grief of the educators in these institutions, namely the withdrawal by parents of more than half of the children from the institutions prematurely and against the explicit wish of the institutions themselves. In their opinion, there was only one way to stop this blockage of re-education, namely to develop laws, with the possibility of withdrawing parental authority from parents in case of bad pedagogical behaviour. The editors of the above named report, as well as the Minister of Justice, Cort van der Linden (member of the liberal party and future Prime Minister) distinguished between the public interest — protection of the society against criminal and abnormal children — and the children's interest — protection of children against their pedagogically failing parents. Forty years later, the famous Dutch pedagogue J.H. Gunning Wzn was to consider the Child Acts only from a pedagogical point of view, laying all emphasis on the effects for child protection[66]. The authors of these Acts, however, were less naive[67].

In fact, the Child Acts passed in 1901 and which became effective in 1905, consisted of three individual acts. The first Act, part of the Civil Code, arranged for the protection of deprived and abandoned children. Parental authority could be withdrawn, and by imposing such a measure, residential re-education could be continued — if necessary against the will of the parents. And so, a solution was found for the blockage of re-education, which was seen as a main problem in the 1898 publication of *Nut*. Moreover, private institutions were awarded guardianship directly by the State, with growing influence of private initiative as a consequence. The second Act, part of the Penal Code, arranged for the treatment of young criminals. Finally, in a third Act, practical conditions, necessary for the execution of these two laws, were detailed[68].

As a result of the parliamentary debates, the religious parties gained an amazing victory. For parliament voted unanimously, including the socialists[69], in favour of a series of laws that not only arranged for child protection, but also caused further enlargement of Christian philanthropy, and consequently of Christian political power. Not only the guardianship of children whose parents, had demonstrated bad pedogogical behaviour was awarded directly to private philanthropical institutions, but private institutions gained responsability for criminal children. This was a consequence of the position of the Minister of Justice, who argued that a principal and strict difference between punishment of criminal children and re-education of children at risk was not possible. Originally, the punishment of criminal children was a task for the State, while re-education of deprived children was private initiative's responsibility. When admitting that the treatment of criminal children not only consisted of punishment but also of education, the Minister of Justice (a member of the Liberal Party) gave the religious parties paths to victory, since education was in principle a private responsibility, punishment being one of the exclusive tasks of the State. In mixing both activities, private institutions had to be engaged in punishment as well; this was the winning argument of the religious parties. Their victory was at the same time a political, juridical, moral, pedagogical and financial one[70].

These Children Acts form an important part of the new social politics of the end of the nineteenth century, comparable with the Compulsory Education Act of the same year, and the Acts against Child Labour from 1874 and 1889.[71] Together, these Acts form an answer to the growing problems, caused by an accelaration of economic and demographic growth and rapid industrialisation and which consequently became a series of drastic social problems. On the other hand, however, the Children Acts form an exception, being characterised by a 'marriage between private and public'. At the same time they created instruments for social policy and for the modernisation of already existing philanthropy, while taking into account the very significant influence awarded to private institutions in applying these Child Acts.

4. Conclusion

Philanthropy is a very ancient phenomenon indeed, charity being a relatively modern one. It is an illusion to try to trace the birth of philanthropy in modern times. Nevertheless, the philanthropy of the Enlightenment differs from ancient philanthropy in a fundamental way. The philanthropy of the Enlightenment is founded on the idea of the elevation of the poor, including their children, by a pedagogical and educative strategy. Antique philanthropy, on the other hand, was focused exclusively on the individual, while charity, being a Christian virtue, was founded on performing the seven acts of charity for the marginals in order eventually to reach God.

Ultimately, then, Christian philanthropy was born, being a combination of ancient charity and modern philanthropy. It united the vertical goals (directed to God) of traditional charity with the horizontal goals (directed to the well-being of other people) of modern philanthropy.

Dutch philanthropy lay somewhere between traditional charity, liberal philanthropy, and Christian philanthropy. In addition to *Nut*, the philanthropical society with national ambitions, Catholics and orthodox Protestants developed their own philanthropical societies and networks, characterised by a combination of goals related to traditional charity but by means of modern philanthropy.

Children at risk formed a social reality; a result of the effects of the Napoleonic wars in continental Europe, of the rapid economic development in England, and of the more generally social and economic crisis of the forties. At the same time, however, children at risk became a category, and a complex one. This group of children was described in very different terms, such as dangerous children (criterion: social order), children in danger (criterion: pedagogical care), criminal children (criterion: juridical), fallen children, especially girls (religious criterion), and finally, sub-normal children (in terms of pedagogical pathology).

Choice of category depended on choice for the interpretation of social reality. For the early Dutch liberal philanthropists, the juridical and social criteria were dominant, while Christian philanthropists made all criteria dependent on religion. At the end of the century, the impact of the scientific criterion had also increased.

The relation between 'Children at risk' and the role of philanthropy in nineteenthcentury Holland was very close indeed. Firstly, we have seen that almost all residential re-education was a philanthropical enterprise until the Children's Acts became effective, in 1905. Secondly, Dutch philanthropy did not withdraw herself from the field of children at risk after 1905. On the contrary, these Acts provided the private initiative for more funds to increase the work, while at the same time stimulating a certain influence of the State. The Children's Acts were an example of a fragile compromise between State and Private initiative; two institutions with responsibility towards children at risk. Therefore, we can speak of a real victory for philanthropy, especially the Christian branch, by the passing of these Acts.

Indeed, we can say that the protection of children at risk in the Netherlands in the nineteenth century was dominated by the philanthropical connection. Can we, however, conclude the reverse as well? In other words, was Dutch philanthropy dependent on, or at least would it not have been so successful, if this philanthropical connection with the problem of children at risk had not existed? We believe that the very nature of Dutch philanthropy itself (Christian as well as Liberal) namely to become a driving force of pedagogical and evangelic mission, was the main reason for their very great interest in, and consequently dependency on, the problem of the protection of children at risk.

References

1. David Owen (1964), *English Philanthropy* 1660-1960 (Cambridge, Mass.: The Belknap Press of Harvard University Press), p. 1.
2. B. Kirkman Gray (1905), *A History of English Philanthropy. From the dissolution of the monasteries to the taking of the first census* (London: Frank Cass & Co Ltd., reprint 1967), p.viii.
3. See Owen (op.cit.) and for the French situation C. Duprat (1993), *Le temps des philantropes*, tôme 1 (Paris: Editions du Comite des Travaux historiques et scientifiques); for the rôle of women in English Philanthropy, see F.K. Prochaska (1980), *Women and philanthropy in Nineteenth-century England* (Oxford: Clarendon Press).
4. F.W. Grosheide / G.P. van Itterzon (1956), *Christelijke Encyclopedie* (Kampen: J.H.Kok).
5. See: 1 Joh 4: 16; Rom. 5: 5; 2 Cor.1: 3,4; Eph.3: 1,2; 1 Cor. 13: 13.
6. *New Catholic Encyclopedia* (1967) (New York: McGraw-Hill Book Company), vol. III, pp.464-465. Cf. *Brockhaus Enzyclopädie in zwanzig Bänden* (1967) (Wiesbaden: F.A. Brockhaus), 17. Auflage, dritter Band, p.610: 'Caritas [...] die göttliche Tugend der Liebe (Agape)'.
7. *Algemeene Nederlandsche Encyclopedie voor den beschaafden stand. Woordenboek van kunst, wetenschap, nijverheid, landbouw en handel* (1867), (Zuthpen/Leiden: P.B. Plantenga & A.W. Sythoff), Volume ll.
8. Idem, pp.300-301.
9. *La Grande Encyclopédie, inventaire raisonné des sciences, des lettres et des arts, sous la direction de André Berthelot* (s.a.), (Paris: Librairie Larousse), Volume 10, pp. 651-656; Volume 26, pp. 642-645.
10. *The Encyclopaedia Britannica* (1910-1911) (Cambridge: Cambridge University Press), eleventh edition (first edition: 1768-1771), pp. 860-861.
11. *The Encyclopaedia Britannica*, (1947), (Chicago/London/Toronto: The University of Chicago / Encyclopaedia Britannica, inc.), pp. 709-710.
12. For example Jeremy Bentham, Adam Smith, Shaftesbury, Hutcheson and Hume. See: D. Owen (op.cit.); F. Barret-Ducrocq (1991), *Pauvreté, charité et morale à Londres au xixe siècle. Une sainte violence* (Paris: Presses Universitaires de France).
13. *The Grande Encylopédie* (op.cit.), Volume 26, pp.642-645.
14. *Encyclopédie ou Dictionnaire raisonné des arts et des métiers*, par une société de gens de lettres, mis en ordre et publié par M. Diderot [...] et, quant à la Partie Mathématique, par M. D'Alembert, Paris, 1751-1780, Volume XII, p. 504. I made use of the microprint edition (1969) (New York:), 4 volumes. See also Pierre Larousse (1867), *Grand Dictionnaire Universel du XIXe siècle* (Paris: Librairie Classique Larousse et Boyer), for the two concepts.

15. Cf. J.J.H. Dekker (1990), The Fragile Relation between Normality and Marginality. Marginalization and Institutionalization in the History of Education. In: D. Van Damme, F. Simon, B. Kruithof and J. Dekker (editors), Beyond the Pale, Behind Bars. Marginalization and Institutionalization from the 18th to the 20th Century, special issue *Paedagogica Historica,* (XXVI), New Series, pp. 13-29; B. Geremek (1989), Le marginal. In: J. Le Goff, *L'homme médiéval* (Paris: Seuil), pp.381-413; D. Van Damme (1990), *Armenzorg en de staat* (Gent: Rijksuniversiteit Gent); for the Dutch Republic in the 17th century, see S. Schama (1987), *The Embarrassment of Riches. An Interpretation of Dutch Culture in the Golden Age* (London: William Collins), with a critical comment in J.J.H. Dekker & L.F. Groenendijk (1991), The Republic of God or the Republic of Children? Childhood and Child-rearing After the Reformation: an appraisal of Simon Schama's thesis about the uniqueness of the Dutch case. In: *Oxford Review of Education*, Vol. 17, No. 3, pp. 317-335.

16. The ancient orphanages, originating in the Middle Ages, were not meaned for criminal and deprived children, but for orphanages, mostly children of citizens of the city. See A. Hallema (1964), *Geschiedenis van het Weeshuis der Gereformeerden binnen Delft te Delft* (Delft: Regentschap), 446-455; J.Th. Engels (1989), *Kinderen van Amsterdam* (Zutphen: De Walburg Pers); J.J. Dankers & J. Verheul (1991), *Als een groot particulier huisgezin. Opvoeden in het Utrechtse Burgerweeshuis tussen caritas en staatszorg 1813-1991* (Zutphen: De Walburg Pers).

17. See Henri Gaillac (1971), *Les maisons de correction, 1830-1945* (Paris: Editions Cujas), 26 f.f. and the title of the first chapter.

18. See E.C. Wines (1880), *The State of Prisons and of Child Saving Institutions in the Civilised World* (Cambridge: Cambridge University Press), p. 693; A.J.Th. Jonker (1882), 'Johann Hinrich Wichern', *Bouwsteenen* (1), 288-315; Th. Nolen (ed.) (1898), *Het Vraagstuk van de verzorging der verwaarloosde kinderen, in opdracht van de Maatschappij tot Nut van 't Algemeen* [Society for the General Good] (Amsterdam: Maatschappij tot Nut van 't Algemeen), p. 17; See M. Perrot (1980), '1848. Révolution et prisons', in M. Perrot, *L'impossible prison. Recherches sur le système pénitentiaire au XIX siècle* (Paris: Seuil), pp. 277-312; J. Petit (1990), *Ces Peines obscures. La prison pénale en France (1780-1875)* (Paris: Fayard); C. Duprat (1993), *Le temps des philanthropies, tôme 1* (Paris: Editions du Comité des Travaux historiques et scientifiques).

19. 'Les jeunes détenus, en vertu des articles 66 et 67 du code pénal appellent plus particulièrement notre sollicitude. [. . . .] *C'est donc de leur éducation qu'il, faut spécialement s'occuper'* (my italics), 29 January 1830. In Gaillac (op.cit.), p.41.

20. M. Carpenter (1851), *Reformatory Schools for the Children of the Perishing and Dangerous Classes, and for Juvenile Offenders* (London: reprint 1968).
21. In H.A.Frégier (1840), *Des classes dangereuses de la population dans les grandes villes, et des moyens de les rendre meilleux* (Paris), p. v.
22. Benjamin Disraeli (1845), *Sybil; or, the two nations* (Harmondsworth: Penguin Books, edn. 1980), p. 96.
23. See on Germany: F.F. Röper (1976), *Das verwaiste Kind in Anstalt und Heim: ein Beitrag zur historischen Entwicklung der Fremderziehung* (Göttingen).
24. For Belgium, see M-S. Dupont-Bouchat (1991), Saint Hubert, pénitencier modèle au XIXème siècle, in *Mélanges L. Hannecart, Saint Hubert d'Ardenne, Cahiers d'histoire*, t. VIII, pp. 143-160; J.J.H. Dekker (1994), Rituals and reeducation in the nineteenth century: ritual and moral education in a Dutch children's home. In: *Continuity and Change*, 9 (1), pp.121-144.
25. See J. Gélis (1988), *La sagefemme ou le médicin. Une nouvelle conception de la vie* (Paris: Fayard).
26. M. Depaepe (1989), *Meten om beter te weten? Geschiedenis van de experimenteelwetenschappelijke denkrichting in de Westerse pedagogiek vanaf het einde van de 19de eeuw tot aan de Tweede Wereldoorlog* (Leuven: Afdeling Historische Pedagogiek, K. U. Leuven).
27. L. von Strümpell (1890), *Die Pädagogische Pathologie etc.* (Leipzig: Georg Böhme), pp. 16-17. See also J.F.G. Közle (1893), *Die pädagogische Pathologie in der Erziehungskunst des 19 Jahrhunderts* (Gütersloh: Bertelsmann).
28. J. Geluk (1882), *Woordenboek voor opvoeding en onderwijs* (Groningen: Wolters).
29. Von Strümpell (op.cit.), p.74. See also K. Andriesse, (1905), Kindergebreken. In: C.F.A. Zernike (red.), *Paedagogisch Woordenboek* (Groningen: Wolters), pp.597-612; J.J.H. Dekker (1990), Witte jassen en zwarte toga's. Medici, juristen en de opvoeding van verwaarloosde en achtergebleven kinderen in Nederland in de tweede helft van de negentiende eeuw. In: *Paedagogisch Tijdschrift* (15), nr.2, special issue on medicalization of educating in Belgium and The Netherlands in the 19th. and 20th. century, pp. 111-121; Th. Jak (1988), *Armen van geest. Hoofdstukken uit de geschiedenis van de Nederlands zwakzinnigenzorg* (Amsterdam: Pedagogisch Aviesbureau), chapter 5, on the initiative of Van Koetsveld in the Hague; J. Klootsema (1904), *Misdeelde kinderen. Inleiding tot de paedagogische pathologie en therapie* (Groningen: Wolters). On Klootsema, see Th.R.M. Willemse (1993), Jan Klootsema (1867-1926), architect van de residentiële orthopedagogiek. In: *Handboek Orthopedagogiek*, 1026.

30. Cf. H.F.J.M. van den Eerenbeemt (1977), *Armoede en arbeidsdwang. Werkinrichtingen voor 'onnutte' Nederlanders in de Republiek, 1760-1795. Een mentaliteitsgeschiedenis* ('s-Gravenhage: Martinus Nijhoff).
31. See B. Kruithof (1990), *Zonde en deugd in domineesland. Nederlandse protestanten en problemen van opvoeding zeventiende tot twintigste eeuw* (Groningen: Wolters-Noordhoff), ch.3; *Gedenkboek Maatschappij tot Nut van 't Algemeen 1784-1934* (1934) (Amsterdam); E.S. Houwaart (1991), *De Hygiënisten. Artsen, staat en volksgezondheid in Nederland 1840-1890* (Groningen: Historische Uitgeverij Groningen).
32. S. Schama (1977), *Patriots and Liberators. Revolution in the Netherlands 17801813* (New York: Alfred A. Knopf), pp. 532-533.
33. W.W. Mijnhardt (1988), *Tot Heil van 't Menschdom. Culturele genootschappen in Nederland, 1750-1815* (Amsterdam: Rodopi), p.265.
34. Mijnhardt (op.cit.), p.270
35. Mijnhardt (op.cit.), p.289.
36. Mijnhardt (op.cit.), p.376.
37. See Dekker & Groenendijk (op.cit.), p. 320.
38. Cf. Barret-Ducrocq (op.cit.); M.E. Kluit (1970), *Het protestantse Réveil in Nederland en daarbuiten 1815-1865* (Amsterdam: Paris).
39. The Protestant Réveil was against obligatory smallpox vaccination and against dechristianisation of the public school, amongst other issues, see Kluit (op.cit.).
40. Cf. Kluit (op.cit.); J.J.H. Dekker (1985), *Straffen, redden en opvoeden* (Assen/Maastricht: Van Gorcum). ch. 2; B. Kruithof (op.cit.), ch. 4.
41. W.H. Suringar (1842), *Redevoering over de gepastheid en noodzakelijkheid van een patronaat over de armen en de wijze waarop hetzelve behoort te worden uitgeoefend* (Leeuwarden: G.T.N. Suringar).
42. See C. Duprat (1980), *Punir et guérir. En 1819, la prison des philanthropes.* In: M. Perrot (op.cit.), pp. 64-12; and Duprat (1993: op.cit.).
43. See J.M. van Bemmelen (1923), *Van zedelijke verbetering tot reclasseering. Geschiedenis van het Nederlandsch Genootschap tot zedelijke verbetering der gevangenen 1823-1923* ('s-Gravenhage: Martinus Nijhoff); W.H. Suringar (1828), *Godsdienstig en zedekundig Handboek voor Gevangenen; geschikt voor zon- en feestdagen* (Amsterdam: Maatschappij tot Nut van 't Algemeen); see Chr. Leonards (1993), *Residential Care for Juvenile Offenders in the Nineteenth Century Netherlands: bourgeois Ideas and experiments in a European Context,* paper, University of Limbourg, Maastricht.
44. Cf. Dekker (1990, Paedagogica Historica, op.cit.), pp.13-29.
45. L-F. Huerne De Pommeuse (1832), *Des colonies agricoles et de leurs avantages* (Paris: Huzard), p. 155.
46. Cf. H. Gaillac (op.cit.) p. 77; C.A. Kloosterhuis (1981), *De bevolking van de vrije kolonin der Maatschappij van Weldadigheid* (Zuthpen: De Walburg Pers).

47. Cf. Kluit (op.cit.), passim.
48. D.Th. Kuiper (1972), *De Voormannen, Een sociaal-wetenschappelijke studie over ideologie, konflikt en kerngroepsvormig binnen de gereformeerde wereld in Nederland tussen 1820 en 1930* (Amsterdam: Vrije Universiteit); J.C. Sturm (1988), *Een goede gereformeerde opvoeding. Over neo-calvinistische moraal,pedagogiek (1880-1950), met speciale aandacht voor de vieuw-gereformeerde jeugdorganisaties* (Kampen: Kok).
49. *Bouwsteenen. Tijdschrift voor inwendige zending* (1882-1894 and 1895-1897) (Utrecht: C.H.E. Breyer).
50. *Pius Almanak. Jaarboekje voor katholieken en inzonderheid voor de leden der katholieke verenigingen in het jaar des Heeren ....* (1875-) (Amsterdam).
51. Cf. Dekker (1985, op.cit.); J.J.H. Dekker (1990), Punir, sauver et éduquer: la colonie agricole 'Nederlandsch Mettray' et la rééducation résidentielle aux Pays-Bas, en France, en Allemagne et en Angleterre entre 1814 et 1914. In: *Le Mouvement Social,* numéro 153, pp. 63-90.
52. See W.H. Suringar (1828: op.cit.); W.H. Suringar (s.d., c. 1850), My visit to Mettray [i.e. the French Mettray] (Rotterdam); a bibliography of Suringar's publications can be founded in E. Laurillard (1873), 'Levensschets van W.H. Suringar', *Handelingen en mededeelingen van de maatschappij der Nederlandsche Letterkunde, over het jaar 1872-1873* (Leiden), pp. 215-246.
53. See M.L. -F. Huerne de Pommeuse (op.cit.); M. Carpenter (op.cit.), especially on the German Rauhe Haus near Hambourg, pp. 335-338; Matthew Davenport Hill, follower of M. Carpenter, wrote about his impressions after a visit to the French Mettray as follows: 'No Mahommedan [...] believes more devoutly in the efficacy of a pilgrimage to Mecca, than I do in one to Mettray', cited in Owen (op.cit.), p. 153.
54. E.C. Wines (op.cit.), p.400; see also Dekker (1985, op.cit.); J.J.H. Dekker 1990, *Le Mouvement Social*), J.J.H. Dekker (op.cit. 1994, *Continuity and Change*).
55. See Dekker (op.cit. 1985), pp. 36-55
56. Cf. chart 2 in Dekker (1990, *Le Mouvement Social*) p.70.
57. See P.A. van Toorenburg (1918), *Kinderrecht en Kinderzorg in de laatste honderd jaren* (Leiden: Leyden University); Herman Franke (1990), *Twee eeuwen gevangen. Misdaad en straf in Nederland* (Utrecht: Aula / Het Spectrum), pp. 85-87.
58. See L. Dasberg & J.W.G. Jansing (1978), *Meer kennis meer kans. Het Nederlandse onderwijs 1843-1914* (Haarlem: Fibula-Van Dishoeck); Hans Knippenberg (1986), *Deelname aan het lager onderwijs in Nederland gedurende de negentiende eeuw* (Amsterdam: Koninklijk Nederlands Aardrijkskundig Genootschap); P.Th.F.M. Boekholt & E.P. de Booy (1987), *Geschiedenis van de school in Nederland. Vanaf de*

middeleeuwen tot aan de huidige tijd (Assen/Maastricht: Van Gorcum); M. van Essen (1990), *Opvoeden met een dubbel doel. Twee eeuwen meisjesonderwijs in Nederland* (Amsterdam: SUA).

59. See J. van Drongelen (1990), *De ontwikkeling van de arbeidsinspectie in een veranderende wetgeving* (Zoetermeer: Van Drongelen), ch. 2 et 3; J.C. Vleggeert (1964), *Kinderarbeid in Nederland* 1500-1874 (Assen: Van Gorcum); S.Sr. Coronel, Geschiedkundig overzicht van het vraagstuk van den kinderarbeid in Nederland. In: *De Tijdspiegel*, II, 1888, pp. 29-58.

60. See P.A. van Toorenburg (op.cit.), ch.2; Franke (op.cit.), ch. VI.

61. See Boekholt (op.cit.), Van Essen (op.cit.), J.C.M. Wachelder (1992), *Universiteit tussen vorming en opleiding.- De modernisering van de Nederlandse universiteiten in de negentiende eeuw* (Hilversum: Verloren), ch. 2.

62. See Dekker 1985 (op.cit.), ch.2, p.149.

63. Cf. A. De Graaf (1920), *Het vraagstuk van de salarisregeling en de rechtspositie van personeel in christelijk-philanthropische inrichtingen* (Utrecht: Centraal-Bond van Christelijk-Philanthropische Inrichtingen in Nederland), p. 11.

64. F. Coenen Jr. (1892), *De Fransche Wet ter bescherming van Verwaarloosde en Mishandelde kinderen* (Amsterdam: doct. thesis University of Amsterdam); H.L. Asser (1897), *Bescherming van minderjarigen. Eene Studie over het ouderlijk gezag en de voogdij. Bekroonde beantwoording van de prijsvraag, uitgeschreven door het gesticht 'Talitha Kûmi'* (Haarlem: De Erven F. Bohn); J. Simon van der Aa (1890), *De Rijksopvoedingsgestichten in Nederland* (Amsterdam: doct. thesis University of Amsterdam); L. del Baere (1891), *De invloed van opvoeding en onderwijs op de criminaliteit* (Amsterdam: doct. thesis University of Amsterdam); Jhr. D.O. van Engelen (1895), *De verwaarloosde jeugd en de jeugdige misdadigers met betrekking tot onze wetgeving* (Haarlem: Bohn); M.C. Nijland (1895), *Rijksweldadigheidsscholen in België* (Utrecht: doct. thesis University of Utrecht).

65. Nolen (ed.), Het Vraagstuk (op.cit.).

66. J.H. Gunning Wzn (s.a., c. 1938), *De studie der paedagogiek in Nederland gedurende de jaren 1898-1938. Een Schets* (Amsterdam), p.38.

67. Cf. Nolen (ed.), Vraagstuk (op.cit.), p.5 et p.11; P.A. van Toorenburg (op.cit.), p.72; the Minister of Justice, P.W.A. Cort van der Linden, in A.D.W. de Vries / F.J.G. van Tricht (1905), *Geschiedenis der wetgeving op de misdadige jeugd (Wetten van 12 Febr. 1901 (S 63) en 12 Febr. 1901 (s 64). Verzameling van regeeringsontwerpen, gewisselde stukken, gevoerde beraadslagingen enz., bijeengebracht, gerangschikt en bewerkt door A.D.W. de Vries en F.L.G. van Tricht* (Haarlem), Volume I, p.37.

68. Probation and children's courts were arranged by law in 1922. See J. Doek (1972), *Vijftig jaar ondertoezichtstelling* (Zwolle: Tjeenk Willink); M.S. Dupont-Bouchat, J-G.Petit, J. Trepanier, B. Schnapper, J.J.H. Dekker et al. (editors) (1993), *Enfants corrigés, enfants protégés. Genèse de la protection de l'enfance (Belgique, France, PaysBas, Québec) 1820-1914, rapport intermédiaire* (Paris: Ministère de la Justice).
69. See M. Brinkman (1983), De S.D.A.P., de kinderzorg en de kinderwetten 18891905. 'Voor de schipbreukelingen van het kapitalisme'. In: *Pedagogische Verhandelingen* 6, pp. 5-52.
70. De Vries et Van Tricht (op.cit.), p. 28, p. 32, p. 43, p. 52.
71. Cf. A. De Swaan (1988), *In Care of the State. Health care, education and welfare in Europe and the USA in the Modern Era* (Cambridge/Oxford: Polity Press).

'CORRUPTING THE YOUNG'? POPULAR ENTERTAINMENT AND 'MORAL PANICS' IN BRITAIN AND AMERICA SINCE 1830

John Springhall

'Unparalleled evil and barbaric killers says judge bud did horrific video nasty trigger James's murder?' queried a tabloid headline on the day after the conviction of two eleven-year-old boys for the murder in February 1993 of two-year-old James Bulger in Bootle, Merseyside. While the capacity of new technology to deliver striking visual images has increased dramatically in recent years, present-day worries about the impact of crime and violence in the mass media on young people are not without precedent. They have their roots in nineteenth-century fears about the ill effects of popular forms of entertainment on poor urban youth and they stretch in an almost unbroken line through successive 'moral panics' in both Britain and America, once popular culture was transformed into urbanised commercial entertainment from the early Victorian years onwards. A common denominator in the fears excited by each successive technological and commercial innovation was and is their tendency to be consumed by the young, a significant audience for the violent and sexual imagery which for centuries has saturated popular culture.[1] *Ipso facto*, the most popular mediums of entertainment among the young at any given historical moment tend also to provide the focus of the most intense social concern.

Thus each new technological break-through, from the rotary printing press to the computer, provides a focus for social anxiety, particularly if exploited commercially to market a new form of amusement for the young. From this perspective, the fear of 'video nasties' or of violent interactive computer games and the fear of mass consumer society often go hand in hand. The frightened would like to disinvent the new technology that has created the video recorder and the home computer and return society to an imaginary, non-violent popular culture, a mythical golden age of tranquil behaviour. To understand properly how such fears have arisen in both Britain and America, forms of cultural production need to be studied in relation to other cultural practices and to social and historical structures. What follows makes some attempt to contextualise the 'moral panics' aroused since the 1830s by various ephemeral forms of purchased entertainment, locating hostility to the amusements of childhood and youth within the prevailing construction of cultural values. This historical perspective excludes 'moral panics' over specific elements in the modern mass media, such as the cinema, television, and popular music, focusing mainly upon so-called 'commercial culture' in printed form directed at the young, samples of which can be seen in collections of children's literature.[2]

Patently, adult disapproval of market-based entertainments intended for young, primarily working-class, consumers has a lengthy historical pedigree, extending over time from the arrival of penny theatres ('gaffs') in the 1830s, to the 'penny dreadfuls' and 'dime novels' of the 1860s and after, from the Hollywood 'gangster films' of the 1930s, to the American 'horror comics' of the early 1950s, the 'video nasties' of the early 1980s, and the violent computer games of the early 1990s. The ideologues of cultural standards writing in the newspaper and periodical press consistently labelled the antecedents of mass culture directed at the urban youth market in the nineteenth-century as 'pernicious' or corrupting. Historical studies might usefully attempt to determine the nature of the interrelationship between the generally unrestrained and sensational content of this 'commercial culture', its predominantly youthful audience, and society's moral guardians. Campaigns to censor youth's diversions in Britain alone have resulted in such anti-libertarian legislation as: the licensing provisions of the Metropolitan Police Act (1839), encouraging the police to close down 'penny gaffs' popular with the young; the Children and Young Persons (Harmful Publications) Act (1955), outlawing American 'horror comics' from Britain; and the Video Recordings Act (1984), the product of a fabricated 'moral panic' over so-called 'video nasties', giving the British Board of Film Classification the strictest powers in Europe to certify and censor purchased home entertainment.[3]

'Moral panic' occurs when the official or media reaction to a deviant social or cultural phenomenon is 'out of all proportion' to the actual threat offered. This problematic and much-devalued term was popularised in 1972 by sociologist Stanley Cohen to represent a press outcry in the 1960s against rampaging teenage gangs of 'mods' and 'rockers'. In this context, 'moral panic' implied a periodic tendency towards the identification and scapegoating of 'folk devils' whose activities were regarded by hegemonic groups as indicative of imminent social breakdown. Similarly, Rob Sindall, writing about street violence in nineteenth-century England, has drawn attention to the newspaper 'panic' in 1856, and again in 1862, over 'garrotte' attacks in London, involving footpads choking their victims. By 1863 any form of street theft accompanied by violence (even jostling) was referred to in the contemporary press as a 'garrotte' attack. These events coincided with a dramatic growth in newspaper circulation, in which 'garrotters' and 'cornermen' were routinely conceived as 'folk devils'. Although street violence was probably on the increase, it was distorted and exaggerated to create sporadic 'moral panics', followed by harsh penalties, throughout the second half of the nineteenth-century.[4]

The 'moral panic' formulation, used here for convenience, needs to be interrogated. For while it usefully draws attention to themes of social apprehension and their association with censorship campaigns, it groups all such 'panics' under a single generic heading, representing them as a consequence of some endlessly cyclical feature of media manipulation. The academic notion of 'moral panic' also comes close to being obsessed by the debunking notion of 'demystification', reaching a preordained conclusion before examining the precise historical evidence. 'Moral panic' is one of those deflating phrases used by allegedly impartial sociologists and historians to condescend to excitements among the general populace. It usually comes equipped with research which demonstrates that alcohol consumption was in fact much larger in the 1870s, or that football hooliganism actually began in 1898. The academic's message is a reassuring one, 'do not worry, we have been here before, your concerns are an ersatz compound manufactured by the media, a few odd bishops, strident voices from the left and the right, moralists and nostalgists of all kinds'. There is a danger of minimising the contemporary sense of worry and crisis, in other words, by an account of its repetitious and historically relative character. People may be right to feel 'panic' about rising crime levels, for example, and hence undeserving of academic disdain.[5]

From 'Penny Gaff' to 'Penny Dreadful'

Improvised out of empty shops or abandoned warehouses, 'penny gaffs' excited one of the earliest Victorian 'moral panics' directed against amusements primarily intended for wage-earning children and adolescents. Offering harmless forms of staged melodrama and pantomime, in mime to avoid prosecution after the 1843 Theatre Regulation Act, these unlicensed theatres provided a rehearsal for subsequent campaigns against incitement to criminality in the mass media, convenient scapegoats to account for the errand boy who robbed his employer. Prosecutions of unlicensed 'gaffs' were largely the result of a widespread early-Victorian belief that they were somehow linked with an apparent rise in the rate of juvenile crime. In 1841 the Report of the Inspector of Prisons for the NE District of England cited an examination of nearly a hundred boys held in Liverpool Prison 'with the view that the mischievous tendency of such productions [as *Jack Sheppard*] may be placed beyond doubt . . . that attentiion may be excited to the subject, and some means may be suggested for the extension and purification of those pleasures which the poorer classes of society are entitled to in the intervals of labour'.[6] Victorian prison inspectors, firm believers in 'rational recreation', were convinced that an interest in Dick Turpin and Jack Sheppard made juveniles into offenders, whereas present day criminologists would probably argue that their way of life turned these boys towards criminal or violent heroes.

From 1839-40 London theatre managers transformed Sheppard, a burglar and jail-breaker hung at Tyburn in 1724 aged twenty one, into a Cockney folk hero, exploiting the serialisation in *Bentley's Miscellany* of middlebrow-novelist William Harrison Ainsworth's melodramatic *Jack Sheppard* (1839). The stage play's 'very popularity with juvenile audiences (who might be so easily swayed by its specious morality) was seen as an index of the danger to society in general and to the moral health of the theatre in particular', writes an historian of English theatrical censorship. Ainsworth's eponymous 'Newgate novel' was also dramatised for the 'penny theatres', reaching youngsters excluded from London's minor theatres by admission price and appearance. On 17 November 1839 a magistrate in SE London heard that the 'respectable' shoemaker father of eighteen year-old Richard John Bayne, arrested for burglary, was convinced that 'bad company' and frequenting a 'penny gaff' in Woolwich had contributed to his son's crime. Characteristically, the ill-informed magistrate, Mr. Broderip, did not know what was meant by a 'penny gaff', so the prisoner's father helpfully explained to the Bench that it was an unlicensed theatre in temporary premises popular with the young, 'which he was convinced did serious mischief in the town. The principal attraction was a new version of the adventures of Jack Sheppard, the housebreaker, and the ''gaff'', as it was termed, was crowded nightly by children. It was here that his son first met Lindsay, the thief'. Broderip recommended that this theatrical 'nuisance' be 'looked after' by the local authorities and was told by the police that measures would immediately be taken for its suppression.[7]

The label 'penny dreadful', constructed from above by middle-class journalists and widely adopted in the 1870s, also came to be equated with juvenile delinquency. It served as a general term of abuse for working-class and lower-middle-class youth's cheap instalment or periodical fiction. Late in 1877 the Society for the Suppression of Vice took out summonses, under Lord Campbell's 1857 Obscene Publications Act, against those responsible for a reissue of *The Wild Boys of London; or, The Children of Night*, an improbable but hardly pornographic mid-1860s 'dreadful'. Reformist sections of the middle class tended to be particularly susceptible, when a rising crime rate was invoked, to a desire to improve the morals and leisure habits of the less privileged. Penny fiction was a particular target because it was felt that expanding literacy had led to the corruption of literature until, among street boys, reading had become an almost criminal pastime. Highwaymen titles were singled out, in what was otherwise an all-embracing indictment of the 'penny dreadful', largely because these popular serials offered an heroic and romanticised image of criminals on horseback defying ineffective Hanoverian law officers. In 1874 crusading journalist James Greenwood urged fellow scribblers to use their pens lance-wise 'in assaulting and killing the hideous dragon that, in the shape of "Boy Highwaymen" and "Knights of the Road", of late years has been nestling with our boys, growing every day more daring and pestilential'.[8]

The flimsy basis for scapegoating 'penny dreadfuls' in relation to juvenile crime becomes fully evident when press reports of late-Victorian trials specifically naming such reading as a criminal accessory are examined. Thus a fourteen-year-old boy was charged on 22 May 1868 before the Worship Street magistrates in Finsbury, NE London, with the theft of two sacks from his employers and sent to prison for a fortnight on hard labour. Issues of Edwin Brett's long-running but harmless periodical *Boys of England* (1866-99) and reprints of the weekly instalment series *Tales of Highwaymen, or, Life on the Road* (1865-66) were discovered on the prisoner, both supposedly 'referring to the achievements of notorious malefactors, which were invested with alluring colours of heroism and magnanimity'. In 1872 seventeen-year-old solicitor's clerk Joseph Bennett and his younger confederate, George Constable, were charged at Bow Street magistrate's court with breaking and entering Messrs. Wigg and Oliver, a firm of architects in Bedford Row, Holborn. Constable told the chief clerk that his office drawer had been cut into and robbed of five pounds and ten shillings. On arrival, the arresting policeman found some weekly numbers of *Tales of Highwaymen* amongst the papers in George's desk. Guilt was inferred ('that looks bad to read such things as these') from mere possession of a 'penny dreadful'. The boy clerk's reported confession ('I have been tempted to do this by reading the tales and by a young man named Bennett') bears all the signs of an attempt to mitigate a crime before a credulous policeman.[9]

Tales of Highwaymen proves to be entirely imaginary and not the Newgate Calendar-style compendium of real-life criminal biographies that these court reports would lead one to expect. It looks back to the Edward Lloyd-style 'penny bloods' of the 1840s, as well as forward to juvenile fiction which presented the highwayman as some kind of charismatic Robin Hood figure. A young reader's weekly penny purchased such far-fetched continuous stories as 'Captain Macheath, the Daring Highwayman and the Black Rider of Hounslow'; 'The Shadowless Rider; or, The League of the Cross of Blood. A Mystery of the King's Highway'; and 'Black Hugh; or, the Forty Thieves of London'. The text relies strongly upon sensational Gothic elements, typical of the 'dreadfuls' put out by the Newsagents' Publishing Company (NPC) in the mid-1860s, rather than the fully realised iconography of the highwayman tale evident in publisher Edward Harrison's best-selling *Black Bess; or, The Knight of the Road* (1863-68), reputed to have sold two million copies over thirty years of constant reissue. If Victorian critics and moralists had taken the trouble to examine the publications of the NPC and its rivals without prejudice, they would have discovered that, far from recommending the values of a criminal or oppositional subculture, their 'point of view' was consistently aligned with support for the established order. In common with other forms of mid-Victorian 'commercial culture', the outwardly sensational melodrama of serialised 'penny dreadfuls' concealed a remarkable degree of moral and social conservatism.[10]

From 'Dime Novel' to 'Horror Comic'

Across the Atlantic, 'dime novels' directed mainly at adult readers flourished between 1860 and 1885, usually Western or detective adventures complete in each monthly part. Smaller folio-sized 'half-dimes', gaining in popularity in the 1880s, were aimed at a larger replacement market of adolescent boys. Anthony Comstock, a name synonymous with American prudery, portrayed 'half-dimes' as 'corrupting the young, glamorising criminal behaviour', and as responsible for the 'fearful increase of youthful criminals in our cities in recent years'. A prodigious moral crusader, Comstock was Secretary and Chief Special Agent of the New York Society for the Suppression of Vice (NYSSV), bankrolled by the Y.M.C.A. and multimillionaire J.P. Morgan, in which capacity he campaigned until his death in 1915 to put 'dime novel' publishers out of business. Under the Federal Anti-Obscenity or 'Comstock' Law of 1873, the NYSSV lobbied strenuously to suppress sensation fiction; tightening restrictions on the second-class postage rate and arresting publishers sending 'pernicious literature' through the mails. While the career of a 'vice ideologue' like Anthony Comstock cannot be taken as fully representative of American culture, he was still part of a much larger reforming and temperance endeavour in the late-nineteenth century which obtained the support of both rural-puritan and urban-philanthropic groups. The NYSSV's major campaign against 'half-dime' novels centred on the Western outlaw stories of the late 1870s and early 1880s, converging with the Postmaster-General's threat to remove the economic privilege of mailing under 'second-class matter' to publications not meeting with Comstock's approval. This assault on American freedoms met with surprisingly little unfavourable publicity, as compared to Comstock's more ludicrous campaigns against 'obscenity' in painting and statuary.[11]

'Dime novels' were superceded after World War One by the short-story 'pulps', adventure, sport, science-fiction, and detective magazines with lurid covers. They, in turn, were overtaken by the paperback book and the comic book, evident among American servicemen during the Second World War. The comic book was developed by Max C. Gaines in the early 1930s out of the Eastern Color Printing Company's 'premium books' or free promotional inducements. Once the initial market-led demand for superhero comic books subsided after 1945, left-wing publisher Lev Gleason, a former Eastern Color employee, found he had initiated a lucrative trend with the earliest and most successful 'crime comic' book, *Crime*

Does Not Pay (1942-55), edited and drawn by Charles Biro. In 1946 the House Committee on Un-American Activities accused Gleason of being 'Communist party influenced', arising out of an investigation into a New York anti-fascist refugee organisation. He was charged with contempt of Congress, along with a group including *Spartacus*-author Howard Fast. Ironically, the preoccupation of Gleason's best-selling comic books with violent crime may have provided a catharsis for the pent up fears and supercharged aggression generated by anti-communist hysteria. In 1948 Gleason's influential market leader and its companion title, *Crime and Punishment* (1948-55), achieved sales of over one and a half million copies each month. The rapid growth of 'crime comics' soon attracted the attention of the media and educators worried about 'copycat' crimes apparently carried out by their younger readers.[12]

The combined monthly circulations of Gleason's titles ranking tenth among all American magazines, by 1950 he was president of the Association of Comic Magazine Publishers. A readership survey taken in the late 1940s determined that 57% of the readers for *Crime Does Not Pay* were over twenty-one, overlapping with young men who read the fading 'pulps'. 'Not intended for children' was displayed on early 'crime comic' covers but, as time went on, they were read by the non-adult. More than 40 comic book publishers issued over 150 new 'crime comic' titles from 1947 to 1954, among them *Justice Traps the Guilty, True Crime Comics, Crimes By Women, Murder Incorporated, Lawbreakers Always Lose* and *Crime Must Pay the Penalty*. Comic book historians tend to emphasise their more sensational qualities, suggesting the escapist appeal of violence to the law-abiding suburban reader. 'Drug addiction, prostitution, kidnapping, murder, violence by women, violence to women, infanticide, torture, whippings, mutilations, bloodletting, and bad attitudes ran throughout the crime comics', according to Mike Benton. 'There were few good role models — the police were ineffectual or brutal, just like the criminals they killed. Children in crime comics were helpless victims or aspiring juvenile delinquents'.[13]

Early in 1950 Max Gaines's son William, the young publisher of Entertaining Comics (E.C.), and his creative partner, artist-editor Al Feldstein, inaugurated a series of innovative 'New Trend' comic books from their Manhattan offices. Together they changed the face of juvenile reading in America, but were also viewed by their critics as debauching the young. Bill Gaines first dropped his 'crime comics', *War Against Crime* and *Crime Patrol*, by renaming them as two 'horror comics', *The Crypt of Terror* (later retitled *Tales from the Crypt*) and *The Vault of Horror*, hosted by a Vault Keeper and a Crypt Keeper with origins in American radio. The celebrated E.C. horror trilogy was made complete when Gaines axed his remaining Western comic, *Gunfighter*, and in May 1950 started *The Haunt of Fear*, filled with 'illustrated suspence stories that we dare you to read'.

E.C. comics now began a boom for graphic horror fantasy that in the next four years would see comic-book publishers circulate over 100 new titles and 2,400 separate issues. The sales peak for comic books was reached in 1953-54, by which time a staggering 75 million ten-cent copies were being read all over America every month. A massive collapse in sales swiftly followed, partly because E.C.'s 'New Trend' horror titles, along with equally gory and violent Marvel, Ace, Harvey, Story, and D.C. imitations, created a massive backlash against the entire comic-book industry. In 1954 this recoil helped publicise New York psychiatrist Dr. Fredric Wertham's tendentious indictment *Seduction of the Innocent: The Influence of Comic Books on Today's Youth*. When he testified on how comic-book reading could teach children to commit crimes, Wertham's characteristically obsessive and incoherent views were received with great deference by the Senate Subcommittee to Investigate Juvenile Delinquency.[14]

William Gaines followed Wertham to the stand on 21 April 1954 and soon became engaged in a heated exchange about the boundaries of 'good taste' with Senator Estes Kefauver of Tennessee, two years before a candidate for the Democratic presidential nomination:

Senator Kefauver: Here is your May 22 issue [of *Crime SuspenStories*]. This seems to be a man with a bloody ax holding a woman's head up which has been severed from her body. Do you think that is in good taste?
Mr. Gaines: Yes, sir; I do, for the cover of a horror comic. A cover in bad taste, for example, might be defined as holding the head a little higher so that the neck could be seen dripping blood from it and moving the body over a little further so that the neck of the body could be seen to be bloody.
Senator Kefauver: You have blood coming out of her mouth.
Mr. Gaines: A little.
Senator Kefauver: Here is blood on the ax. I think most adults are shocked by that.
The Chairman: Here is another one I want to show him.
Senator Kefauver: This is the July one. It seems to be a man with a woman in a boat and he is choking her to death here with a crowbar. Is that in good taste?
Mr. Gaines: I think so.
Mr. Hannoch: How could it be worse?[15]

The preoccupation with the boundaries of 'good taste' evidenced by Senators and Chief Counsel on this Senate Subcommittee is significant, because the process of establishing taste differentials ('most adults are shocked by that') here becomes a symbolic weapon in the struggle for ideological domination between established cultural arbiters and the commercial harbinger of a new generation.

A majority of intimidated comic book publishers, responding to Washington's strictures, formed the Comics Magazine Association of America in September 1954. This body created a strict set of editorial standards for their comic books called the Comics Code Authority, with its own independent review board. The Code made it difficult for horror and crime titles to continue, since after October those that did not abide by its over-zealous guidelines ('no comic magazine shall use the word "horror" or "terror" in its title') would not get distributed. Whereas in 1952 about 500 comic book titles were available, by 1955 the number had dropped to around 300. The monthly sales of Lev Gleason's crime titles fell from 2,700,000 in 1952 to around 800,000 in 1956. Boom times were over for the profit making but competitive and under-capitalised American comic-book industry. While the tremendous growth of television had certainly played its part, so too had a 'moral panic' driven by the anti-comic book crusaders and amplified by the media. The mid-1950s also saw the collapse of every one of E.C. publisher Bill Gaines's comic-book titles. He announced that he was stopping publication 'because of a premise, that has never been proved, that they stimulate juvenile delinquency. We are not doing it so much for business reasons as because this seems to be what the parents want — and the parents should be served'. Privately, he confessed: 'I'd been told that if I continued publishing my magazines, no one would handle them. I had no choice'. Wholesalers and retailers refused to take E.C. titles, with the exception of satirical former comic book *Mad*, converted into a 25-cent bimonthly magazine to avoid the Code. *Mad* eventually became one of the best selling magazines in America and Gaines died a wealthy man.[16]

Britain Bans the 'Horror Comic'

American 'horror comics' reached Britain in the early 1950s as ballast in ships crossing the Atlantic, unsold copies were also imported from Canada and Australia. Few penetrated much further than the environs of the great ports of Liverpool, Manchester, Belfast and London. One anti-comic-book member of the Comics Campaign Council (C.C.C.) sought out elusive copies from London's East-End street markets, 'I must confess that I put on an off-white accent and an old coat before I won the vendor's confidence'. Using blocks made from imported American matrices, subsequent British versions were printed in Leicester and London to be sold in small back-street shops. On 17 May 1952 *Picture Post*, the popular Hulton Press photo-magazine, drew widespread public attention to the British 'horror comic' trade in a provocative article ('Should U.S. "Comics" Be Banned?') by Peter Mauger, a communist teacher anxious to exploit anti-American feeling. 'Who can look at these comics and escape the conclusion that there is a connection between them and the increasing volume of juvenile delinquency?' queried a reader's letter. If Hulton, publishers of the irreproachable *Eagle* range of British comic papers, feared American competition for the juvenile market, parliamentary deputations of teachers and churchmen feared American mass culture invading Britain. All gave voice to an orchestrated groundswell of opinion demanding urgent government action.[17]

'The problem which now faces society in the trade that has sprung up of presenting sadism, crime, lust, physical monstrosity, and horror to the young is an urgent and a grave one', thundered *The Times* on 12 November 1954. 'There has been no more encouraging sign of the moral health of the country than the way in which public opinion has been roused in condemnation of the evil of horror comics and in determination to combat them'. Yet the relatively small sales of American 'horror comics' in comparison to home-grown British comics was openly admitted by Dr. Sam Yudkin, an active British Communist Party (C.P.) lobbyist and force behind the C.C.C. During a somewhat disingenuous address to the Tory Education Committee, Yudkin estimated that perhaps only ten per cent of British school children bought 'horror comics'; albeit because of 'swopping' their circulation was somewhat wider. This small circulation did not prevent such unlikely allies as the C.C.C., the British C.P., the Established Church, and the National Union of Teachers (N.U.T.) from vigorously campaigning against their diminishing sales. The N.U.T. eventually distanced itself from the C.C.C., made aware of the political affiliations of many of those active in the anti-comic book campaign. Instead, the teachers' union organised their own exhibition of gruesome 'horror comic' illustrations which was allowed in the Palace of Westminster for two weeks, before touring the country attracting publicity and intensifying the demand for action.[18]

Ultimately, Britain's Conservative government could not afford to ignore the swelling chorus of 'moral panic' amplified through the press. The new Home Secretary, Major Gwilym Lloyd-George, told the Tory cabinet, meeting at Premier Winston Churchill's office in the Commons on 6 December 1954, that a bill to outlaw 'horror comics' would be difficult to frame. Yet if the government failed to take the initiative, 'there was a risk that legislation might be brought forward in the form of a Private Member's bill, which would involve the Government in even greater embarassment'. To forestall such a move, Lloyd-George received authority to make an early statement in the House that legislation was being considered, restricted to the type of publication which had 'aroused so much public concern in recent weeks'. On 27 January 1955 the cabinet expressed general support for legislation along the lines of a draft bill that banned the sort of comic book which, as a whole, 'would tend to incite or encourage to the commission of crimes or acts of violence or cruelty, or otherwise to corrupt, a child or young person into whose hands it might fall'. It would become an offence to sell or publish 'horror comics', punished by up to four months in prison or a fine not exceeding £100, with the option of trial by jury. The Home Secretary wished to avoid a delay in announcing proposals because he wanted to avoid an impression that the government had been pushed into legislation by pressure from the opposition. Furthermore, the Eisenhower administration was concerned, according to the Foreign Office, 'about the extent to which American participation in the production of horror comics is being used to foster ill-feeling between the United States and this country'. The Commander of American Forces in England even attempted to get American P.X.'s to stop bringing 'horror comics' into the country, so desperate was the threat to basic British values.[19]

Civil servants produced an avalanche of papers, once official authority to proceed with legislation had been received, passing on and correcting the views of their respective political masters as regards definition of terms, amendments, redrafting of clauses, and possible penalties. The Children's Department of the Home Office, a liberal bastion, felt that the original draft bill was misconceived because it laid too much emphasis upon 'horror comics' as an incitement to juvenile delinquency, statistically declining in mid-1950s Britain. 'First, there is no evidence that the kind of publication aimed at does incite to the commission of crimes by juveniles and, second, crimes of violence, cruelty or horror . . . are definitely infrequent among children and young persons'. A general tendency for such reading to corrupt through 'the lowering of moral standards, rather than causing particular acts on a particular occasion', was considered preferable wording. This proposal was rejected, despite receiving support from the Tory Attorney-General, Sir Reginald Manningham-Buller, who felt that the cumulative effect of 'horror comics' on the young was the real evil, leading to 'contempt for the law and an entirely wrong view of adult society'. The Home Office also condemned 'crime comics' for glorifying the criminal and 'holding the forces of law and order up to ridicule'. A century earlier, the Lord Chamberlain's office had used similar language to justify banning stage plays portraying prison-escaper Jack Sheppard as a glamorous criminal. The subversive content of 'horror comics', particularly those of the E.C. stable, clearly made some contribution to the 'moral panic' in Establishment circles.[20]

According to Treasury Counsel, Mervyn Griffith-Jones, the real evil of 'horror comics' lay in the false picture they gave children and young people 'of the way in which the grown-up world thinks and behaves'. One particularly shocking feature was the 'horror comic' representation of family life as dysfunctional. Not long before the Home Secretary began drafting parliamentary legislation, Griffith-Jones offered the following sententious remarks on his 'horror comic' reading to the Director of Public Prosecutions:

The characters are ordinary human beings with ordinary faces and clothed in ordinary clothing. These usually normal people are represented as being selfish, violent and filled with greed and hate. Husbands and wives are continually shown as unfaithful; parents as hating their children and vice versa. Almost as a matter of course and without there being anything unusual about it, many of them are in possession of guns and all are prepared to relieve themselves of their immediate troubles by the simple expedient of murder.[21]

E.C.'s stories of internecine strife, adulteries, and murderous impulses, presented a forcefully paranoiac critique of America's most hallowed social institution, the contemporary family.

Pushed through Whitehall and the Tory cabinet in just a few months, fuelled by the 'moral panic' over 'horror comics', the Children and Young Persons (Harmful Publications) Bill was piloted through the House of Commons by Major Lloyd-George and the Attorney-General. The bill's second reading on 22 February 1955 was attended by a full house and the debate lasted for over six hours, with strong views being presented both for and against. The Commons traditionally got excited whenever a question of the liberty of the subject was involved and this debate was no exception. Roy Jenkins and Michael Foot for Labour took up the cudgels in defence of freedom of expression, seeing no apparent contradiction in arguing that a more comprehensive measure should have been introduced to reform the 1857 Obscene Publications Act (eventually modernised by the 1959 'Jenkins Act'). Tory backbenchers who caught the Speaker's eye protested an ardent desire to protect children from being corrupted by the sort of reading matter so graphically exposed in the N.U.T.'s highly selective exhibition of 'horror comic' illustrations. Several M.P.'s were worried that legislation against 'horror comics' could be given a wider application than intended by the bill's framers. On the other hand, Parliament's interference in liberty of publication was justified by both government spokesmen and Labour's Shadow Home Secretary, Sir Frank Soskice, as necessary to plug gaps in existing obscenity legislation.[22]

'It is true that the public outcry last autumn and the decision to introduce this bill have stopped the publication of ''horror comics'' in this country', confessed Major Lloyd-George, 'but I am convinced that, if the House had not been resolute in its determination to deal with this evil, we would have been faced with a much more serious problem'. The redundant bill passed its second reading by a unanimous majority and became law on 6 May 1955. Six months later, only one complaint had reached the Home Secretary and of three other comic books brought to the attention of the Attorney-General none were proceeded against. The sledge-hammer of parliamentary legislation had been brought to bear in order to crack a very small nut indeed. The Act was renewed without discussion in 1965 and is still on the statute books. The first, and possibly only, prosecution under this legislation came on 22 October 1970, when W.L. Millers and Co. of Stepney, East London, was charged at Tower Bridge Court with importing from America 25,000 copies of *Tales from the Tomb, Weird, Tales of Voodoo, Horror Tales* and *Witches Tales*. Part early-1950s reprints, part poorly drawn originals, they had been allowed past customs. Despite being fined only £25 with £20 costs, the firm closed down soon after.[23]

Concluding Remarks

The preceding survey of recurrent adult 'panic' reactions to forms of commercial entertainment that attracted the young has been underpinned by the language used to determine the 'social construction' of cultural values and their contestation. This methodology explores the way in which certain tastes, values, and hierarchies are established by the academy, literary periodicals, and the authorities as 'respectable' or preferential and others not. The way in which culture is constructed, according to Pierre Bordieu, is ideological and the consequences of discrimination in taste are that aesthetic distinctions become operations of domination and subordination. Cultural consumption is predisposed, consciously or not, to fulfil a social function of legitimating both social and age differences. The process of establishing taste differentials thereby becomes a symbolic weapon in the struggle between classes and generations for ideological domination. How cultural and taste hierarchies were established is relevant to this paper because the construction process allowed cultural authorities to amplify social anxiety or rejection over products of the 'commercial culture' that threatened established 'good taste'. In this sense, the manufacture of labels like 'penny dreadful' and 'video nasty' represent the struggle between middle-class moralism and popular demand, assigning taste for the sensational or melodramatic to a permanent lower-class or, as here, juvenile ghetto.[24]

Intellectual rigour and honesty are in short supply on all sides of the current debate about the effects of violent forms of entertainment on a young audience. There can be no easy answers based on inconclusive evidence. Scapegoating then censoring the media offers little solution to juvenile delinquency, primarily a complex structural and pathological problem. On the other hand, sociologists like Geoffrey Pearson who debunk the idea that we live in an age of unprecedented 'falling standards' and rising crime tend to ignore the historical lineage of cultural pessimism. The very fact of a recurring historical cycle might suggest not so much a persistent irrationality or media-induced 'crisis tendency', rather the expression of fundamental contradictions in relations between classes and generations. Assigning each successive 'crisis' to the inclusive category of 'moral panic' risks disregarding particular features of historical context, new technology, or social anxiety. We should, perhaps, give more emphasis to the *continuity* of the fear and loathing of modernity which such fears represent and the specificity of the various constituencies, populist, conservative, and fundamentalist, from which they emerge. Violent or sensational forms of popular culture can be offered in any historical age but the public reaction to them is that age's alone.[25]

References

1. 'Unparalleled evil. . .', *Today*, 25 Nov. 1993, pp.2-3; James B. Twitchell, *Preposterous Violence: Fables of Aggression in Modern Culture* (New York, 1989), pp.48-89.
2. Those consulted include: the Opie, John Johnson and Frank Pettingell Collections, Bodleian Library, Oxford; the Barry Ono Collection, British Library, London; the Renier Collection of Children's Books, Bethnal Green Museum of Childhood, London; the Hess Collection, Walter Library, University of Minnesota, Minneapolis; and the Osborne Collection of Early Children's Books, Toronto Public Library.
3. Graham Murdock, 'Disorderly Images: Television's Presentation of Crime and Policing', C. Sumner, ed., *Crime, Justice and the Mass Media* (Cambridge, 1982), p.104; J.J. Tobias, *Crime and Industrial Society in the Nineteenth Century* (Harmondsworth, 1972 edn.), p.53.
4. Stan Cohen, *Folk Devils and Moral Panics: The Creation of the Mods and Rockers* (London, 1972), pp.9-10; Les Levidow, 'Witches and Seducers: Moral Panics for Our Time', Barry Richards, ed., *Crises of the Self: Further Essays on Psychoanalysis and Politics* (London, 1989), pp.181-215; Rob Sindall, *Street Violence in the Nineteenth Century: Media Panic or Real Danger?* (Leicester, 1990), pp.29-36.
5. 'The Hammer Blow to Our Conscience', *The Independent on Sunday*, 21 Feb. 1993, p.21; Richard Sparks, *Television and the Drama of Crime* (London, 1992), pp.65-66.
6. John Springhall, 'Leisure and Victorian Youth: The Penny Theatre in London, 1830-1890', John Hurt, ed., *Childhood, Youth and Education in the Late Nineteenth Century* (Leicester, 1981), pp.101-24; *Report of the 1852 Select Committee on Criminal and Destitute Juveniles*, pp.515, VII, Appendix 2.
7. John Russell Stephens, *The Censorship of English Drama, 1824-1901* (Cambridge, 1980), p.77; 'A Candidate for the Glory of Jack Sheppard', *The Examiner*, 17 Nov. 1839, p.6. The new Metropolitan Police Act (1839) gave the Chief Police Commissioner power to order the arrest of all those operating an unlicensed theatre.
8. Alan Bristow, *Empire Boys: Adventures in a Man's World* (London, 1991), p.32; 'Police Reports', *The Times*, 13 Dec. 1877, p.11; James Greenwood, *The Wilds of London* (London 1874), p.246.

9. Cited: J.H. Friswell, *Modern Men of Letters Honestly Criticised* (London, 1870), p.268; J.P. Harrison, 'Cheap Literature — Past and Present', *Companion to the [British] Almanac of the Society for the Diffusion of Useful Knowledge or Year Book of General Information for 1873* (London SDUK, 1872), pp.75-76.
10. Anon., *Tales of Highwaymen; or, Life on the Road* (London, NPC, 1865-66); John Springhall, ' "A Life Story for the People"? Edwin J. Brett and the London "Low-Life" Penny Dreadfuls of the 1860s', *Victorian Studies*, Vol.33, No.2 (Winter 1990), pp.223-246.
11. Antony Comstock, *Traps for the Young*, (Cambridge, Mass., 1967 edn.), pp.28-29; *Annual Reports of the New York Society for the Suppression of Vice* (New York, 1883-86); Lydia Cushman Schurman, 'Anthony Comstock's Lifelong Crusade Against "Vampire Literature"', *Dime Novel Round-Up*, Vol.58, No.6 (Dec. 1989), pp.82-83; Michael Denning, *Mechanic Accents: Dime Novels and Working-Class Culture in America* (London, 1987), pp.51, 159-60, 233, fn.9.
12. Lee Server, *Danger Is My Business: An Illustrated History of the Fabulous Pulp Magazines, 1896-1953* (San .Francisco, 1993); David Caute, *The Great Fear: The Anti-Communist Purge Under Truman and Eisenhower* (London, 1978); Ron Goulart, *Over Fifty Years of American Comic Books* (New York, 1991), pp.204-205.
13. Mike Benton, *The Comic Book in America: An Illustrated History* (Dallas, 1989), p.155; idem., *The Illustrated History of Crime Comics* (Dallas, 1993), p.69.
14. Mike Benton, *The Illustrated History of Horror Comics* (Dallas, 1991), pp.13-23; Ron Goulart, *Over Fifty Years, op.cit.*, pp.174-182; James Gilbert, *A Cycle of Outrage: America's Reaction to the Juvenile Delinquent in the 1950s* (New York, 1986), pp.109-126; testimony of Dr. Fredric Wertham, *Hearings before the Subcommittee to Investigate Juvenile Delinquency of the Committee on the Judiciary*, United States Senate, Eighty-Third Congress, Second Session, S. 190 (Washington, 1954), pp.79-96.
15. Testimony of William M. Gaines, *Hearings, op.cit.*, p.103. Gaines' testimony was analogous to that of the guitarist Frank Zappa at the Senate Commerce Committee hearings in September 1985 on pornography in rock music.
16. Mike Benton, *Horror Comics, op.cit.*, pp.49-51; Ron Goulart, *Over Fifty Years, op.cit.*, p.217; Maria Reidelbach, *Completely Mad: A History of the Comic Book and Magazine* (Boston, 1991), pp.8-9; Frank Jacobs, *The Mad World of William M. Gaines* (New Jersey, 1972), pp.112-113.

17. P.M. Pickard, *I Could A Tale Unfold: Violence, Horror and Sensationalism in Stories for Children* (London, 1961), p.118; George H. Pumphrey, *Comics and Your Children* (London, 1955); Sara Selwood and Diana Irving, *Harmful Publications: Comics, Education and Disenfranchised Young People* (London, 1993); Peter Mauger, 'Should U.S. "Comics" Be Banned?', *Picture Post*, 17 May 1952, pp.33-35.

18. 'A Horrible Trade', *The Times*, 12 Nov. 1954, p.6; PPS to Home Sec., 'Horror Comics', report of meeting on 22 Nov. 1954, HO 302 (15), PRO, Kew; Martin Barker, *A Haunt of Fears: The Strange History of the British Horror Comics Campaign* (London, 1984), pp.18-55.

19. Cabinet Conclusions, 6 Dec. 1954, 27 Jan. 1955, CAB 128/27/28; Major Lloyd-George to Viscount Kilmuir, 2 Feb. 1955, LCO 2/5638;(?) to Mr. Pittam, 8 Dec. 1954; HO 302 (15), PRO, Kew.

20. C.P.H. to A.W. Peterson, Home Office, 14 Jan. 1955; A.W. Peterson to Hutchinson, Scottish Office, 15 Jan. 1955; A.W. Peterson to Sir A. Strutt, 20 Jan. 1955; Alistair Macdonald, Law Officer's Dept., to Chorley, Parl. Counsel's Office, 26 Jan. 1955; A.W. Peterson to Chorley, 26 Jan. 1955: HO 302 (15), PRO, Kew; John Russell Stephens, '*Jack Sheppard* and the Licensers: The Case Against Newgate Plays', *Nineteenth Century Theatre Research*, Vol.1, No.1 (1973), pp.1-13.

21. Mervyn Griffith-Jones to DPP, 11 Nov. 1954, HO 302 (15), PRO, Kew. Griffith-Jones became notorious in 1960 as the prosecuting counsel who asked whether Englishmen wanted their wives and servants to read the Penguin paperback edition of D.H. Lawrence's *Lady Chatterley's Lover*.

22. *Children and Young Persons (Harmful Publications) Bill*, 1954-55, Second Reading, *Hansard*, Vol.538, 1072-1186.

23. 'Notes for Third Reading', A.W. Peterson to Home Sec., HO 302 (16), PRO, Kew; 'Comics That Can "Lead To Murder" ', *The Daily Mail*, 23 Oct. 1970, p.9.

24. Pierre Bordieu, *Distinction: A Social Critique of the Judgement of Taste* (London, trans. 1984); Lawrence W. Levine, *Highbrow/Lowbrow: The Emergence of Cultural Hierarchy in America* (Cambridge, Mass., 1988); Michael Denning, 'The End of Mass Culture', *International Labour and Working-Class History*, No.37 (Spring 1990), pp.4-18.

25. Geoffrey Pearson, 'Falling Standards: A Short, Sharp History of Moral Decline', Ed. Martin Barker, *The Video Nasties: Freedom and Censorship in the Media* (London, 1984), pp.88-103; Sparks, *Television and the Drama of Crime, op.cit.*, pp.65-66.

AT-RISK CHILDREN AND THE COMMON SCHOOL IDEAL*

Barry M. Franklin

I

During the first two decades of this century, American urban school administrators had established an implicit accord among themselves, their clients, and certain private philanthropies which involved a recalibration of the mid-nineteenth century common school ideal. According to this reconstituted ideal, public schools would be accessible to all children. Once inside the school, however, these children would not necessarily enjoy a shared educational experience. Rather, they would be channeled to any of a number of different programmes on the basis of their abilities, inclinations, and interests. Among them were an array of remedial and special education programmes which were made possible by the emergence of a medicalized discourse for talking about childhood learning difficulties. The evolution of this medicalized discourse during the next seventy years would produce by the early 1960s the so-called handicapping condition of learning disabilities.[1] Similarly, a series of events during the 1970s would lead to a further shift in this discourse producing the so-called at-risk child. The purpose of this paper is to explore those events and to consider what they tell us about the present status of efforts to educate at-risk pupils.

The decade of the 1970s would see an apparent challenge to this recalibrated common school ideal. A number of civil suits in the Federal and State courts questioned in virtually the same way as had the 1954 case of Brown v. the Board of Education the constitutionality of excluding children, in this case disabled children, from the public schools.[2] Among the issues raised in these suits was the appropriateness of placing these children in special classes and other separate settings. In the majority of the cases, as it turned out, the courts ruled against segregation, arguing that the most suitable placement for most handicapped children was the regular classroom.[3]

Coincidental with these legal challenges were legislative efforts to ensure

*An expanded version of this paper appears as the epilogue in Barry M. Franklin, *From Backwardness to At-Risk: Childhood Learning Difficulties and the Contradictions of School Reform* (Albany: State University of New York Press, 1994).

that disabled children had access to the nation's public schools. In a series of amendments to the Elementary and Secondary Education Act that were enacted between 1966 and the passage of the Education for All Handicappd Children Act (Public Law 94-142) in 1975, Congress mandated that virtually all of the nation's disabled children be guaranteed a free, public education. Among the issues raised in this legislation was the placement of disabled children once they were admitted to the public schools. Not surprisingly, Congress took a position in favour of integration and mandated that all disabled children be educated in the so-called least restrictive environment. Although this provision did appear greatly to restrict the ability of school administrators to remove handicapped children from regular classrooms, it did not abolish segregated placements. Rather, the provision required that the States establish a 'continuum of alternative placements' for handicapped children, which included the regular classroom, special classes and schools, and an array of non-school settings.[4] Public schools under this provision were to place disabled children in environments that provided them with an appropriate education while maximizing contact with their non-handicapped peers. For many disabled children, the least restrictive placement was the regular classroom. For others, however, it would be a separate classroom or school or even a residential setting.

Neither the legal challenges to the exclusion of handicapped children from the public schools and certainly not the least restrictive placement provision of P.L. 94-142 abolished the segregation of disabled children. In 1976, the year before P.L. 94-142 was implemented, about sixty-seven percent of all handicapped children and about eighty percent of learning disabled children spent some time, although we do not know precisely how much, in regular classrooms. Six years later in 1982, the percentages were virtually unchanged.[5] Although large numbers of learning disabled and other handicappd children spend some time in regular classrooms, the refurbished common school ideal, at least at present, remains intact.

II

There are, however, indications of a coming sea change in the understanding of childhood learning difficulties that may have the effect of undermining what currently passes for common schooling. Despite the Congressional enactment of the least restrictive environmental provision, there were those who doubted its efficacy in reducing the segregation of disabled children. In an April 1974 letter to the House Subcommittee on Education, which was then considering the series of amendments that would become P.L. 94-142, Lloyd Dunn, a former president of the Council for Exceptional children, attacked this provision on the grounds that it 'does not move us toward the normalization and integration of services for children with learning problems but will have the reverse impact.' Instead, he went on to say, it will create 'special education domains at the expense of many other professionals equally competent and ready to serve children with school problems.'[6]

By the mid-1980s Dunn's doubts about least restrictive placements had spurred on a full scale oppositional movement known as the Regular Education Initiative, or, simply, REI. Like Dunn, proponents of REI argue that the least restrictive environment provision has not done away with segregated special education. Disabled children, they claim, remain as segregated as they were before the implementation of P.L. 94-142. REI supporters differ among themselves on how to reduce this isolation. Some call for increased cooperation between special and regular educators to enable more mildly handicapped and even some severely handicapped children to be placed in regular classrooms. Others recommend the virtual merging of regular, special, and compensatory education so that all children will receive instruction in regular classrooms. Most supporters of this movement take positions somewhere in-between.[7] Proponents of REI have certainly provoked those who support the practice of least restrictive placements. One such advocate depicts the Regular Education Initiative as the educational equivalent of the so-called 'trickle-down' economic practices of Presidents Reagan and Bush. Just as this economic strategy has been criticized for aiding the most prosperous at the expense of the poor, this critic claims that REI will aid those students who have little difficulty at the expense of those with the greatest problems.[8] It is not clear at this point if REI is having any impact on school practice. Nevertheless, the very presence of this movement and the rancour it has engendered among educators does point to an uncertain future for segregated programmes for children with learning difficulties.

III

The establishment of special classes for low achieving children has been one phase of the larger effort of early twentieth century school administrators to differentiate the curriculum. Along with an array of other schemes, including vocational education, grouping arrangements of various sorts, and the introduction of terminal, non-academic curricular tracks, it has become a practice that throughout this century has stimulated extensive research and precipitated highly charged debates.[9] Not surprisingly, research findings concerning this practice are often inconsistent and inconclusive and almost always cloaked in partisan rhetoric. In so far as we can reach any conclusions from this conflicting collection of research, it would appear that the bulk of opinion, certainly current opinion, is weighted against curriculum differentiation. From the vantage point of most contemporary researchers, differentiation is viewed as doing little to enhance the educational achievement of students, except for those who are placed in the highest tracks, to lead to the disproportionate placement of poor and minority group children in lower level classes, and to have a negative impact on the overall improvement of educational quality. In short, it is a long standing practice that has done more to exacerbate the problems of American public schooling than to resolve them.[10]

Our most recent round of educational reform, the so-called 'excellence' movement, has been particularly unkind to curriculum differentiation. Almost uniformly, the array of reports and proposals emanating from this movement have called for the introduction of a common, academically oriented curriculum for all students and the elimination, or at least reduction, of existing differentiated programmes.[11] As the most prominent sponsors of this campaign see it, a common, academic curriculum built on the disciplines of knowledge offers the best education for all American youth. It provides the best model for conveying to children their cultural heritage, the best background for participating in democratic politics, and the best preparation for life and work in a technologically advanced society. Curriculum differentiation, they go on to say, legitimates the creation of non-academic courses of study that lack standards and rigour. Further, they argue, this practice is routinely used to segregate poor and minority group children from their peers, thereby consigning them to an inferior education and a subordinate place in adult society. These reformers are not opposed to some informal and temporary in-class grouping arrangements to accommodate the ability and skill differences that exist among children. They insist, however, that despite the use of different pedagogy to teach children of varying abilities, the content of education should remain the same for all children.[12] Curriculum differentiation is certainly a common feature of today's schools. Yet, current criticisms of this practice suggest that we may be about ready to rethink this taken-for-granted scheme for accommodating diverse students.

IV

In the decade following the implementation of P.L. 94-142, the number of learning disabled children who were served in special education programmes increased by 134 percent from 796 thousand to over 1.8 million. By 1980, learning disabled children became the largest group of exceptional students served in the public schools.[13] Despite this growth, the same doubts that have always existed about learning disabilities remain. The evidence for its neurological origins is just as elusive today as it was when Alfred Strauss and Heinz Werner first postulated the existence of the supposed brain-injured child in the early 1940s.[14] Similarly, many contemporary researchers appear as sceptical about the neurological roots of this condition as was Seymour Sarason in his 1949 criticism of Strauss and Werner's brain injury research.[15] As a consequence, the field's

114

current experts seem preoccupied with trying to figure out precisely what a learning disability is. They certainly seem as divided as were their counterparts during the 1960s in settling on a definition of this condition.[16]

Between 1977 and 1982, the U.S. Department of Education funded research centres at five universities to investigate a variety of issues related to the education of learning disabled children and adolescents. In a special issue of *Exceptional Education Quarterly*, published in the Spring of 1983, representatives of the institutes, located at the Universities of Illinois at Chicago, Kansas, Minnesota, Virginia, and at Teachers College, Columbia University, offered assessments of their research efforts. Taken together, the five essays painted a positive picture, noting particular successes in identifying important characteristics of learning disabled children and in developing some apparently promising instructional techniques.[17] In addition to the review essays, the journal published commentaries by two learning disabilities researchers who were not affiliated with the institutes. While these commentators were generally positive in their assessment of this body of research, they did point to certain problems. As Barbara Keogh saw it, the institutes did little to explain the actual nature of learning disabilities as a handicapping condition.[18] Similarly, James McKinney noted that despite their collective efforts, these institutes were not able to provide much guidance for differentiating learning disabled children from other low achievers.[19] Notwithstanding, his recognition of this weakness, McKinney singled out the Minnesota institute for criticism precisely because so much of its work highlighted this difficulty. He charged the Minnesota researchers with undermining public confidence in the viability of learning disabilities as a diagnostic category.[20] In a response to McKinney, a number of members of the Minnesota Institute noted how vague the concept of learning disabilities was. Learning disabilities is, as they put it, 'whatever society wants it to be, needs it to be, or will permit it to be.'[21]

Despite the current size of the learning disabled student population, its rate of growth appears to be declining. Between 1977 and 1981, the percentage of learning disabled children served in public school special education programmes increased about fifteen percent a year. Between 1981 and 1985, the percentage increased only about three and a half percent a year. Some of this decline is undoubtedly because of the increasing success of the nation's public schools in identifying learning disabled children. Whereas about a quarter of children with learning disabilities were being accommodated in the nation's public schools before the enactment of P.L. 94-142, about eighty percent of these children were being served by the mid-1980s.[22] Yet, this diminishing growth rate may also reflect persisting doubts about learning disability itself. With the development of a medicalized discourse for talking about low achievement, learning disabilities came to supplant backwardness as a public school vehicle for accommodating low achieving children. Likewise, continuing uncertainties about the soundness of learning disabilities as a diagnostic category may undermine its existence.

V

The events we have just considered did not occur in isolation. Rather they took place in the midst of major social and economic changes. In its 1989 report, the U.S. House of Representatives Select Committee on Children, Youth, and Families painted a rather dispiriting picture of the present status of these groups. During the 1980s, the Committee noted:

> . . . the most profound influence on American families has been the mounting economic pressures which have diminished their resources and made more children more vulnerable. The combind effects of persistently high rates of poverty, declining earnings, underemployment, and single parenting have made childhood far more precarious and less safe for millions of American children . . .[23]

The report itself details an array of indicators which taken together point to a deterioration in the well-being of children and families. Between 1970 and 1985, the median family income of children when adjusted for inflation has declind some $1,700 from $29,943 to $28,210. Since 1985, income has increased slightly but remains below the 1970 figures. During the same period the rate of childhood poverty has increased from about fifteen percent of all children to a little over twenty percent. And again, during these years, the percentage of children living in female-headed single households, the families most likely to live in poverty, has increased from about eight percent to fourteen percent.[24]

These demographic changes, not surprisingly, have had their impact on childhood learning and school achievement. About one quarter of the nation's twenty eight million 10-17 year olds, are behind the expected grade for their age. A 1985 study by the Centre for Educational Statistics that compared the number of the nation's high school graduates that year with the number entering high school as freshmen four years earlier indicated a dropout rate of twenty-nine percent. Fourteen percent of all adolescents are functionally illiterate. In assessments of mathematics and science achievement, American thirteen year olds scored near or at the bottom in comparison with their peers from other industrialized nations. And according to a 1985 report from the National Assessment of Educational Progress, only eleven percent of the nation's thirteen year olds were sufficiently proficient at reading to understand written material of a complex nature.[25]

It does not take more than a cursory reading of these data to recognize that the contemporary American state, not unlike its turn-of-the-century counterpart, lacks the administrative capacities to address its most pressing problems. The recent appearance on the scene of public school programmes for at-risk children may signal that those who manage at least one sector of the state, namely the public schools, are attempting to develop some of those missing capacities. Yet, whether such programmes represent an immanent sea change in our understanding of childhood learning difficulties is less certain.

The problem is that programmes for at-risk children come in so many shapes and varieties that it is difficult to tell precisely what this apparent movement espouses. Some recommendations depart from our longstanding reliance on segregating low achieving children and call instead for restructuring schools to better serve all children, including those thought to be at-risk of school failure.[26] In this vein, Henry Levin and his associates are advocating such a restructuring plan under the rubric of accelerated schooling. Accelerated schools, as these researchers see them, are sites where teachers have a decision making rôle in the school's operation, where administrators are facilitators rather than managers, and where parents are active participants in the education of their children. With respect to curricular and instructional practices, Levin and his associates appear to take their cues not from remedial programmes but from those for the gifted and talented. Accelerated schools offer an enriched, common programme for all students that, among other things, involves children in the use of higher order cognitive processes and problem-solving, encourages creative thinking, integrates the teaching of language throughout the curriculum, and provides for experiential learning.[27]

The majority of initiatives currently being advanced for at-risk students, however, appear to continue an historic reliance on differentiation. Many of these programmes, including various forms of individualized instruction and tutoring, Upward Bound, the Job Corps, and numerous Chapter 1 initiatives, represent recycled special programmes from the compensatory education efforts of the 1960s.[28] Others are apparently new, but they, too, rely on offering at-risk children something different from that provided to the majority of students. They can involve the introduction of special curricula, such as basic life skills, that provide these children with capabilities which they often lack. If at-risk children are explicitly taught, among other things, how to relate appropriately to their peers, how to make decisions, how to avoid intimidation, and how to assert themselves, they can, according to advocates of this curricular offering, attain the kind of social competence that typically characterizes academically successful youth.[29] Or they can involve the establishment of alternative schools and schools-within-schools. Typically these alternative institutions are smaller and allow for more intimate relationships among students and faculty. They provide an environment that is designed to nurture psychological well being. And they offer a curriculum thought to be more relevant to the interests and abilities of at-risk children. Such a school could link academic course work to career preparation. It could, with the inclusion of courses in media technology, computer applications, and photography emphasize the kind of experiential learning often ignored by regular schools. Or, it could serve a particular at-risk population, say American Indians or adolescent mothers.[30]

Most proposals for accommodating at-risk children in today's schools are, then, strikingly similar to the efforts during the early years of this century for educating backward children and to more recent programmes for the learning disabled. Proponents of these initiatives, like their earlier counterparts, see no real need to alter schools as they are presently constituted. What they want to do is to devise special programmes that are directed to at-risk students. Such special programmes may, as their promoters often claim, be more responsive to the needs of at-risk children than the regular curriculum. And they may, again as their supporters maintain, be more attractive to at-risk students and more likely to keep them in school. Yet, not unlike most remedial and special education programmes, they have the effect of segregating low achieving students in programmes that are less academic and less demanding than those offered to most students. They are in effect efforts to maintain a recalibrated common school ideal that channels different students to separate programmes and ultimately to decidedly different and unequal life destinies.

How contemporary school administrators choose to deal with the presence of at-risk students will ultimately affect the resolution of the century-long dilemma over common schooling. Almost uniformly, those promoting the cause of today's at-risk students claim, in stark contrast to their counterparts earlier in this century, to oppose tracking and other forms of curriculum differentiation.[31] In fact only those, like Levin, who have advanced re-structuring strategies directed to all students can make this claim. Those who recommend creating special programmes and alternative schools for at-risk children are in reality advocating segregated education for children with learning difficulties.

From the first, the efforts of American school administrators to provide for students with learning difficulties have pulled them in contradictory directions. Not certain as to whether they wanted to provide for the individual needs of these children or to ensure the uninterrupted progress of the regular classroom, these educators embraced a recalibrated common school ideal that resolved their dilemma through curriculum differentiation. The result has been the creation of an array of special programmes to remove these children from regular classrooms. Throughout this century we have viewed children with learning difficulties differently. Early in the century, we thought of them as being backward. By mid-century, we saw them as being learning disabled. Today, we label them as being at-risk. Our labels, it seems, have changed, but our reliance on segregation has persisted.

Although never completely realized, the ideal of common schooling first spelled out by mid-nineteenth century school reformers provides a moral compass for our efforts to improve education. Whether we are talking about inequities in school financing, unfair allocations of curricular and instructional resources, or racial and ethnic segregation, to name but a few, this ideal has directed us, often unwillingly, toward solutions that embody our most democratic and egalitarian impulses. If those impulses are to serve us today in both addressing the needs of children with learning difficulties and more broadly in dealing with the contradictions in our efforts at school reform, we must go against the grain and reassert an authentic version of the common school ideal.

References

1. For a discussion of this history, see Barry M. Franklin, *From Backwardness to At-Risk: Childhood Learning Difficulties and the Contradictions of School Reform* (Albany: State University of New York Press, 1994).
2. Alan Gartner and Dorothy Kerzner Lipsky, 'Beyond Special Education: Toward a Quality System for All Students', *Harvard Educational Review* 57 (November, 1987): 368-369; H. Rutherford Turnbull and Ann Turnbull, *Free Appropriate Public Education: Law and Implementation* (Denver: Love Publishing Company, 1978), 12-16, 255-263.
3. Alan Abeson, *A Continuing Summary of Pending and Completed Litigation Regarding the Education of Handicapped Children*, No. 6 (Arlington: Council for Exceptional Children, 1973).
4. *The Education for All Handicappd Children Act (P.L. 94-142)*, 20 U.S.C., Sec. 1412; *Federal Register* 42 (August 23, 1977): sec. 121a.550-121a.551.
5. The way in which State education officials reported their placement data to the Federal government before 1984 made it difficult to assess the actual extent of integration. Children were counted as being placed in one of four settings, regular classes, separate classes, separate schools, and other environments. Using such categories, children who spent some time of the day outside the regular classroom in so-called resource room programmes were often counted by States as being placed in regular classrooms. Beginning in 1984, Congress mandated a more detailed reporting of placements by increasing the number of environments to include, among others, resource rooms. With the resource room included, it appears that only twenty-six percent of all handicapped children and sixteen percent of learning disabled children were being served in regular classrooms. Over sixty percent of all handicapped children and eighty percent of learning disabled children were removed from regular classrooms at least part and perhaps all of the day. See Department of Education, *Third Annual Report to*

Congress on the Implementation of Public Law 94-142: The Education for All Handicapped Children Act (Washington, D.C.: U.S. Department of Education, 1981), 54; Department of Education, *Seventh Annual Report to Congress on the Implementation of Public Law 94-142: The Education for All Handicapped Children Act* (Washington, D.C.: U.S. Department of Education, 1985), 232-233; Department of Education, *Ninth Annual Report to Congress on the Implementation of the Education of the Handicapped Act* (Washington, D.C.: U.S. Department of Education, 1987), 17-21.

6. Congress, House of Representatives, Subcommittee on Education, *Hearings Before the Select Cubcommittee on Education of the Committee on Education and Labour on H.R. 70*, 93rd Cong., 2nd sess., March 6, 7, 8, 22, 1974 (Washington, D.C.: GPO, 1974), 364.

7. The literature on the Regular Education Initiative is extensive. I have drawn my account from the following: Dorothy Kerzner Lipsky and Alan Gartner, 'The Current Situation', in *Beyond Separate Education: Quality Education for All*, ed. Dorothy Kerzner Lipsky and Alan Gartner (Baltimore: Paul H. Brookes Publishing Company, 1987), 255-289; M. Stephen Lilly, 'The Regular Education Initiative: A Force for change in General and Special Education', *Education and Training in Mental Retardation* 23 (December, 1988): 253-260; Maynard Reynolds and Margaret C. Wang, 'Restructuring "Special" School Programms: A Position Paper', *Policy Studies Review* 2 (January, 1983): 189-212; Susan Stainback and William Stainback, 'The Merger of Special and Regular Education: Can It Be Done? A Response to Lieberman and Mesinger', *Exceptional Children 51 (April, 1985): 517-521; Madeleine C. Will*, 'Educating Children with Learning Problems: A Shared Responsibility', *Exceptional Children* 52 (February, 1986); 411-415. For a review and evaluation of REI, see Thomas M. Skrtic, *Behind Special Education: A Critical Analysis of Professional Culture and School Organization* (Denver: Love Publishing Company, 1991), 51-84.

8. James M. Kauffman, 'The Regular Education Initiative as Reagan-Bush Education Policy: A Trickle-Down Theory of Education of the Hard-to-Teach', *The Journal of Special Education* 23 (Fall, 1989): 256-278. For another critique of REI, see Glenn A. Vergason and M.L. Anderegg, 'Preserving the Least Restrictive Environment', in *Issues in Special Education*, ed. William Stainback and Susan Stainback (Boston: Allyn and Bacon, 1992), 45-53.

9. Barry M. Franklin, 'Progressive and Curriculum Differentiation: Special Classes in the Atlanta Public Schools, 1898-1923', *History of Education Quarterly* 29 (Winter, 1989): 571-573.

10. Jeannie Oakes, Adam Gamoran, and Reba N. Page, 'Curriculum Differentiation: Opportunities, Outcomes, and Meanings', in *Handbook*

of Research on Curriculum, ed. Philip W. Jackson (New York: Macmillan Publishing Company, 1992), 570-608.

11. Gail P. Kelly, 'Setting the Boundaries of Debate About Education', in *Excellence in Education: Perspective on Policy and Practice*, ed. Philip G. Altbach, Gail P. Kelly, and Lois Weis (Buffalo: Prometheus Books, 1985), 35-37.

12. William Bennett, *The De-Valuing of America: the Fight for Our Culture and Our Children* (New York: Summit Books, 1992), 61-62; Chester E. Finn, Jr. *We Must Take Charge: Our Schools and Our Future* (New York: The Free Press, 1991), 218-219; Diane Ravitch, *The Schools We Deserve: Reflections on the Educational Crisis of Our Time* (New York: Basic Books, 1985), 58-74, 277-278; Diane Ravitch and Chester E. Finn, Jr., *What Do Our 17-Year Olds Know?* (New York: Harper and Row, 1988), 168-172.

13. Judith D. Singer and John A. Butler, 'The Education for All Handicapped Children Act: Schools as Agents of Social Reform', *Harvard Educational Review* 57 (May, 1987): 130.

14. For a good example of how difficult contemporary researchers find it to make a compelling case for the neurological origins of learning disabilities, see Carl W. Cotman and Gary S. Lynch, 'The Neurobiology of Learning and Memory', in *Learning Disabilities: Proceedings of the National Conference*, ed. James F. Kavanagh and Tom J. Truss, Jr. (Parkton: York Press, 1988), 1-69.

15. Barry M. Franklin, 'From Brain Injury to Learning Disability: Alfred Strauss, Heinz Werner, and the Historical Development of the Learning Disabilities Field', in *Learning Disability: Dissenting Essays*, ed. Barry M. Franklin (London: Falmer, 1987), 29-42.

16. Barry M. Franklin, 'Introduction: Learning Disability and the Need for Dissenting Essays', in *Learning Disability . . .*, 1-3; Kenneth A. Kavale, 'On Regaining Integrity in the LD Field', *Learning Disabilities Research* 2 (Summer, 1987): 60-61. For the difficulties facing educators in trying to identify the nature of this condition, see Barbara K. Keogh, 'Learning Disabilities: In Defense of a Construct', *Learning Disabilities Research* 3 (Winter, 1987): 4-9 and Heinz-Joachim Klatt, 'Learning Disabilities: A Questionable Construct', *Educational Theory* 41 (Winter, 1991): 47-60.

17. Rebecca Daily Kneedler and Daniel Hallahan, ed., 'Research in Learning Disabilities: Summaries of the Institutes', *Exceptional Education Quarterly* 4 (Spring, 1983): 1-114.

18. Barbara Keogh, 'A Lesson from Gestalt Psychology', Ibidem, 122.

19. James D. McKinney, 'Contributions of the Institutes for Research on Learning Disabilities', Ibidem, 139.

20. Ibidem, 136-139.

21. Ibidem, 145.

22. Frederick J. Weintraub and Bruce A. Ramirez, *Progress in the Education of the Handicapped and Analysis of P.L. 98-199: The Education of the Handicapped Act Amendments of 1983* (Reston: The Council for Exceptional Children, 1985), 8.

23. Congress, House of Representatives, Select Committee on Children, Youth, and Families, *U.S. Children and Their Families: Current Conditions and Recent Trends, 1989*, 101st Cong., 1st sess., September, 1989 (Washington, D.C.: GPO, 1989), x.

24. Ibidem, 54-55, 100-101, 108-109.

25. Joy G. Dryfoos, *Adolescents at Risk: Prevalence and Prevention* (New York: Oxford University Press, 1990), 82-88; David A. Hamburg, *Today's Children: Creating a Future for a Generation in Crisis* (New York: Time Books, 1992), 41-43; Carnegie Council on Adolescent Development, *Turning Points: Preparing American Youth for the 21st Century* (New York: Carnegie Corporation, 1980), 27-32.

26. Gary Natriello, Edward McDill, and Aaron M. Pallas, *Schooling Disadvantaged Children: Racing Against Catastrophe* (New York: Teachers College Press, 1990), 157-180.

27. Wendy S. Hopfenberg and Others, *Toward Accelerated Middle Schools for Disadvantaged Youth*, Stanford University, February, 1990, 43-47; *Accelerated Schools* I (Winter, 1991): 1, 10-11, 14-15.

28. For a description of these programmes see Natriello, McDill, and Pallas, 71-137; and Nancy A. Madden and Robert E. Slavin, 'Effective Pullout Programs for Students At Risk', in *Effective Programs for Students at Risk*, ed. Robert E. Slavin, Nancy L. Karweit, and Nancy A. Madden (Boston: Allyn and Bacon, 1989), 52-72.

29. Hamburg, Ibidem, 240-244; Fred M. Hechinger, *Fateful Choices: Healthy Youth for the 21st Century* (New York: Hill and Wang, 1992), 53-56.

30. Gary Wehlage and others, *Reducing the Risk: Schools as Communities of Support* (London: Falmer Press, 1989), 75-112.

31. Natriello, McDill, and Pallas, 15, 84; Dryfoos, 137, 216-217; Hamburg, 212-213.

ASPECTS OF CHILD EMPLOYMENT, 1890-1914: CONTINUITY AND CHANGE

Pamela Horn

During the nineteenth century there was a significant shift in public opinion from the common view, in the early years, that where possible children had a duty to contribute to family earnings, to a growing belief among many at the century's end that labour in childhood was undesirable and 'a society stood condemned by its existence'.[1] However, the course of that change was uneven, with greater prominence given to the issue at some periods than others.

In the 1860s child employment had been widely discussed and there was general approval when the Factory and Workshop Acts were extended during the decade to include a broad range of new industries. Even agriculture was covered in part by the 1867 Public Gangs Act. Then in the 1870s and early 1880s, with some exceptions, such as the Factory Acts of 1874 and 1878, which raised the minimum employment age for half-timers from eight to ten, the legislation to regulate children working in brickfields, and certain ineffective measures like the 1873 Agricultural Children Act and an 1877 Act concerned with children on board canal boats, the debate lost momentum. Attention was switched instead to the broader issues of educational reform and school attendance. However, this latter was itself often linked to juvenile employment and the desire of parents not to lose their children's earnings through the imposition of compulsory schooling, especially in time of economic hardship. Symptomatic of the ambivalent attitude of many was a case brought in 1884 by the London School Board, concerning a twelve-year-old labourer's daughter, who had been earning 3s. a week as a nursery maid. She had not achieved the Board's exemption level for employment, but there were several children in the family and her earnings were a useful contribution to household income. The magistrate dismissed the case and when it went to appeal not only was the original verdict upheld but the judge declared approvingly that the girl has been

> discharging the honourable duty of helping her parents, and, for my own part, before I held that these facts did not afford a reasonable excuse for her non-attendance at school, I should require to see the very plainest words to the contrary in the [Education] Act.[2]

In a similar spirit the Cross Commission in 1888 admitted that although premature employment disrupted school attendance, 'the poverty of . . . parents, both in towns and in country districts, makes it . . . exceedingly difficult to remove, and demanding very considerate treatment . . . Home needs, such as sickness in the family, the absence of the mother at work and nursing babies, keep many girls away, sometimes for long periods.' Only in the case of children working in the theatre was a sterner line taken, with the Commission calling for this to be brought under the regulation of the Factory Acts. That was partly because it considered the health, morals, and education of the children involved were being damaged, but also because 'we are told that it is not the poorest parents who send their children on the stage.'[3]

Within a decade, however, juvenile employment had re-emerged as a major issue, with a delegation from the Women's Industrial Council going to the Education Department in March 1898 to draw attention to the long hours worked by London school children engaged in home industries. They were received sympathetically by Sir John Gorst, Vice-President of the Committee of Council on Education. He favoured raising the school leaving age to thirteen, fourteen, or even fifteen, and criticized those who still argued that mass education was unwise because it might unfit 'boys and girls for those humbler employments . . . in which . . . they think . . . the greater part of the people . . . should remain.'[4] A few years later, now out of office, he condemned government inertia on the juvenile employment question. 'The obligation of public authority to protect the health of children and young persons in establishments of organised industry is . . . admitted by every civilised nation of the world', he declared.

Until twenty or thirty years ago Great Britain enjoyed the illustrious position of guiding all countries which had betaken themselves to factory industry in establishing laws for this purpose: she is now a good way behind many of her disciples.[5]

Gorst also lamented the large number of school children whose health was being injured by working out of school hours as street traders, newspaper vendors, shop assistants, domestic servants and errand boys and girls.

It is the purpose of this paper to examine why there was renewed interest in child employment between 1890 and 1914, how representative it was, and what steps had been taken by 1914 to remedy the deficiencies identified by Gorst.

The issue arose, interestingly, at a time when the proportion of children of school age in employment was in sharp decline. According to the 1891 census, 26 per cent of boys and 16.3 per cent of girls aged 10-14 were in occupations. By 1911 those figures had fallen to 18.3 per cent and 10.4

per cent, respectively. Similarly, if the number of half-timers is taken into account (including those exempted both under the Factory legislation and under the Education Acts), the totals had dropped from 172,363 in the year ended 31 August, 1892, to 70,255 by 1911-12. There were, of course, many children still working out of school hours — almost a quarter of a million of them by 1911-12, according to one estimate (see Appendix 2). It was their plight which was to cause particular concern at the beginning of the twentieth century. But such employment was not new and as early as 1878 the Scottish Education Act had sought, unsuccessfully, to regulate street trading by children. What was new in the 1890s was the increasing attention paid to the matter.[6]

Even the long-established half-time system came under critical scrutiny, with contemporaries like Allen Clarke condemning its deleterious effect on the health and welfare of young workers:

It is a sad fact that the majority of parents in Lancashire regard children only as commercial speculations, to be turned into wage-earning machines as soon as the child's age and the law will permit. For this they oppose the raising of the age of half-timers; for this resent all legislative interference, either educational or hygienic, in the matter of their children . . . [A] great many human beings in Lancashire — and elsewhere — are eager to turn their young to the most advantage by sacrificing them . . . for paltry pecuniary gain.[7]

Clarke's allegations were supported by the results of an 1897 ballot organized by the Northern Counties Amalgamated Association of Weavers over the possible ending of child labour under fifteen years of age. Almost 80,000 workers voted against the proposal, compared to less than 3½ thousand who supported it. Among the towns covered was Blackburn, where 399 voted in favour and 10,510 against, and Burnley, where the 480 in favour were swamped by 9,053 against. A decade earlier over a quarter of Blackburn's school children had been half-timers, as were a fifth of those in Burnley.[8] Custom clearly helped to perpetuate this use of young workers.

Clarke's criticism of the half-time system in the late 1890s contrasted sharply with the view expressed more than twenty years earlier by Karl Marx, who had seen in half-time working a positive educational and economic benefit. Marx, indeed, in 1875 had maintained that a prohibition on child labour would not only be incompatible with 'the existence of large-scale industry' but would be reactionary, 'since, with a strict regulation of the working time . . . and other safety measures . . . an early combination of productive labour with education is one of the most potent means for the transformation of present day society'. To later commentators it was merely a device for reducing the educational opportunities of the children involved without providing any adequate compensation.[9]

The reminiscences of half-timers suggest that most accepted their lot with resignation and sometimes also with pride, seeing it as a way of helping to support the family. Harry Pollitt, who became a half-timer helping his mother in a Lancashire weaving mill when he was twelve, in 1902, remembered that he and his friends were concerned they would not be able to pass the examination which permitted half-time working.

> We need not have worried. The mill-owners who controlled the educational bodies took previous good care that the biggest dunce in the school could pass it. . . . Within a very few days, the certificate came saying that Harry Pollitt had passed and could now work half-time.
>
> I was delighted, but not so my mother. She bitterly regretted the step which had to be taken, but it saved her from paying half a crown a week to some other half-timer to help her with her four looms.[10]

Similarly Ethel Saggerson, who started work — illegally — in an Oldham mill in 1909 when she was only eleven, recollected being told to go in by the back entrance to avoid being seen. 'But nobody seemed to bother. They didn't ask how old you were — they knew you needed the money . . . I don't know how much I got, but it weren't much more than a shilling.'[11]

William Williams, who began work in a Bradford worsted mill in 1898, aged eleven, also recalled the long hours. One week the half-timers went in in the mornings and the next in the afternoons. They attended school during the other half of the day. The morning shift lasted from 6 a.m. to 12.15 p.m., with a half-hour break for breakfast, each week-day and on Saturday morning, too, when the finish was at 1 p.m. That meant a total of 35 hours a week. On the afternoon shift the time was shorter, from 1 p.m. to 5.15 p.m., making 21 hours in all. However, so attractive was half-time working to some parents that they even moved house in order that their offspring could take advantage of it. One girl, the seventh child of an impoverished Yorkshire smallholder, recalled that in about 1910 her parents decided to settle in Bradford, 'where with a large family like ours the children could work in the mills. At least we would be fed . . .'[12] She herself became a half-timer as soon as she was old enough.

It was in these circumstances that Jocelyn Dunlop in 1912 condemned the 'unenviable legacy' bequeathed by the Victorians in the matter of child employment:

> The nineteenth century . . . raised juvenile labour to a fresh dignity, and regarded it as an independent factor in the labour market. As such, . . . it stood in need of special regulations, and accordingly an impressive array of regulations were duly formed. An employer must not employ a

child for unlimited hours, nor imperil his life and limbs. But the nineteenth century, content with its superficial diagnosis, made no attempt to prevent a child from spending years in work that made no call upon its intelligence, and from undertaking occupations that fitted it only for unemployment.[13]

That applied to some boy half-timers in worsted weaving, since the adult weavers were predominantly female and there was no place for many of the lads when they grew up.[14] In 1911, males comprised less than a fifth of the Bradford weaving workforce, although among those aged 10-14 inclusive they contributed over two-fifths of the total.

Alongside this were anomalies arising from the legislation itself. The 1878 and 1901 Factory and Workshop Acts, for example, made it optional only for workshop owners to have prospective juvenile employees examined by a certifying surgeon before they were appointed, whereas for factory children this was obligatory. As a result certification for workshops became virtually a dead letter even though the conditions under which youngsters had to labour were often far worse than in factories, especially as regards ventilation.

Other critics, like Robert Sherard, appealed to their readers' emotions. In 1905 Sherard wrote of the 'most helpless amongst the helpless, . . . the weak, hungry little children of the poor, who because of the utter poverty of their parents are put to toil and labour, the Child-Slaves of Britain.'[15]

Meanwhile, the government, despite initial reluctance, especially at the Home Office, was becoming involved in the debate, not merely through the reports of the factory inspectors, whose role was already well established, but through the issuing of specialist reports. These included the 1899 *Elementary Schools (Children Working for Wages) Return*: the 1902 *Report of the Inter-Departmental Committee on the Employment of School Children*; the 1909 *Report of the Inter-Departmental Committee on Partial Exemption from School Attendance*; and the 1910 *Report of the Departmental Committee on the Employment of Children Act, 1903*. All provided evidence of the kinds of work children carried out. The 1899 *Return*, for example, dealt with youngsters employed outside school hours, selling in the streets, caddying on golf links, helping on farms, taking dinners to adult workers, delivering milk, working in 'sweated' industries, and many other jobs. One school reported it had 70 pupils engaged in selling newspapers, carrying out domestic work, and running errands, for about 3d. to 8d. a week each, while in another school, 49 boys between eight and thirteen were employed selling newspapers, matches, and other goods on the streets for between 4 and 35 hours a week.[16]

The domestic employment taken up by the girls included looking after babies, scrubbing floors, and laundry work, as well as such 'sweated' home tasks as boxmaking, shirt-making, beading, and making belts, often to assist parents. But the number of girls recorded — about a quarter of the total — is undoubtedly an underestimate. In all, 147,349 working children were identified in the 1899 return, and of these around a quarter were aged ten or under (with about 130 less than seven). Approximately 28 per cent of the youngsters worked more than 20 hours a week, and 0.5 per cent worked 50 or more hours weekly.[17] Many of these tasks were *regular* part-time commitments.

Other reports, like the 1913 *Report of the Departmental Committee on the Hours and Conditions of Employment of Van Boys and Warehouse Boys*, although primarily concerned with those over fourteen, included evidence on casual employment among school children. In Birmingham, in particular, school boys were employed illegally until 10.30 p.m. by parcel delivery companies, and the city authorities apparently made little effort to control the trade.[18]

Such casual juvenile occupations were, of course, not new. Mayhew's investigations half a century earlier had revealed a similar range of child workers. Why, then, was so much attention concentrated on them in the 1890s and beyond? There seem to have been six major causes of this revival of interest, which was, significantly, more than matched by contemporary anxiety about the newly identified 'boy labour' problem among adolescents, and particularly the fact that many young male school leavers went into 'blind alley' employment. It came, too, at a time when the apprenticeship system was on the decline and when, as the Webbs pointed out in 1902, 'hundreds of thousands of youths, between fourteen and twenty-one' were taken on to do unskilled work, at relatively high wages, only to be turned adrift without a trade as soon as they required a man's pay.[19] Part of the child labour debate was concerned with the potential link between the premature employment of school children and the rising problem of the unskilled adolescent, who would, in turn, contribute to growing adult male unemployment. The fact that the occupation expanding most rapidly among ten to fourteen-year-olds, according to the census returns, was the 'blind alley' employment of messenger and porter, reinforced these anxieties. By 1911, over a quarter of boy workers aged ten to fourteen worked as messengers and porters (including Post Office messengers); a further 3.2 per cent were involved in the equally 'blind alley' occupation of newspaper vending (see Appendix 1).

Against this background we must now examine the main reasons for the growing urgency of the child labour debate.

First, there was the influence of the education legislation between 1870 and 1880, which by the 1890s was isolating perennial truants, especially in the larger towns. As Nigel Middleton has written

the daily assembly of a large portion of the nation's children for a legally enforced activity lasting several hours gave an unavoidable opportunity to understand the needs and deprivement of the children of the poor. . . . Once children had been called to the attention of the country by assembling them in schools, measures to improve their depressed state followed in profusion.[20]

These included special provision for blind, deaf and other handicapped children, the setting up of charitable school meals schemes, and concern for children's welfare on a wider basis, such as the 1885 legislation to outlaw juvenile prostitution by raising the age of consent from thirteen to sixteen, and, four years later, a measure to protect children against cruelty by parents as well as by other adults. (Even the thorny subject of incest was tackled in 1908). Premature child labour came under scrutiny as part of the same process, and that applied to exhausted half-timers who fell asleep at their desks after their stint in the factory as well as to youngsters who were working long hours while attending school full-time. The 1899 *Elementary Schools (Working for Wages) Return* included many examples of this latter kind, like the boy who began work for his father at 3 a.m. each day and continued in the evening until 9 p.m. 'He often goes to sleep during morning school from sheer weariness.' Another boy who placed skittles for 34½ hours a week, from 6 p.m. to 11 p.m. daily, frequently slept during afternoon lessons. In other cases children were kept away for days to carry out casual labour, particularly land work or, for the girls, domestic chores. Reformers claimed that this not only damaged their education but wasted public money, since they were unable to benefit from the schooling provided. In an era preoccupied with 'value for money' that was a particularly cogent argument.

A second factor contributing to the debate was Britain's declining economic position compared to that of some of her competitors, notably Germany, and the extent to which this was due to a shortage of skilled labour. In 1898 Gorst warned that without efficient elementary schooling youngsters could not take advantage of technical instruction. Later, in the 'national efficiency' controversy which followed recruitment for the Boer War, there was anxiety about the future physical fitness of the nation, and its effect on Britain's ability to defend the empire. In 1902 Sidney and Beatrice Webb identified as perhaps the 'gravest social symptom at the opening of the twentieth century' the 'lack of physical vigor, (sic) moral self-control, and technical skill of the town-bred, manual-working boy'. They demanded the introduction of compulsory part-time day continuation schools for working adolescents. Other reformers pressed for the implementation of welfare initiatives like the provision of school meals and medical inspection to improve the health of younger children. The newly expanding eugenics movement added to this general atmosphere of concern about the future of the race.[21]

In 1902 the *Report of the Inter-Departmental Committee on the Employment of School Children* reflected some of these preoccupations when it declared that

> the too early employment of children may, like the premature work of horses, injure their future capacity, and . . . what is gained at the commencement of life is much more than lost at a later stage. . . . Even on the lowest ground . . . of financial interest, it is not cheap to work a child so as to cause him to be prematurely worn out. It is more economical to start him in life after a healthy childhood with powers that will last longer, and keep him to a later age from being dependent on others for his support.

The Committee was not opposed to all child employment, however, for the old fear that the devil finds work for idle hands had not entirely died away. Instead it argued in favour of 'moderate work under healthy conditions', since 'the poor boy, if he has no work to fill up his spare time has in most large towns only the alternative of playing or loafing in the streets or of moping in dull rooms in a crowded tenement. We think that, quite irrespective of anything he may earn, it is better for him, mentally, morally and physically to be engaged for a few hours a day in regulated labour rather than to spend his whole leisure in the public thoroughfares or in the penny music-hall'. In evidence to the Committee, a member of the London School Board echoed this view by claiming that if children were prevented from working for wages they would spend their time 'in gambling for buttons on the kerb-stone.'[22]

For the Committee, appropriate employment was a useful part of a boy's education. 'It would be well if a larger number of children could at an early age be introduced to some of the practical work of the carpenter, the shoemaker, or the blacksmith; but if it is impossible, even the running of errands or the selling of newspapers, helps to make them alert and industrious and prepares them for the part they have to take in after life'. It was not child labour, particularly boy labour, *per se* which was at fault, but merely some of the jobs children performed.

A third aspect of the debate was the degree to which cheap juvenile workers were undermining the job security of adults. By using more machinery and sub-dividing tasks, it was possible for youngsters to be used in routine, 'dead-end' occupations from which they could be dismissed when they became too costly. Many trade unionists and their sympathisers believed that the only solution was to keep youngsters out of the labour market for as long as possible. Henry Hyndman of the Social Democratic Federation demanded an 'absolute prohibition of all child labour for wages up to the age of 14 at least', while the Webbs in 1897 argued that the 'industrial parasitism' involved in using child workers must be ended. This meant immediately raising the age at which youngsters could enter industrial life 'to the fourteen years already adopted by the Swiss federal code, if not to the fifteen years now in force in Geneva, and eventually to the sixteen years demanded by the International Socialist and Trade Union Congress of 1896'.[23] They also favoured changing the half-time system so that full factory hours would be worked only when a youngster had reached eighteen years.

Such radical policies found little favour with either government or employers, and in the textile districts, as we have seen, proposals to raise the age for child employment were fiercely opposed by the workers. In 1891, the Bolton Operative Spinners' Union even rejected a proposition to raise the minimum working age for half-timers from ten to twelve, condemning it as an 'entirely uncalled for' step; 'we . . . assert that a child does not suffer, either physically or intellectually, as a result of becoming a half-timer'.[24] In the event, the 1891 Factory Act raised the minimum employment age for half-timers to eleven; a further decade was to elapse before it was raised to twelve. Many of the half-timers were, of course, directly recruited and paid by adult workers who wished both to minimize their outlay on pay and to maximize the children's output, if necessary by using them illegally to clean machinery while it was still in motion.[25] Since their own pay was based on piecework, to stop the machines would have reduced their earnings.

In 1904 the MP David Shackleton, who was secretary of the Darwen Weavers' Union, frankly admitted that whatever his personal opinion might be on child labour, 'if he was to be the nominee of the textile workers, he was bound to answer in harmony with the decision of the textile workers, and the result was that he could not support the raising of the age of children going to work to sixteen.' As late as 1909, when the Amalgamated Association of Operative Cotton Spinners held a ballot on raising the exemption age for half-time working to thirteen, 151,000 of the 185,000 who voted opposed the measure.[26] In that same year a government survey revealed that the accident rate among half-timers was nearly double that for adults and young persons.

A fourth factor in the child labour discussion had an international dimension. Already in the 1880s the Swiss Federal Government had sought to promote international labour agreements, while in 1890 a Congress was held in Berlin under German auspices to consider the question. From the juvenile point of view its most notable recommendations were the prohibition of child labour in factories under the age of twelve and below ground in mines under fourteen. Germany, Austria, Belgium, France, and several other countries voted for a minimum age of twelve for factory work, but the United Kingdom, Spain and Italy initially abstained, although later the United Kingdom acceded to the proposal.[27] In practice, it was not until 1901 that twelve became the legal minimum age for half-time working in British factories.

Meanwhile Cardinal Manning, in an article in the *Contemporary Review* in 1891 supported the Berlin recommendation of twelve as the minimum age for factory employment. In so doing he stressed the importance of protecting the child's individual rights, even against parents: 'children are not chattels. . . . And if parents fail to protect . . . their children, the Commonwealth is bound to do so'. This view that the child was entitled to State protection had been advanced in the early days of the factory reform movement.[28] It was also taken up by Henry Dunckley, another contributor to the half-time question in the *Contemporary Review*. Dunckley linked it to the 'value for money' arguments put forward by certain educational reformers by noting that although children 'belonged' to their parents they also belonged to the nation:

> In a few years they will enter into the material of which adult society is made, and we have to be on our guard against a damaged article. The nation has recognized its interest as well as its obligations by devoting millions of money every year to the instruction of the young, and it has a right to see that the utmost possible amount of benefit is derived from the outlay.[29]

It was enlightened self-interest that demanded the State intervene if a child's welfare were being jeopardised.

Fifthly, there was the contribution of the 'anti-cruelty' lobby. This developed in the 1880s, with the setting up in Liverpool of the first English Society for the Prevention of Cruelty to Children, in April 1883. It was based on a New York model and was followed in July 1884 by a similar body in London. Both societies were concerned primarily to protect children from physical ill-treatment by adults, including their parents, but interest also extended to what the London Society called 'Child Slaves' — children sent out to beg or hawk on the streets until late at night. Special officers were appointed by the Society in an effort to curb these activities, but the lack of an effective legal framework outlawing them made the attempt unavailing. In these circumstances the London Society pressed for the passage of legislation which would extend the protection already afforded to young workers in factories, mines and brickfields to those who made a living in the streets. Largely as a result of these efforts the Prevention of Cruelty to Children Act was passed in 1889. It not only laid down penalties for the mistreatment and neglect of children but prohibited any boy under fourteen, or girl under sixteen, from singing, acting, performing for profit, or offering goods for sale in the streets or on licensed premises (other than those licensed for public amusement) between 10 p.m. and 5 a.m. Children under ten were prohibited from carrying on these activities at any time. Fines or a term of imprisonment could be imposed on those who caused children to break the regulations.

In 1894 the Act was further tightened, but enforcement proved difficult, even in cities like Liverpool and Manchester, which introduced a system of licensing child street traders. In 1914 a critic could observe of Liverpool, where licensed youngsters had to wear special badges, that the 'evils of street trading by children are . . . perhaps more obvious . . . than in any other English town.'[30] Yet as early as 1884 the City Council had issued regulations under the Municipal Corporations Act, 1882, prohibiting children under nine from trading in the streets at all, or those under thirteen from trading after 9 p.m. in summer and 7 p.m. in winter. These regulations were rendered invalid by a decision of the High Court in 1887 which declared *ultra vires* similar regulations drawn up by Newcastle-on-Tyne Corporation. In 1893 Liverpool made fresh bye-laws under the 1889 Prevention of Cruelty to Children Act and these were extended five years later, when in addition to the licensing system the Council agreed to provide homes for licensed children where this seemed necessary. In 1895 a Police-aided Clothing Association was set up in the city to provide clothes for destitute youngsters, including those engaged in street trading.[31] Later that duty was taken over by the Watch Committee itself.

The Liverpool initiatives were considered models of their kind, and were adopted by other towns and cities, including Manchester, Bolton, Bradford and Halifax. But any hope that child street traders would be regulated effectively by them was soon dashed. In Bradford, the Watch Committee complained in March 1896 that the laxity of JPs made it difficult to enforce the restrictions of the Prevention of Cruelty to Children Act on hawking: '27 cases out of 38 in the past year [have] been discharged by the magistrates'.[32] Eighteen months earlier the Bradford School Attendance Committee had refused to allow half-time exemption from school for any child intending to hawk in the streets. But the problem persisted. Even efforts to ensure that youngsters were decently clad were often thwarted by the children themselves. They found business more lucrative when they appealed to the charitable dressed in rags.

The practice of arresting children found trading without a licence was virtually abandoned in Liverpool after 1904. Instead they were brought before the Street Trading Sub-Committee and cautioned. On rare occasions the parents of children trading without a licence were prosecuted under the 1894 Prevention of Cruelty to Children Act. But much unlicensed trading remained. In 1912, while 505 boys and 32 girls were reported as holding licences on 31 December, a further 235 children had been trading without a licence during that year. Of these, 165 were cautioned and 35 summoned, while proceedings against parents were taken in four cases; 324 of the licensed children also received clothing from the Watch Committee. The pressure of family poverty, in a city where casual labour connected with the port was widespread, ensured that juvenile street trading was a continuing feature of Liverpool life.[33] The anti-cruelty lobby and its associated legislation were unable to eliminate it.

The final influence leading to the renewed attention paid to child employment during the 1890s arose from the actions of individual reformers, among whom Mrs. Edith Hogg and the committee of the Women's Industrial Council were particularly prominent. In an article in the *Nineteenth Century* in 1897 Mrs. Hogg publicised the problems connected with the employment of school children. She pointed to evidence collected by a committee of the Women's Industrial Council upon fifty-four London schools, catering for about 26,000 pupils from differing economic and social backgrounds. Of these, 729 boys and 523 girls, i.e. about five per cent of the total, were working for wages. That took no account of those working at home for parents or relatives without pay. In a series of case studies Mrs. Hogg detailed not only the wide range of tasks carried out by the children and the long hours many of them worked, but the paltry pay most received. For delivering newspapers and milk about 1d. to 1¼d. an hour was earned; for street trading ¾d. an hour; for running errands, ½d. an hour, and for shop work 1d. to 1¼d. an hour. 'Sometimes food is given in addition, but this and the rate of payment seem to be purely an arbitrary arrangement'. That applied to both boys and girls. Of the 729 boys in Mrs. Hogg's survey, 102 worked as newspaper sellers, 313 were in shops, and 134 ran errands, while 56 were involved in street selling and hawking. Of the 523 working girls, 140 ran errands, 135 were baby-minders and 115 did domestic cleaning.[34]

Mrs. Hogg argued that not only were the children often overworked but they were prevented from benefiting from their education, and their remuneration was 'too small to be taken into account'. She called for fresh legislation to protect those working children not covered by the Factory Acts.

In November 1897 the Women's Industrial Council organized a conference on London home industries, which again provided examples of child overwork. Details were passed to the Home Office and the Education Department. The Home Office was unenthusiastic, with the Chief Inspector of Factories pointing to the difficulty of policing child employment in the home. 'Detailed inspection, of a minuteness and frequency sufficient to constitute any effective check, could hardly be,' he wrote.

> . . . In a workshop or factory the mere presence of a child raises presumption of employment, but at home it suggests anything. Home work could often be packed away out of sight at a moment's notice.[35]

A colleague in the Home Office agreed: 'To inspect homes generally to see how children are employed would require such an enormous staff and require such an interference with family life as would not be tolerated'.[36]

The Education Department, under Sir John Gorst, was more sympathetic and arranged for the collection of data on child employment which were published in the 1899 *Return* on *Elementary Schools (Children Working for Wages)*. Also active was the Committee on Wage Earning Children, set up in December 1898 to organize its own inquiries and to lobby Parliament for protective legislation. Partly as a result of this pressure the Inter-Departmental Committee on the Employment of School Children was appointed in 1901. The Committee, whilst opposed to the prohibition of all child labour, recognized that further regulation was needed. As a result, after some delay, the Employment of Children Act was passed in 1903.[37]

The Act laid down five prohibitions designed to safeguard the health and morals of working children and to prevent their labour interfering adversely with their education. These were:

1. an end to the employment of any child under fourteen between 9 p.m. and 6 a.m., with local authorities empowered to vary these times if they thought fit, so as to cut working hours still further; girls were restricted from street trading under sixteen;
2. no child could trade on the streets under the age of eleven;
3. factory or workshop half-timers were not allowed to take up any additional occupation;
4. no child was to lift or move heavy weights likely to cause injury;
5. no child was to be employed in an occupation likely to injure its life, health or education.

Unfortunately the Act's vagueness on certain points and the permissive nature of other aspects reduced its value. In 1907 the Home Office admitted that even local authorities which considered it beneficial merely stated this 'as a pious opinion without any further particulars being given'.[38] By that date sixty-six local authorities had drawn up bye-laws under the legislation. They included just two County Councils — Gloucestershire and London. Even in 1913, out of 329 local authorities only 131 had produced bye-laws relating to street trading, which was considered the form of employment which most threatened children's moral and physical welfare. On the question of general employment, a mere 98 authorities had made regulatory bye-laws, compared to 231 which had not.[39] Their laggardliness was partly due to fears of incurring expenditure by employing staff to implement the regulations. But a further difficulty was the hostility of the employers of child workers.[40] These included newspaper proprietors, milk dealers, grocers, barbers, and shopkeepers of all kinds, many of whom were well-represented on local councils. They used their influence on the councils to discourage the adoption of bye-laws.

What, then, was the harvest from this renewed agitation on child labour between 1890 and 1914? First, as more and more parents saw the value of delaying their children's entry on to the job market, the minimum employment age of most full and half-time child workers was raised

135

progressively from ten in 1890 to twelve by the beginning of the twentieth century. Under some local authorities it was higher still. Yet the lack of enthusiasm to outlaw child labour entirely was demonstrated in 1911 when a proposal to end half-time working and to raise the minimum leaving age to thirteen was withdrawn by the government, without discussion, 'owing to pressure of time'.[41] Despite some encouragement to reintroduce it, no action was taken until the 1918 Education Act.

Second, there was the effect of the 1894 Prevention of Cruelty to Children Act and the 1903 Employment of Children Act which sought to limit the employment of school-age children, especially after dark; a minimum age of eleven was also established for children trading on the streets. But these provisions were of limited value only. They did little to help those engaged for long periods working at home, like children encountered in 1904 by Robert Sherard in Birmingham. They included youngsters earning 2¼d. for making up a thousand packages of hair-pins, a task which took four of them two days; in other cases children earned 1d. a day bending the tin clasp round safety pins.[42] Many of these unprotected home workers were likely to be girls.

Ten years later Frederic Keeling considered it 'optimistic to assume that the total number of wage-earning school children had been diminished by more than 10 to 15 per cent as the result of the regulation of child labour by the Employment of Children Act and kindred Acts'. He also pointed to the anomalies which arose when some local authorities chose to ignore the bye-law issue entirely or, like Cambridge, Norwich and Northampton, drew up bye-laws which they had little intention of enforcing. Others again, following Birmingham's lead, implemented certain aspects of the legislation only, while neglecting the rest, and some, like Bradford, Liverpool and London, endeavoured to operate a comprehensive programme of regulation. On a rough estimate, Keeling concluded, there was

something approaching fairly effective all-round administration of child labour regulations in areas containing about a fifth or a sixth of the population of the United Kingdom, while in areas containing something like a quarter of the population, the various laws might as well not exist.[43]

The net effect of this uneven treatment was to breed resentment among some parents and employers in areas of strict enforcement and thereby to encourage them to adopt strategies to evade the regulations where they could.

The confused and often ambivalent response to the juvenile labour question was exemplified in 1912 when Devon County Council proposed introducing a bye-law to prevent any child liable to attend school full-time from working on school days between 8.30 a.m. and 4.30 p.m. It evoked such a storm of protest that a government inquiry had to be held. This revealed that a 'substantial number of children' aged eleven or less worked regularly within the county. From Honiton, for example, the poor law guardians complained that the proposed restrictions would

> entail great hardship and injustice to poor parents, especially to widows, whose children between the hours . . . mentioned, are often able out of school hours to earn their dinners and a few pence per week by doing odd jobs at the homes of farmers and others residing near the schools without affecting their school studies or in any way injuring or exhausting themselves.[44]

In the north of the county labourers' children frequently lodged with farmers while they were at school, and paid for their bed and board by land work.

In the end a modified bye-law was put forward. This allowed the children to work during their midday break and declared that a pupil would not be deemed to be employed 'within the meaning of [the] byelaw' if he or she were engaged in driving cattle to pasture or taking horses to and from the farrier while on the way to or from school. Also permitted was the delivery of small quantities of milk and farm produce on the way to school and the carrying of meals 'to any person or persons'.[45] With these loopholes there was little danger of casual child labour in Devon being much affected.

In 1912, Jocelyn Dunlop referred bitterly to the sympathy accorded the 'paternalist', who urged the importance of child labour in helping families meet 'temporary and accidental misfortune'.[46] What was needed, she argued, was not this parasitic dependence by the family on juvenile employment, thereby sacrificing a youngster's long-term prospects to the exigencies of the present, but a more generous provision of public assistance, in the form of sickness and unemployment benefit and the like which would render it unnecessary. Even in 1914 that was a view which was certainly not universally accepted, while casual rural tasks like hop-picking and fruit gathering were regarded virtually as holidays by many poor families in London and the Midlands.[47]

APPENDIX 1

a. *Occupations of children aged 10-14 inclusive in England and Wales as shown in Census Reports.*

Percentage of children aged 10-14 in England and Wales in occupations:

	Boys	Girls
1871	32.1	20.4
1891	26.0	16.3
1901	21.9	12.0
1911	18.3	10.4

b. *Individual occupations of boys 10-14* as recorded in 1891 and 1911 censuses.

Of those occupied:

1891		*1911*	
Messenger, porter &c.	18.6%	Messenger, porter, &c.	24.2%
Ag. lab. & farm servant	16.3%	Coalmining	9.5%
Cotton manufacture	8.6%	Ag. lab. & farm servant	8.3%
Coalmining	7.5%	Cotton manufacture	7.7%
General labourer	3.1%	Woollen & worsted	3.4%
Worsted manufacture	2.5%	Newspaper vending	3.2%
Shoemaker	2.2%	Commercial clerks	2.1%
Clerks	2.0%	Farmers' sons	1.7%
Grocer, &c.	1.4%	Post office messengers	1.6%

c. *Individual occupations of girls 10-14* as recorded in 1891 and 1911 censuses.

Of those occupied:

1891		*1911*	
Domestic service	40.9%	Domestic service	24.0%
Cotton manufacture	18.7%	Cotton manufacture	19.8%
Dressmaking, tailoring, millinery, &c.	9.1%	Dressmaking, tailoring, millinery, &c.	11.5%
Worsted manufacture	5.4%	Woollen & worsted	7.2%
Teaching	2.3%	Messengers, porters, &c.	2.4%

APPENDIX 2

SUMMARY OF THE POSITION OF THE EMPLOYMENT
OF CHILDREN UNDER 14 IN ENGLAND AND WALES IN 1912

Children employed *full-time* under Factory Act   55,000
Children employed *part-time* under Factory Act   31,140
Children employed under Mines Acts   4,740
Children employed *full-time outside* Factory & Mines Acts   136,424
Children employed *part-time outside* Factory Act   8,961
Children *attending school full time* employed out of school hours   240,000

From: F. Keeling, *Child Labour in the United Kingdom* (1914), p.xxviii.

References

1. Carolyn Steedman, *Childhood, Culture and Class in Britain: Margaret McMillan, 1860-1931* (London, 1990), 109.
2. David Rubinstein, *School Attendance in London, 1870-1904* (Hull, 1969), 102; Lionel Rose, *The Erosion of Childhood* (London, 1991), 52-53.
3. *Final Report of the Commission on the Elementary Education Acts in England and Wales*, P.P.1888, Vol. XXV, 110.
4. *The Times*, 3 March, 1898.
5. Sir John E. Gorst, *The Children of the Nation* (New York, 1907), 216.
6. Frederic Keeling, *Child Labour in the United Kingdom* (London, 1914), 16 and 22; Hugh Cunningham, *The Children of the Poor* (Oxford, 1991), 176-179.
7. Allen Clarke, *The Effects of the Factory System* (Littleborough, 1985 edn.), 105-106. The book was first published in 1899.
8. For the ballot see H.O. 45/9919/B.22933 at the Public Record Office (PRO). For the number of half-timers see Bradford School Board: School Attendance Committee Minutes, BBT.13/2/21, 8 March, 1887, at Bradford Record Office.
9. *Report of the Inter-Departmental Committee on Partial Exemption from School Attendance*, P.P.1909, Vol. XVII, 4 and 12. (Hereafter *Cttee. on Par. Exemp.*)
10. Harry Pollitt, *Serving my Time* (1940), extract at the National Museum of Labour History, Manchester.
11. Freda Millett, *Childhood in Oldham 1890-1920* (Oldham, 1989), 27.
12. Reminiscences of William Williams at Bradford Record Office, ID.77/1. Maggie Newbery, *Reminiscences of a Bradford Mill Girl* (Bradford, 1980), 22.
13. O. Jocelyn Dunlop, *English Apprenticeship and Child Labour* (London, 1912), 309-310.

14. *Cttee. on Par. Exemp.*, 10-11.
15. Robert H. Sherard, *The Child-Slaves of Britain* (London, 1905), xvi.
16. *Elementary Schools (Children Working for Wages) Return*, Cd. 205 (HMSO, 1899), Part I, 12. (Hereafter *1899 Return*).
17. *1899 Return*, 4 and 25.
18. *Report of the Departmental Committee on the Hours and Conditions of Employment of Van Boys and Warehouse Boys*, P.P.1913, Vol. XXXIII, *Minutes of Evidence*, Q.1818-1830.
19. S. and B. Webb, *Industrial Democracy* (London, 1902 edn.), 483.
20. Nigel Middleton, 'The Education Act of 1870 as the Start of the Modern Concept of the Child', *British Journal of Educational Studies*, Vol. 18 (1970), 177.
21. G.R. Searle, *Eugenics and Politics in Britain 1900-14* (Leyden, 1976), 21-32. G.R. Searle, *The Quest for National Efficiency* (Oxford, 1971), 236. Harry Hendrick, *Images of Youth* (Oxford, 1990), 26.
22. *Inter-Departmental Committee on the Employment of School Children*, P.P. 1902, Vol. XXV, *Report*, 19 and *Minutes of Evidence*, Q.143.
23. Hugh Cunningham, op. cit., 183.
24. Allen Clarke, op. cit., 104-105.
25. *Annual Report for 1912 of the Chief Inspector of Factories and Workshops*, P.P.1913, Vol. XXIII, xxv and 92. Allen Clarke, op. cit., 98-99. S. and B. Webb, op. cit., 811.
26. Edmund and Ruth Frow, *A Survey of the Half-time System in Education* (Manchester, 1970), 67; Chris Wrigley, *Arthur Henderson* (Cardiff, 1990), 37-38.
27. Hugh Cunningham, op. cit., 176. B.L. Hutchins and A. Harrison, *A History of Factory Legislation* (London, 1966 edn.), 270. Interestingly in Germany under an Imperial Law of 1891, 13 was the minimum age for factory employment.
28. Clark Nardinelli, *Child Labor and the Industrial Revolution* (Bloomington and Indianapolis, 1990), 14. Henry Edward Cardinal Manning, 'Child Labour: Minimum Age for Labour of Children', *Contemporary Review*, Vol. 59 (1891), 796.
29. Henry Dunckley, 'The Half-Timers', *Contemporary Review*, Vol. 59 (1891), 799-800.
30. Frederic Keeling, op. cit., 256. George K. Behlmer, *Child Abuse and Moral Reform in England, 1870-1908* (Stanford, Cal. 1982), 53, 55, 90 and 199. *Tortured Children: Third Year's Experience in their Defence* (London Society for the Prevention of Cruelty to Children, 1887), 14.
31. Frederic Keeling, op. cit., 256.
32. Bradford School Board: School Attendance Committee Minutes, BBT.13/2/22, at Bradford Record Office, 23 March, 1896.
33. Frederic Keeling, op. cit., 261 and 264.

34. Edith F. Hogg, 'School Children as Wage Earners', *Nineteenth Century*, Vol. 42 (1897), 235, 238, 239 and 241.
35. Comment dated 10 February, 1898 in H.O.45/9929/B.25717/1 at PRO.
36. Comment dated 11 March, 1898 in H.O.45/9929/B.25717/1 at PRO.
37. Hugh Cunningham, op. cit., 181.
38. Replies to Home Office circular, 20 September, 1907 in H.O.45/10502/122671 at PRO.
39. Frederic Keeling, op. cit., 31-32. *Return of Local Authorities making Byelaws under the Employment of Children Act*, 1903, P.P.1907, Vol. LXXII.
40. O. Jocelyn Dunlop, op. cit., 345.
41. Edmund and Ruth Frow, op. cit., 67.
42. Robert H. Sherard, op. cit., 131.
43. Frederic Keeling, op. cit., 57-59.
44. *Employment of Children Act, 1903: Report on the Byelaw made at the Devon County Council*, P.P.1913, Vol. XXIII, 5.
45. Ibid., 15.
46. O. Jocelyn Dunlop, op. cit., 348.
47. Frederic Keeling, op. cit., 56 and 65. David Rubinstein, op. cit., 64. Harry Hendrick, *Child Welfare, England 1872-1989* (London, 1994), 73-74.

SUBURBS AND SCHOOLS: THE GENERATION OF AT-RISK CHILDREN IN POST-WAR BRITAIN

Roy Lowe

This paper brings together several recent pieces of research which are seemingly not closely related to each other, in an attempt to offer a view on the nature of modern English society and the uses it makes of its schools. It seeks to analyse the links which have developed between schools and their suburbs in modern England and argues that patterns of suburbanisation are a key element in determining the social functions of schooling and the recent politics of education. Not least, the maldistribution of opportunity which follows from suburbanisation has resulted in the generation of whole groups of children who are, through no fault of their own, 'at risk' of being unable to partake fully of the opportunities which ought rightly to accrue to all citizens.

My own interest in this has two starting points: the first is at the anecdotal level but is perhaps the most strongly felt. As a tutor to students on school practice, I became increasingly aware, over a number of years, as I moved around the West Midlands conurbation, of the extent to which sections of society seemed to be closed off from each other. As an extreme variant of this I would occasionally take students directly from work in an inner city Birmingham comprehensive to visit a well-known public school. The contrast was vivid, shocking, and needed no commentary.

At another level, I was increasingly drawn, in writing *Education in the Post War years*,[1] to consider the linkages between suburbanisation and schooling at the moment when the first comprehensive schools were being built. I argued there that the new comprehensives may in some senses have been a vehicle for the heightening of social contrasts rather than an ameliorative agency, as their apologists would claim: I finished that book with a strong sense of the need to pursue this issue when looking at more recent trends.

Schooling and Social Stratification in Late-Nineteenth Century England

What then are the issues raised by recent research for those looking at education in modern England? The work of Bill Marsden has brought home to historians of education in England the importance of an approach which

142

is essentially ecological and which draws on a variety of disciplines.[2] He emphasizes in his recent book on the *Unequal educational provision in England and Wales*[3] his debt first to that group of urban historians based at Leicester. He singles out David Reeder as the only one of the group who has given any priority to the investigation of urban schooling: It was Reeder, among these urban historians who drew attention to the 'taken for granted'[4] attitude of historians of education towards the urban context of schooling. The second important element informing Marsden's work is historical geography, deploying techniques which are essentially geographical to tease out the spatial significance of school within their suburbs. Finally, the debt to urban sociology, and in particular the Chicago school is evident and is fully recognized by Marsden. He emphasizes too the way in which much recent work in this field, although still deeply influenced by the thinking of Robert Park and his associates, has moved beyond an emphasis on competition as the driving force behind the changing structure of cities, towards a recognition of the importance attaching to what Marsden calls the 'cultural values and attitudes attached to particular locations',[5] which might conceivably exercise a stronger influence than economic forces, such as changing land values. These then are the techniques which Marsden has sought to apply to the study of nineteenth century schooling, and he is not alone among historians of education in stressing the need for an essentially ecological approach. Michael Katz has called for an 'historical ecology of school systems'[6] and Kaestle and Vinovskis have emphasized the need to study schooling 'in relationship to the evolving social structure, economic system, and cultural relationships of community, region and nation'.[7] Marsden has attempted, with considerable success in my view, to deploy these techniques at both national and suburban level, but so far this has always been done in the context of the nineteenth century. He draws a vivid picture of the interconnections of variegated land use, differing school systems, local entrepreneurial decisions, differing views of what constituted a good education to conclude that 'the want of equality in the distribution'[8] which was first compained of in a correspondent of 1846, proved to be an enduring characteristic of nineteenth century urban schooling. The challenge is to relate these techniques, and the issues they raise to the recent period to grasp the texture and reality of schooling in post-war England.

This challenge is heightened by the work of Fritz Ringer and his associates who are also primarily concerned with the late-nineteenth and early-twentieth century, but who also raise issues and set out to establish hypotheses about schooling in industrial society which are just as significant for more recent times. It was in his powerful introduction to *Education and society in modern Europe*[9] that Ringer first developed his theory that what marked the emergence of education as a system in the full sense of the term was its becoming segmented or tracked, so that the upturn in numbers passing through the education systems of Europe in the late-nineteenth century was mediated through either institutional barriers (i.e. different types of school for pupils from different social origins) or else curricular ones, by which different pupils received different curricula. He suggests that the segmented systems which actually developed during the high industrial phase of development worked in practice to 'legitimate and perpetuate the existing class structure'. He points out that in England the coming of universal secondary schooling merely resulted in the reappearance of the old elementary/secondary divide within the secondary system. He argues that the battles over differentiated curricula are critical in determining the social functions of schooling systems. These ideas were refined and developed in the more recent *Rise of the modern educational system*,[10] a book which attempted to apply Ringer's ideas more directly within real historical contexts, but which was also deeply influenced by Bordieu's views on social reproduction, and by Detlef Muller's work on schooling in the Prussian gymnasien which stressed the concept of systematisation. Put together, and crudely summarised, what these ideas in combination led to was the view that during the second phase of industrialisation, from about 1870 to 1930, the extension of State education in England may have involved the formation of a self-perpetuating system, with clear boundaries between different types of institution and differing curricula. Pre-existing schools may have played the rôle of 'defining institutions'[11] whose curricula were widely copied in a scramble for status: in brief, a socially hierarchical system built up through what the authors called 'a conflict-ridden exercise in social demarcation',[12] which once established exercised a dominant rôle in the formation of social classes, and which was unlikely to be easily dislodged. These controversial ideas, which merit a much fuller explanation than is possible here, also raise pressing questions for the historian of recent and near-contemporary education in England. For, if these characteristics may be perceived in early-twentieth century English education, it follows that they are likely to be characteristic of more recent developments, particularly in view of the extent to which Muller, Ringer & Simon emphasize the power of these systems of schooling to elf-perpetuate. Are there any characteristics then of schooling in England in recent years which would tend to substantiate, or to deny these segmentation theories?

The importance of suburbanisation as a key factor to be taken into account by recent historians has been brought home even more forcibly by Harold Perkin's recent book on *The rise of professional society*,[13] which repeatedly emphasizes the extent to which suburbanisation meant a re-definition and reworking of social class distinctions. Perkin sees the coming of the suburbs in the late-nineteenth century as being the moment when, for the first time, what he calls 'segregated classes' were created in England. He argues that 'it was the late-Victorian age, with its trams, buses and suburban railways, which began the commuter age of modern times and

with it the height of inequality between the classes'.[14] Perkin sees the turn
of the century as the moment when, historically, these social class
distinctions were most marked: he calls this era 'the zenith of class
society'.[15] Perkin introduces, too, a new element to which I will return
later when I come on to the post-war years. He distinguishes clear political
and cultural implications arising from this suburbanisation. He writes of
'the "villa Toryism" of the new outer suburbanites . . . which became
a pillar of Conservative Party organisation. . . . In the inner city suburbs
too the growth of the lower middle-class of clerks, teachers and small
business men, with their morbid fear of the working class, reinforced that
division into Liberal/Labour inner-city islands in a suburban and county
Tory sea which became the major feature of twentieth century political
geography'. Perkin comes back to this theme repeatedly, and emphasizes
what he calls 'the minutely refined gradations of status, expressed not only
in dess, style and location of house, number of servants, and possession
of personal transport' (he is writing here about horses, though the consideration might equally apply to cars at the close of the century). 'Sometimes
we ought to speak of urban hamlets rather than villages, since there were
differences of status beteen single streets, or between two ends of the same
street. Segregation was as strong within the working class as between
them'.[16] Snobbery, claims Perkin, was geographical: a phrase which he
lifted, with proper acknowledgement, from a contemporary source. He
argues that the obsessive attempt of the new lower-middle class of Edwardian
England was desperately to try to get away from the working class, in
income, in status, in appearance and in physical residence. Further, Perkin
claims, in this desperate quest for status this new middle class seized every
educational opportunity, whether formal or informal, even those intended
for the working class, whether it was Sunday schools, youth clubs, the
WEA or the developing school system itself. The model could not be clearer.
Perkin goes on, if only briefly, to apply it to the new suburbs of the 1930s.
He calls this a period when 'England was more visibly graded into discrete
social layers . . . The suburbs were only classless in the sense that each
catered for the class that could afford that price of house and no more,
or that level of rent on a housing estate'. In fact, he continues 'the classes
and subclasses sorted themselves out more neatly than ever before into
single-class enclaves which did not know or speak to each other'.[17]

And there Perkin stops. Although he goes on to write about the post-
war years, and brings his account up to date, he does not return to this
question of suburbanisation: he says nothing about the new towns that were
built after the second world war, nothing about the vast post-war council
housing estates, nothing about the housing boom of the sixties nor that
of the eighties. It is a strange omission, but he has already done enough
to lay out a further part of the agenda for any serious analysis of schooling
after the Second World War.

It is worth dwelling on this theme of late-nineteenth century schooling to consider what these analyses might mean in practice when we look at an actual urban context. In this case I use Birmingham as an example of a swiftly growing industrial city. During the final thirty years of the nineteenth century, a schooling system developed in Birmingham which can be seen in retrospect to have served a society divided in these ways, and which was in a real sense also segmented. But part of this segmentation derived from the fact that what we are considering is a schooling system which was set up within, and as part of a society which was itself being born out of suburbanisation. It is vital to conceive of this historically as a living, constantly-changing set of organic relationships rather than as a static phenomenon. So, in reality, the first board schools appeared during the mid-eighteen seventies at the edge of the growing town, only about a half mile or at most a mile distant from the urban centre. They were built on the schoolroom principle and were little more than large schools designed on the model that had evolved in rural settings. By 1880 new and then prestigious suburbs were appearing one and two miles from the centre. Balsall Heath, one mile and a half south of the urban centre was one of them. It was here that the first multi-storey central hall school was built to cater for up to 1,000 pupils, and here that the skilled artisans who were doing well out of the Brummagem trades came to live and built their new homes. By the end of the century, the expansion of the minor professions and the tertiary sector of the economy, was leading to the appearance of new, more distant suburbs, made possible only by the coming of rail and tram routes into the city. Selly Oak, Moseley, Kings Heath, Aston, were among them. In these new suburbs, which by their very creation supplanted the earlir suburbs as prime locations for habitation and the cultivation of a semi-rural lifestyle, there appeared a new kind of board school, typically more spacious, usually in a neo-Georgian style of architecture, and in some cases involving three separate schools situated alongside each other within a large playground space. So, three phases of board school building, and three stages of suburbanisation within a single city. By the end of the century rent levels and house prices, together with commuting costs, were determining which social groups frequented these contrasting locations. Even within the elementary sector, the expansion of the board schools worked to confirm social class contrasts. This is a picture which was replicated elsewhere.[18]

What emerged in Birmingham had all the hallmarks of a system in the sense intended by Ringer and Muller, and it was a system which not only mirrored social class but which helped to define it. The schools themselves, with their differing architecture, internal organisation and differing coded messages for their clientèle actually helped to define the classes which were emerging. There was an important sense in which the school was its suburb. The work of Marsden suggests that this may well have been generally true, and that not dissimilar patterns and relationships developed elsewhere in England, obviously differing in detail in response to local variations in social structure, to accidents of school foundation, and particular circumstance, but bearing broad signs of this interlinkage between suburbanisation and schooling. If this typology of schooling in one city during the late-nineteenth century is accurate, then the question which naturally follows is whether we can start to discern similar patterns in more recent years. What have been the links between schooling and suburbanisation in post-war England and what have these linkages meant for the children who frequent these schools?

Post-War Developments

The parallels between late-nineteenth and late-twentieth century developments in the distribution of housing stock are striking. From the late-thirties, with the war as a brief interruption, there was a sustained growth in new housing which extended until the early 1970s. The eighties saw another spurt, but this time even more regionally concentrated on the south and south east. In England this was complicated by the fact that from 1919 until the late-1970s there was some kind of balance between new privately-owned housing and council property (that is housing built by the State and rented to selected tenants). But the two kinds of stock appeared in different locations. So, crudely, if we apply this generalisation to a city such as Birmingham, new council houses appeared in large planned estates on the edge of the city, but did not interfere with the development of Sutton Coldfield, Solihull and even some of the old suburban outer areas like Moseley, Kings Heath, Selly Oak and Northfield, which experienced the full impact of Harold Macmillan's and Antony Eden's drive towards a 'property owning democracy'. It is important to emphasize for those not familiar with housing in England that the private owner-occupied housing is almost always seen as more prestigious than the State-rented 'council' property. That thrust of policy during the fifties, which saw new owner-occupied properties outnumber council houses for the first time in 1958 anticipated an even stronger growth in the owner-occupied market during the sixties. It was then, with the growing professionalisation of society, and new, more efficient transport links, that satellite towns began to grow around the big cities. In the West Midlands this meant Redditch New Town, designated in 1964, but similarly, without being called new towns, Bromsgrove, Droitwich, Lichfield, all about twenty to thirty miles from the city centre (a vast distance to the minds of English commuters!). These had the effect of syphoning off what was in effect a new commuter middle class with house ownership increasingly part of its agenda. The last phase of the new town movement, during the late-sixties, which in the case of the West Midlands saw the designation of Telford, led to the relocation of many working class families from central Birmingham in a location which was to prove potentially disastrous for access to employment opportunities. It would be facile, and wrong to suggest that what was happening here was the creation of discrete new social classes, though it would be fair to say that the particular circumstances surrounding the development of each of these townships and suburbs led to them having their own distinctive social mix, in each case skewed towards a particular layer of society. What happened in Birmingham was not untypical of other big English cities. The final element in this setting of the scene in one part of the country is to recall briefly the evolution of housing policy in Birmingham itself. After the War the demand for further council property was met first by further vast estates on the fringe of the city, a policy which was pursued until the mid-sixties, and finally, during the mid-sixties by an implosion back into the inner city with slum clearance programmes linked to the creation of new high and low rise council housing close to the city centre. So, different phases of council building left differing kinds of housing stock.

Council housing in Britain dates from 1919. By 1975 roughly 30% of the national housing stock was council owned. But the proportion varied widely from area to area. In Bournemouth, at one extreme, there were by 1975 only 34 council houses per 1000 population: in Sunderland there were 141. Further, the nature of council estates was partly dependent on when they were built, and this depended on local circumstances, such factors as inherited patterns of housing stock and slum clearance policies. So, for example, in the mid-seventies in big cities like Birmingham, Manchester and Liverpool, about half of the council houses were post-war; in Sunderland, Portsmouth and Bournemouth, about 80% had been built since the War.

The importance of housing policy for all this is emphasized by B.T. Robson, who in 1975 pointed to a further factor: this was that although private ownership was preferred to living in council property, those members of the working class who were lucky enough to get into council housing were almost always better off than the poorest who were forced into ownership or tenancy in the old, run down inner city suburbs.[19] Robson saw this as a key factor in analysing the distribution of the working classes in modern Britain and it is of importance in this context.

Its significance is intensified by a racial component which cannot be overlooked. By the early seventies, it was becoming clear to researchers that the clustering of immigrant communities in the inner city was directly related to housing policy and to patterns of house ownership. In areas of considerable black immigrant settlement like London and Birmingham, similar patterns emerged. The figures for the even inner London boroughs in the mid-sixties summarize the position well. 33% of the indigenous English population was in council housing, but only 5% of the non-white. This was for obvious reasons, to do with the difficulty of newly arrived immigrants in meeting the criteria for council accommodation. Poor immigrants had difficulty in affording reasonable quality rented accommodation too. 44% of the indigenous English residents were in unfurnished rented accommodation, but only 24% of the new arrivals, most of whom were black. Where then could the newly arrived black population live? The answer lay in low quality owner-occupied property at the bottom end of the market, and unlikely to appreciate in price. So 22% of immigrants were in owner-occupation as against 14% of the indigenous English. Below this 48% of the immigrants were obliged to take unfurnished lodgings, a sector of the market into which only 6% of the English population were forced.

As Robson showed in 1975 this has clear educational implications:

'The difficulty is heightened in the educational sphere, since, given the young age structure of coloured populations, schools in immigrant areas tend to have proportions of coloured children which are much higher than the proportion of coloured households in the area. The dangers are clear; all the ingredients exist for a popular association of black settlement, urban decay and the perception of an educational crisis'.[20]

This all leads to some significant regional variations, and it is worth reflecting on the ways that the drift to the south has impinged on schooling. For example, there are wide regional contrasts in the structure of the population. Research by Moser and Scott showed that during the early fifties Dagenham, at one extreme had only 7% in the Registrar General's Classes 1 and 2, while Coulsdon and Purley had 45%. Hardly surprisingly, this correlated with other phenomena. Only one third of the people in Beckenham left school at 15, but 86% of the people in Stoke did. So, it seems more than likely that these contrasting areas would generate radically differing attitudes to schooling among their local communities. Only 3% of the Dagenham households were one person, but 20% in Hove. In Hove only 15% of the population was aged 0-15: in Huyton, the Liverpool overspill area, the figure was 31%, a striking contrast in the demands these southern and northern areas were making of their education systems. Huyton had 17% living in families of six or more, Southgate only 14%: another index of the fact that the education authorities facing the heaviest demand were also dealing with a significantly greater proportion of working class families. Put briefly, what all this adds up to is that the very areas where there were the greatest demands on the school system were those which were worst placed to benefit from income through the rates. The Local Education Authorities with the biggest problems, whether perceived or actual, were the poorest.

It might be argued against this that what really distinguishes recent suburbanisation is the greater mingling of social groups with similar income levels but differing kinds of employment, as professionals and skilled manual workers are forced into neighbourliness in new housing estates. B.T. Robson is among several researchers who have shown this not to be the case. Robson was one of those who investigated the applicability of the Chicago 'concentric' model to post-war Britain. He concluded that 'the appearance of large areas of local authority housing has made nonsense of the rings or sectors of the Classical ecological theory'. He went on to argue that 'Despite their lower incomes. The white collar families tend to live in the better areas'.[21] Bassett & Short, who produced *Housing and residential structure* in 1980 confirmed this, concluding that what determined the structure of modern British suburban society was 'an underlying concept of social classes . . . and the resultant jockeying for position in urban residential space'.[22] Differing social groups may briefly be forced into neighbourliness during a building boom, but they soon unscramble into differing localities as they gain more control over their housing choice. Heraud, and other researchers have suggested that, even where there has been an attempt at planned social mixing, as in the new towns, it has failed. He showed that there was relatively little social segregation in Crawley as early as the mid-sixties. This was confirmed by John Burnett in his *Social history of housing* which pointed out that 'the social mix in New Towns has been less than expected . . . relatively well paid workers are better represented than semi-skilled or unskilled'. Burnett showed that what was often critical here was the rent level set by the development corporations which were running the new towns.[23]

This coincides with research which throws doubt on earlier theories of the embougeoisement of the working class. Goldthorpe & Lockwood, looking at Luton in the late-sixties, suggest that there was far less convergence, in attitudes and behaviour, of affluent manual workers and those in minor professional occupations than had previously been thought.[24]

Another element in patterns of suburbanisation is a distinctive pattern of age distribution within towns and cities. Although there are not grounds for a direct comparison with USA (Sun City in Arizona has a residential qualification of fifty years of age), but as Robson concludes 'the fact of age segregation in English cities is indisputable'.

All of this was of enormous significance for schooling, and there has been some research which has begun to give credence to this view. Obviously, the famous sociological work of the early-sixties, perhaps most notably that of Jackson and Marsden on Huddersfield, related.[25] Flann Campbell, researching under D.V. Glass in the 1950s showed that one effect of suburbanisation in the South East was to alter the social class composition of the London grammar schools, with schools in a central location taking more working class pupils and those in the outer suburbs recruiting a growing number of middle class pupils as their catchment areas changed in social composition.[26] Robson's research on Sunderland in the 1960s led him to conclude that:

'the area of residence had a strong association with a person's attitudes to education even when occupational status held constant. In other words it appeared that the milieu of the urban social area had an independent effect on the individual's social outlook'.[27]

Steve Guratsky's research at Birmingham University on suburbanisation and schooling in Walsall pointed to the same conclusions: he argued that by the late-Seventies, access to comprehensive schools in Walsall was price rationed. He claimed too that what was happening in Walsall seemed to be the case elsewhere in the country:

'The basic principle is that each school draws its pupils from its immediate neighbourhood . . . a principle applied by 51% of LEAs in 1977 . . . Catchment area allocation does not involve any *direct* price-rationing of school places. . . . However, it seems clear that *indirect* price-rationing may occur through the operation of private housing markets'.

Guratsky showed that when he did his research Sneyd High School was regarded as the prestige comprehensive in Walsall and he found clear evidence of a significant number of potential parents buying in to the housing estate which guaranteed a place at the school. One further finding is worth pointing out before we move on to look at Birmingham. Guratsky found that one criterion which made the school seem attractive to parents was its newness, the fact that it reflected the best recent educational ideas in its design. As one parent put it: 'We've got a brand new school with the best facilities in Walsall'.[28]

If we seek to apply these insights to the development of secondary schooling in a city such as Birmingham during the post-war era, we find an interesting parallel with developments during the late-nineteenth century. Housing policy has shaped the conurbation and has largely predetermined educational opportunities. The concentration of council housing on the fringe of the city and in the inner-ring gave the area a particular socio-economic structure; a predominance of council tenants in the inner and outer rings, together with a ring of middle-class suburbs with relatively few council properties and a preponderance of owner-occupiers.[29] As significant numbers of predominantly white owner-occupiers chose to move out to outlying townships and villages, adopting a commuter lifestyle, a new lower middle class was created with a particular attachment to the new comprehensive schools of these townships. Further, the failure by the mid-1970s of the city's dispersal policy (an attempt begun in 1969 to distribute black council tenants evenly across the city), led to the inner-ring council property becoming the enclave of either the black community or of the poorest whites. The building of schools matched these trends, in much the same way as had been the case in the late-nineteenth century. Several of the more prestigious grammar schools of the King Edward's Foundation were relocated in the better off 'middle ring' areas of white owner-occupation. King Edward's School itself moved to Edgbaston just before the war, to a site adjacent to the University. Camp Hill Schools moved to Kings Heath and Five Ways School to Bartley Green in the post-war years. Interestingly, those lower prestige municipal grammar schools which did not relocate were all, ultimately, drawn into comprehensive reorganisation and became neighbourhood schools drawing from a quite different section of the population.

Birmingham's first commitment to comprehensive education, like many other local authorities, was partial, a decision being made in the late 1950s to serve three quickly growing outer ring residential areas (all with a high proportion of council property) with large schools to cater for the demand for secondary schooling likely to accrue from these large estates. Great Barr, Sheldon Heath and Shenley Court were built in a particular architectural idiom; flat roofed, brick, reinforced concrete and plate glass. They were, in the context of this argument, monoliths for a newly relocated working class.

Hardly surprisingly, the second phase of Birmingham comprehensives which were purpose built served the far flung new housing estates which were appearing on the fringes of the city. As we have seen these were predominantly white too, but involved a different type and quality of housing stock, built during the sixties. Much of it was high rise. And so the process went on around the fringe of the city. To the north the Perry Beeches estate was given the Perry Beeches Comprehensive School. Castle Vale School, Perry Common School and Four Dwellings were all comprehensives of this type serving similar suburbs. A large overspill housing estate at the south end of Kings Norton was given its own new comprehensive, Primrose Hill. These schools were built at the height of the open plan movement. They had a distinctive appearance, often merging with the architecture of the estates in which they were located, and are now clearly redolent of a particular historical moment. Finally, the new high rise inner ring estates of the mid- and late-sixties were given their own new comprehensives too. When in 1969, Birmingham finally went for comprehensive reorganisation, pulling pre-existing secondary modern and municipal grammar schools into the comprehensive sector, they were repeatedly forced into split-site arrangements. These occurred predominantly in the old suburbs, and were evident in parts of the city where a declining suburb had meant a school losing prestige in the post-war years. Significantly, several of the old municipal grammar schools, like Waverley, Yardley, and George Dixon were absorbed into split-site arrangements and suffered disastrously in public perceptions as a result. What developed was a stratified school system serving an increasingly stratified society.

The development of comprehensive schooling in the neighbouring areas tends to confirm this picture. Seen in this light, the campaign of Solihull residents to preserve their best comprehensive school when threatened by a return to grammar school status in 1981 ·was not as Brian Simon has suggested, a triumph for the comprehensive principle, but a middle class community defending a privileged position which would be threatened by the reintroduction of a competitive criterion of merit alongside that of ability to pay for housing in the neighbourhood.

If this is an accurate analysis of what was going on during the post-war era, then it is a phenomenon which helps to explain the political developments of the 1980s. It is usual to point out the ways in which educational legislation is a response to develpments taking place on the ground. Such an analysis has been made of 1902 and 1944. Most comment so far has depicted the 1988 legislation as historically inexplicable, seeing the Radical Right theorists of the sixties and seventies as some kind of historical aberation. Is it possible that the kind of views on the need for a more competitive education system which have emerged in the last twenty years, and the press campaigns which have suggested that education isn't working, are in reality reflections of the differing perceptions of schooling which arise within a society which is stratified in this way? Have those of us working within education been blinded to the realities of what was going on by our own absorption in a peculiarly English egalitarian ethic, redolent of post-war labourism and of much of the sociological research which focused on the maldistribution of educational opportunity?

Was the 1988 Education Reform Act, not as many have seen it, an affront to the English educational tradition, but in reality, a measure which was to be anticipated, which, sooner or later, was inevitable given the ways in which schooling had come to reflect the new social divisions of post-war Britain?

And finally, does this glance at the urban context in which it took place mean that the introduction of comprehensive schooling in England, intended to promote social harmony and a fairer society, was in reality doomed from the start because, in this particular context, the promotion of community schools was as likely to divide society as to reunite it? It certainly suggests that the social divisions which are implicit in this maldistribution of housing stock resulted in many children, particularly in the inner ring and older decaying areas of our cities, entering schools where they were seriously 'at risk', indeed even predetermined not to be full beneficiaries of the affluent society. Higher education, the major professions, even in some cases salaried work, were denied them by the accident of location. The words of the 1963 Newsom report are as true today as when they were written and make a fitting, but sad, epitaph for schooling in modern Britain:

'the social challenge which schools in the slums have to meet comes from the whole neighbourhood in which they work . . . The difference is so great as to constitute a difference in kind.'[30]

That is the gloomy speculation to which I am drawn by this 'ecological' approach to the study of schooling in modern Britain.

References

1. Roy Lowe, *Education in the Post-War years*, Routledge, 1988.
2. See for example W.E. Marsden, *Educating the respectable*, Woburn Press, 1991; also W.E. Marsden, 'Historical geography and the history of education', *History of Education*, vol. 6, no. 1, Feb., 1977, pp.21-42.
3. W.E. Marsden, *Unequal educational provision in England and Wales: the Nineteenth Century roots*, Woburn Press, 1987.
4. Marsden, *Unequal educational provision*, p.3.
5. *Ibidem*, pp.1-17.
6. M.B. Katz, 'Comment', *Hist. Ed. Q.*, vol. 9, 1969, pp.326-7.
7. C.F. Kaestle & M.A. Vinovskis, *Education and social change in Nineteenth Century Massachusetts*, Cambridge, 1980, p.1.
8. Marsden, *op.cit.*, p.1.
9. F. Ringer, *Education and society in modern Europe*, Univ. of Indiana Press, Bloomington, 1979.
10. D.K. Muller, F. Ringer & B. Simon (eds.), *The rise of the modern educational system: structural change and social reproduction, 1870-1920*, CUP, 1987.
11. *Ibidem*, p.8.
12. *Ibidem*, pp.1-12.
13. H. Perkin, *The rise of professional society: England since 1880*, Routledge, 1989.
14. *Ibidem*, p.28.
15. *Ibidem*, p.27.
16. *Ibidm*, p.104.
17. *Ibidem*, p.269.
18. See on this M. Seaborne and R. Lowe, *The English school: its architecture and organisation, 1870-1970*, RKP, 1977.
19. B.T. Robson, *Urban social areas*, Clarendon, Oxford, 1975, 12-15.
20. *Ibidem*.
21. B.T. Robson, *Urban analysis: a study of city structure*, CUP, Cambridge, 1969.
22. K. Bassett and J. Short, *Housing and residential structure*, RKP, London, 1980.
23. J. Burnett, *A social history of housing, 1815-1985*, Methuen, London, 1986.

24. J.H. Goldthorpe, D. Lockwood *et. al.*, *The affluent worker*, CUP, London, 1968.
25. B. Jackson and D. Marsden, *Education and the working class*, RKP, London, 1962.
26. F. Campbell, *Eleven plus and all that*, Watts, London, 1956, p.36.
27. B.T. Robson, *op. cit.*, quoted in Bassett and Short, *op. cit.*
28. On this see J. Henderson and V. Karn, *Race, class and state housing; inequality in the allocation of public housing in Britain*, Gower Press, Aldershot, 1987.
29. S.P. Guratsky, *Owner occupation and the allocation of comprehensive school places: the case of Walsall*, University of Birmingham Centre for Urban and Regional Studies, Working Paper 90, 1982.
30. CAC, *Half our future*, HMSO, London, 1963, p.21.

BOOK REVIEW

Falmer Press Library on Aesthetic Education
Series Editor: Dr. Peter Abbs

Living Powers, edited by Peter Abbs, 227pp., £13.50 paperback; *A is for Aesthetic*, Peter Abbs, 188pp., £14.00 paperback; *The Symbolic Order* edited by Peter Abbs, 300pp., £15.00 paperback; *The Rationality of Feeling*, David Best, 211pp., £13.95; *Film and Television*, Robert Watson, 180pp., £11.50 paperback; *Education in Drama*, David Hornbrook, 181pp., £12.00 paperback; *Dance as Education*, Peter Brinson, 234pp., £12.50 paperback; *Music Education in Theory & Practice*, Charles Plummeridge, 169pp., £12.00 paperback; *Literature in Education*, Edwin Webb, 159pp., £11.95 paperback; *The Visual Arts in Education*, Rod Taylor, 179pp., £12.95 paperback; *The Arts in the Primary Schol*, Glennis Andrews and Rod Taylor, 198pp., £12.95 paperback; *Key Concepts*, Trevor Pateman, 208pp., £14.00 paperback.

The Falmer Press Library on Aesthetic Education is timely in its completion. It is to be hoped that it will have some impact on turning the tide of events that has led to a serious erosion of the position and status of arts education. Its twelve publications, falling within three distinctive yet interrelated sections, can only be of positive benefit in encouraging a serious and informed debate on the values of the arts in education and in society. Four of the volumes provide the historical and philosophical frame for the series, six volumes make up the individual studies of major arts forms, including the arts in the primary school, and a work of reference elaborates on some of the key concepts and movements current in aesthetics, criticism and arts education. Collectively these works reflect the challenge of arts teaching within the context of educational and social change stated in terms of the political and financial constraints that have marginalised the arts and through the fundamental philosophical issues that emanate from within the arts themselves.

The need for intellectual clarification, as the means of defence and affirmation, along with a detectable shift towards a more formal aesthetic in the arts was first registered in the *Gulbenkian Report: The Arts in Schools* over a decade ago. Certain seminal issues from the report provide the main unifying thesis and impetus for many of the works in this cultural project which reflect Peter Abbs's vision to bring the role of the arts to the forefront. In this quest he has been supported by a succession of vibrant and challenging responses from outstanding scholars and teachers who have sought to identify and remedy some of the major problems that currently beset arts education. They have also demonstrated how individual arts relate to and interact with each other in a shared 'aesthetic field'.

The term 'aesthetic field' was first defined by Peter Abbs in *Living Powers* and has gained two distinct meanings. One defines the process of art-making while the second refers to the symbolic system in which all art is made. The former includes the four phases of the creative process — the making, presenting, responding and evaluating, the latter refers to the whole symbolic system of cultural forms within which individual works are created and understood. Crucially, the arts are grouped collectively as a generic community. The interaction and rebound between them occurs at the different stages through which they pass and also between their broader historical and global contexts.

Living Powers, provides historical outlines of several arts within the curriculum. The contributors reveal that time and resources for aesthetic pursuits are being reduced. On a more positive note they launch the key theme of the existence and defence of the 'aesthetic field' on the grounds that society must provide a facilitating environment within which the aesthetic potential of all of its members can find appropriate expression. Peter Abbs's personal contribution is in *A is for Aesthetic*, a work in which he presents two major premises; firstly, that the proper methods of learning are Socratic, dynamic and collaborative, and secondly that the balanced curriculum is constructed on the generic notion of human understanding. These key principles for the renewal of education do not depend on standardised testing, nor on mechanically linking knowledge to 'relevance', neither on the *ad hoc* selection of ideologically favoured subjects, but rather in the coordinated principles of dynamic learning and a plural epistemology.

A major chapter, highlighting the belief in a formal aesthetic for the teaching of the arts, was published in 1985 as the lead paper in *Aspects of Education*, No. 34, when Abbs presented and developed the hypothesis of the shift in the understanding and teaching of the arts from the informal progressive approach. He wrote of the radically pluralistic nature of art as a form of knowing, tracing the development of the rationality of the philosophical tradition that has since led to the acceptance of what he then termed transactional language, information acquisition, quantitive measurement and competitive achievement which, prophetically, has currently resulted in the low status value afforded to artistic accomplishment and experience in our society.

The Symbolic Order, a contemporary reader on the arts debate, is a collection of previously published papers written by a galaxy of art-makers, influential educationists and seminal critics whose common aim is to foster generative conception and to promote the sense of connection between different art forms. These are the means of answering the vital need for new formulations, comprehensive critiques and engendering greater awareness of the plurality of artistic conventions and of expressive possibilities within the arts. The specific application of these basic ideologies in the Library is expounded through the collective wisdom of specialist authors in the fields of dance, drama, film and television, music, literature and the visual arts. They provide more than a vision of good practice for they reinforce, while preserving their uniqueness, the underlying message of the overview texts while individually interpreting and emphasising aspects of the 'aesthetic field'.

Peter Brinson, in dedicating his work to the unity of British Dance Culture and identifying the forces which need to conjoin in order to achieve this unity, considers dance from the point of view of aesthetic imagination and national culture, including the sources of power which condition the uses of this culture. He achieves this by focussing on the manner in which dance is received by society. He provides a cultural overview of the contemporary dance scene set within the constraints of prejudice, hegemony, paucity of resources, and internal divisions. Boldly written, Brinson believes dance to be a liberating agent that can help overcome the guilt, snobberies and constrictions that plague modern society.

The important contextual issues that influence the provision and practice of all the arts, not just music, his own specialist field, are identified by Charles Plummeridge who demonstrates how democratic accountability leads to networks in which all parties in the education system recognise their responsibilities to each other through the sharing of pedagogical successes and failures. Musical understanding enables children to enter the world of sound so that they will come to an awareness of the deep structures which convey meanings across a wide variety of styles and genres. According to Plummeridge, this does not imply conformity of practice, but encourages diversity within a common framework that emphasises the great continuum of music aestheticism through listening, composing, performing and responding.

David Hornbrook also continues this latter and recurring theme in terms of dramatic art, illustrated through reference to various 'texts' whether stage, electronic or social, which in turn constitute the essence of play-making, performance and response. He provides a way of marking out the parameters of attainment and forms the basis of an assessment scheme for drama. This work is a response to the current curriculum state in which there is a real danger that the teaching of drama could slip quietly out of schools. Hornbrook challenges the idea that drama is best thought of as part of English and offers a new theoretical basis for the subject in its own right enabling children to receive a sensitive induction into a culture of theatre with its own conventions and accumulated knowledge and skills that are intended to stimulate creative autonomy.

This approach provides an interesting nexus between literature and film, since drama exists in both worlds — that of words and visual images. Robert Watson traces the development of film in education, examining the technical aspects of creating the 'moving image' and providing insight into the generic antecedents of selected popular forms of television, in the belief that the study of formulaic conventions and anonymity can lead to greater understanding of narrative art. His concluding chapter considers where there are 'slots' for film, as a major contemporary narrative art, in the curriculum and cites General Studies, Integrated Arts courses, Media Studies and English as the main areas.

The ways in which we encounter and experience the arts — through the imagination, the memory, the culture and the medium are also discussed by Edwin Webb. He presents, decisively, without apology, and without subversion to other ulterior or utilitarian purposes, the significance of the arts in education, stating categorically literature's role as art within this. Webb reiterates the message contained within the Library when he asserts that only through an encounter with the cultural forms of the past can we be liberated artistically from the tyranny of the present. He also acknowledges the importance of cross-cultural artistic transactions in order for renewed growth and inspiration to occur.

A characteristic of Rod Taylor's work on visual arts is the value placed on the art of teaching art. Appropriately, he placed pedagogy at the heart of the 'aesthetic field' by expounding how content, form, process and mood are essential elements of a model that has valuable potential for student empowerment, especially when set with the context of historical and critical understanding. He exemplifies his own approaches and professional experiences by incorporating the evidence of case studies that includes the artistry and personal/critical responses of teachers and sixth form students. Empirical reference to the arts in the primary school, and how this relates to the overall philosophy of the series, is revealed in Taylor's collaborative authorship with Glennis Andrews and features work undertaken at Tyldesley County Primary School. This case study emphasises the importance of commitment, funding, value and belief in the establishment and the creation of an arts ethos within a school as part of a policy of entitlement and serves as a worthy exemplar.

The Falmer Press Library on Aesthetic Education pervades a powerful message. Firstly, by exposing the fears of current concerns of neglect, cultural aridity, insensibility and fears of mass standardization it alerts all interested parties to the important tasks that lie ahead in order to overcome these deficiencies. Secondly, by proffering a strong intellectual model for curriculum development in the arts it provides new strategies for future development. It must be realised that the fate of the arts in education is linked with the fate of the arts in society, and if the arts do become subordinated within the curriculum, then their future and that of society's will be grim. *Key Concepts* and *Rationality of Feeling* were reviewed in Aspects of Education No. 49 *Socratic Education*, edited by Peter Abbs.

Anne Bloomfield
Reader in Primary Arts Education,
Nottingham Trent University

NOTES ON CONTRIBUTORS

Dr. Caitríona Clear is Lecturer in History in the National University of Ireland at University College, Galway.

Dr. Hugh Cunningham is Professor of Social History in the University of Kent at Canterbury.

Dr. Leigh M. Davison is Lecturer in Economic History in the University of Humberside.

Dr. Jeroen J.H. Dekker is Professor of the History and Theory of Education in the University of Groningen.

Dr. Barry M. Franklin is Associate Professor at Kennesaw State College, Marietta, Georgia, USA.

Dr. Pamela Horn is the author of a number of important studies in Victorian and Edwardian education.

Dr. Roy Lowe is Reader in the School of Education at Birmingham University.

Dr. V. Alan McClelland is Professor of Educational Studies in the University of Hull.

Dr. John Springhall is Reader in History in the University of Ulster at Coleraine.

GUEST EDITORS AND PREVIOUS ISSUES IN PRINT